AFRO-ATLANTIC FLIGHT

AFRO-ATLANTIC
FLIGHT

Speculative Returns and the Black Fantastic

Michelle D. Commander

Duke University Press • Durham and London • 2017

Printed in the United States of America on acid-free paper ∞
Designed by Heather Hensley
Typeset in Warnock Pro by Westchester Publishing Services

Library of Congress Cataloging-in-Publication Data
Names: Commander, Michelle D., [date] author.
Title: Afro-Atlantic flight : speculative returns and the
Black fantastic / Michelle D. Commander.
Description: Durham : Duke University Press, 2017. |
Includes bibliographical references and index.
Identifiers: LCCN 2016038106 (print)
LCCN 2016039151 (ebook)
ISBN 9780822363118 (hardcover : alk. paper)
ISBN 9780822363231 (pbk. : alk. paper)
ISBN 9780822373308 (e-book)
Subjects: LCSH: African diaspora. | Slave trade—
Africa, West. | Back to Africa movement. | Afrocentrism. |
Blacks—United States. | Blacks—Brazil.
Classification: LCC DT16.5.C63 2017 (print) |
LCC DT16.5 (ebook) | DDC 909/.0496—dc23
LC record available at https://lccn.loc.gov/2016038106

Cover art: Donovan Nelson, *Ibo Landing 7*, © 2010, 54 × 52 in.
(137.16 × 132.08 cm). Charcoal on paper. Collection of Valentine
Museum of Art.

• FOR ETHAN

CONTENTS

ACKNOWLEDGMENTS

On a fateful November day in 1995, my grandfather stood up to lead the St. Paul Pentecostal Church's congregation in a song titled "Running for My Life." The song, like other spirituals, contains interrelated meanings regarding hope, grace, and the opportunity to truly live even after death. I imagine that for my grandfather, it also spoke directly to his unwavering Christian faith as well as to the idea of escaping to an elsewhere—an otherwise existence. He sang, in part:

> I'm running for my life, I'm running for my life.
> I'm running for my life, I'm running for my life.

> If anybody asks you, what's the matter with me,
> Tell them that I'm saved and sanctified,
> Holy Ghost filled and I've been baptized.
> I've got Jesus on the inside and I'm running for my life.

> Won't you come on home with me?
> Won't you come on home with me?

At the end of the song, my grandfather suddenly collapsed and transitioned. The thought that he, who had seen oppression and terror in ways that haunt our moment; prayed with fervor for basic rights that we, perhaps, will never have to; and relocated to the North and then back to the South for a better chance at realizing social life, has returned to the home of his imagination is sustaining. This book has afforded me the wonderful opportunity to reflect on the radical possibilities for disrupting Black social alienation and dispossession by using them as embarkation points from which to take flight.

◆　◆　◆

Afro-Atlantic Flight would not have been possible without the fantastic support of my beloved family, friends, colleagues, and mentors. How lucky I am to have so many generous and kind people around to nurture my work and me. In what follows, I will attempt to thank as many of these individuals as possible.

I completed my dissertation in the Department of American Studies and Ethnicity at the University of Southern California (USC) under the direction of my chair, Ruthie Gilmore, as well as my committee members, John Carlos Rowe (JCR) and Fred Moten. Ruthie, Fred, and JCR helped me become a better researcher, writer, and person. They pushed and challenged me. They push me and challenge me. I am profoundly moved by their continued dedication to supporting me and lifting me up. I thank them for seeing and helping me develop my promise. I also worked with other professors at USC and elsewhere who were supportive of my endeavors and helped me grow as a researcher and academic. To the late great Clyde Woods, Lanita Jacobs, Denise Ferreira Da Silva, Curtis Marez, Marita Sturken, Francille Rusan Wilson, Viet Nguyen, Sarah Banet-Weiser, and Laura Pulido, I appreciate all of you for taking a genuine interest in me early on and for offering kind words and good advice along the way. I had the good fortune to attend the Futures of American Studies Institute at Dartmouth College and the University College Dublin's Clinton Institute's Summer School, where I participated in small group discussions of my work with scholars and received wonderful feedback from them and our dynamic group leaders, Donald Pease and Werner Sollors, respectively. Thanks to all of the participants and leaders for your generous comments and critiques about my project.

While I was in graduate school, I made wonderful friends with whom to share the ever-so-humbling years of coursework and the mostly exciting dissertation experience. I do not know where I would have been without good buddies to engage in many writing sessions, moments of commiseration, coffee, and lots of cake. Thank you for your friendship, Laura Fugikawa, Emily Hobson, Tasneem Siddiqui, Sharon Luk, Orlando

Serrano, Sionne Neely, Jennifer Stoever, Hillary Jenks, Thang Dao, Nisha Kunte, and Jesus Hernandez. While I was in the field, I was fortunate to make new friends with whom I traveled around the world, ate amazing food, discussed my research, and experienced many fun times. For being there to remind me to enjoy myself and take a break, while remaining committed to the work, I express deep appreciation to Victoria Okoye, Abena Annan, Nansata Yakubu, Irene Salia, and Joshua Anny Osabutey. In 2012–2013, I was fortunate to serve as a Fulbright Lecturer/Researcher in Ghana, where I was part of a close-knit Fulbright and study-abroad family. Thanks to Todd Cleveland, Julianna Munden, Suzanne Gott, and Helena Addae for helping to make our little compound on the University of Ghana at Legon's campus into a home. I am also grateful for my friendship with the novelist Leslie Youngblood, who eagerly sought out writing spaces in Accra with me. In addition, I would like to express my appreciation to the faculty and staff in the University of Ghana at Legon's Department of English and Institute of African Studies for hosting me.

I cannot say enough about my amazing colleague-friends at the University of Tennessee (UTK). I still marvel at the fact that there are so many good-natured, funny, and absolutely brilliant people in one place. I would like to acknowledge all of the faculty members in the Department of English and in the Program in Africana Studies with whom I am fortunate to work and serve. For their embrace of me; kind words of encouragement; and their beautiful, smiling faces, I especially would like to acknowledge the following UTK colleague-friends: Margaret Lazarus Dean, Katy Chiles, Christopher Hebert, Bertin Louis, Josh Inwood, Awa Sarr, Dawn Duke, Amadou Sall, Gĩchingiri Ndĩgĩrĩgĩ, Ben Lee, Mary Papke, Lisi Schoenbach, Urmila Seshagiri, Dawn Coleman, Amy Elias, Lisa King, Jioni Lewis, Michelle Christian, Joe Miles, Patrick Grzanka, Chonika Coleman-King, Tom Heffernan, Chuck Maland, Angie Batey, Gerard Cohen-Vrignaud, Tanita Saenkhum, Lisa King, Jessi Grieser, Stanton Garner, and Allen Dunn. I had the great privilege to serve as a Provost's Junior Faculty Fellow for six years, which entailed monthly lunches to discuss my scholarly progress, university happenings, and the academic profession generally with the provost and vice-provosts as well as with other tenure-track faculty members. To Susan Martin and the leadership in the Office of the Provost from 2010–2016, I would like to express my deepest gratitude for the unwavering interest and concern that you have shown for me. It has made a difference.

Over the years, various stages of this project were supported financially by several entities. I am eternally grateful for the generous funding that I received from the Avery Research Center at the College of Charleston; Duke University's John Hope Franklin Research Center for African and African American History and Culture; the Dornsife College of Letters, Arts, and Sciences at the University of Southern California; the Irvine Foundation; the Ford Foundation; the Fulbright Foundation; the University of Tennessee's Hodges Fund in the Department of English; and the University of Tennessee's College of Arts and Science and the Office of Research (especially Alan Rutenberg). I could not have traveled as extensively or researched and written as effectively as I have over the years without each of these funding sources.

My experiences with the editorial staff at Duke University Press have been more than I could ever have hoped for. I first met the fabulous Ken Wissoker at the Ford Foundation's annual conference when I was a recipient of the foundation's dissertation fellowship. Ken always expressed an interest in this project and generously made suggestions—I just had to get it done. Many years of research, writing, and rewriting later, I am luckily publishing with the press of my dreams. Wow. Ken's editorial assistant, Elizabeth Ault, has been such a joy to work with. She is organized, smart, and genuinely kind. Thank you, Ken and Elizabeth, for making the process so easy to bear. I must also thank the two anonymous readers of my manuscript for their feedback and words of encouragement. My work was much improved by their careful handling of my manuscript and obvious desire for me to succeed in this endeavor. If I knew who they were, I would send them a batch or two of my famous Southern pecan cookies. Thank you, readers, truly.

I extend my heartfelt appreciation to the people whose stories inform and inspire me and the actual travel narratives imparted herein: the tourists, expatriates, tour guides, and tour company owners throughout Ghana, Brazil, and the American South; the W. E. B. Du Bois Centre and the Diaspora African Forum in Accra, Ghana; César Nascimento and the staff of Integrare in São Paulo, Brazil; Joel Gondim of Sankofa Tours in Salvador, Brazil; and the staff members at Cape Coast Slavecastle and Elmina Slavecastle in Ghana. Parts of Chapter 2 first appeared in my journal article, "Ghana at Fifty: Moving toward Kwame Nkrumah's Pan-African Dream," *American Quarterly* 59, no. 2 (2007): 421–41.

Wendy Cheng, Ashon Crawley, Imani Kai Johnson, Badia Ahad Legardy, and Koritha Mitchell provided invaluable, honest feedback about this book project, and I am grateful for their kindness. Katy Chiles and Mary Papke read the first draft of the manuscript from beginning to end. Actually, they both approached me at different times and offered to provide me with feedback on the entire book. How selfless! How supportive! How inspiring! I owe them both so much, and I promise to do the same for others. I would like to thank my undergraduate and graduate students for their curiosity about my work; insights that have reinforced the stakes of this project, particularly as we have witnessed the continued devaluation of Black life in almost hypervisible ways given the rise of 24/7 media outlets and social media; and for their willingness to engage with me as I worked through some of the ideas that appear in this book. My graduate research assistants, Heather Williams and Jewel Williams, have been fantastic to work with. Heather and Jewel, thank you for your attention to detail, commitment to meeting deadlines, and for assisting me in producing the best work possible. For their support, (tough) love, and hugs and all of the amazing adventures over the years, I thank my sister-friends: my closest confidante and co-conspirator Terrion Williamson, and Wendy Cheng, Araceli Esparza, Perla Guerrero, Imani Kai Johnson, Schanna Smalls, Karla McKanders, Camille Boyd, Desy Osunsade, and Clarice Phelps.

Without my family, I do not know how I would have managed to endure the many twists and turns of life. I appreciate them for their encouragement, prayers, love, and even their curious glances at me as I described why I was "still" writing this book. Thank you to my ancestors (known and unknown) and to all of my family members, particularly my parents, my late father Otis and beautiful mother Barbara Wingard; the Jacksons—Tommy, Hilda, Natalye, Derrick, Amanda, and Keenan; the Foushees—my late aunt Gwen and Warren; and the Rothers—Joachim (Papa J), Kristina, Lutz, Claudia, Annika, Alexa, and Nicklas. My partner, Gernot, has been gracious, patient, and supportive of my research. When we were dating, he read the bound version of my dissertation for fun in airports and on airplanes as he traveled for work. That was impressive, to say the least. In the final stages of this book, our greatest joy, Ethan, arrived. My hope is that you learn to live speculatively as you navigate this world, my little prince. *Ich liebe dich.* Forever.

At slave castle–dungeons, the surrounds of centuries-old concretized ne-cropolises pique the visitor's imagination. If one actively listens at these sites of memory of the transatlantic slave trade, one will hear the lamentations growled by the sea. Alongside the structures, fishermen attend to their business, and women in the nearby markets prepare smoked fish and sell household supplies and the like. Everyday life seemingly has gone on. The slave castle–dungeons in Ghana's Central Region, despite their more recently erected gift shops and artisans' rooms, remain wretched time capsules. They have become places of diasporan mourning whose overpowering presences mock the relative underdevelopment of the towns over which they hover. In recalling what the death journeys from these sites entailed and that fateful moment at which each ship disappeared into the coalescence of sky and sea, one shudders at how the violent disregard for human life could have ever happened.

On a practical level, it is clear that monetary greed was the principal factor that compelled the slave trade: a sordid system that plucked at least thirty million Africans and nonchalantly dispersed them throughout the New World. In 1781, the crew of the British-owned *Zong* slave ship encountered navigational issues en route to the New World from the Gold Coast (Ghana), resulting in panic about the possibility that they would not arrive in the Americas with viable, living commodities. In response to an

I.1 A view of Elmina, Ghana, from the slave castle courtyard. © Getty Images.

impending water shortage, crew members tossed Africans into the Atlantic; the slave speculators had concluded that the certain way to ensure that they maintained their entire investment was to file insurance claims to recoup the value of their property. The crew members' homicidal actions were very much guided by a capitalistic impulse, an acute individualism that rejected the humanity of others in service of the preservation and economic uplift of the self.[1] The *Zong* massacre is one of the most significant historical moments because it prefigured how speculators and businesspeople have continued to prosper despite Black social alienation and death, and because this incident and others like it spurred a legacy of Afro-Atlantic dissent. Given the continued devaluation of Black humanity and life, it must be articulated that the Middle Passage is alive with the specter of death: "At the bottom of the Atlantic Ocean there's a railroad made of human bones. Black ivory. Black ivory."[2] The expanse of the sea, a pathway marked by rupture, is haunted indeed.[3] What inspires the analysis that follows are the ways in which the enslaved and their descendants took and have continued to take back control over their bodies despite the threat of violence, turning the language of speculation on its head.

In various Afro-Atlantic folkloric tales, Mami Wata or Yemanja/Iemanja, a mermaid-like spiritual goddess of water who heals and liberates those who summon her, often appears. During the slave trade, a group of Igbo Africans who, though shackled together on a slave ship, called on Mami Wata to "carry" them back home to Africa, a plea that she granted, endowing them with the needed strength to leap into the ocean.[4] Their screams, the clinking of metal shackles against the body of the ship, and their impassioned entreaties to Mami Wata are thus fabled to endure in the Atlantic's sonic atmosphere, offering a radical, haunting reverberation.[5] The ocean's very existence as an unwitting accomplice in the slave trade bears witness.[6] Its eternal groans and bellows, which can be witnessed in the landscapes and literaturescapes across the Afro-Atlantic, demand remembrance, articulate sorrow, and express perpetual rage against the shores of dispossession. Reminiscent of the story of Mami Wata and the Igbo slaves, it is noted often that some Africans en route to the New World threw themselves from slave ships with hopes of returning spiritually to their villages. Narratives in the Black American folklore tradition also engage with the speculative through the often retold and re-created story of the Flying Africans; these tales chronicle a group of Africans who, upon setting foot in the West, took a look around at the landscape and their imprisoned selves, and ascended into flight, "stealing away" across the Atlantic back to their homelands.[7]

This book explores how African descendants in the New World have extended the legacy of the Flying Africans. Specifically, I examine how writers, tourists, urban planners, and activists imagined the Africas to which African descendants might return, belong, and feel free through the lens of what I refer to as *Afro-Atlantic speculation*: a series of imaginings, including literary texts, films, and geographic sites, that envision return flights back to Africa. I analyze cultural production in which Black American artists either send their protagonists back to slavery or representative Africas, or chronicle the artists' actual trips to the African continent proper. The examination of these Black American neo–slave narratives and travel accounts are situated alongside acts—multilayered narratives that are performed by a cast of "real" traveling characters: Black American tourists and expatriates, tourism industry workers, traditional faith leaders and healers, and market vendors located across imagined Africas in Ghana, Bahia, Brazil, and the American South. Drawing upon and contributing to the disciplines of American studies, literary studies, diaspora studies, cultural anthropology, geography, and performance studies,

I.2 Donovan Nelson, *Ibo Landing 8*. © 2010, 54 × 52 in. (137.16 × 132.08 cm), charcoal on paper, Collection of Valentine Museum of Art in New York City.

I accumulate this multifaceted archive to examine thoroughly how the speculation that began with the folkloric myth of the Flying Africans endures in the post–civil rights moment.

I describe how this particular set of African-descended peoples creates and performs Africa, and I contend that this multigenre process—at times celebratory and romantic, at times disappointing—helps them attend to the dispossession caused by the slave trade. Each of the Afro-Atlantic sites explored herein is haunted by and promotes particular kinds of narratives about transatlantic slavery and imagined Africas. Along the coastlines and interior regions of these sites sat major embarkation facilities from which human cargo was dispersed to the Americas during the transatlantic slave trade; these artifacts, coupled with cultural elements throughout each region, have become prominent tourist attractions, drawing thousands of Black American travelers each year. I perform the important tasks of mapping and examining the myths that Afro-Atlantic communities perpetuate about slavery and their purported retentions from the original Africa—the imagined, pristine landscape from which their ancestors were stripped—despite temporal and geographic separations. I argue for a more expansive reading of these circuits that not only considers flight and its related outcomes but also contemplates the possibility for increasing Black relations across the globe.

Literal and figurative flights closer to Africa are indicative of the ceaseless reconfigurations of resistance to elide racism and its attendant systems of domination. *Afro-Atlantic Flight* argues that myriad forms of radical cultural production travel among the people of the Afro-Atlantic in the post–civil rights era. I utilize the term *Afro-Atlantic* to account for the flows of a diversity of African-descended peoples and to clarify at the outset that though this analysis is centered primarily on Black American cultural production and migrations, it also interrogates how a range of African-descended groups contemporaneously perform and remember Africa. The folklore and myths that inform imaginaries about Africa are products of a complicated, transnational spectrum of longing; inherently, Afro-Atlantic speculative fictions are the result of collaborative processes whereby African cultural epistemologies are exchanged, imagined, and reconfigured. In the texts and movements explored throughout, Africa emerges as a signifier that is perpetually in flux, reinforcing the impossibility of literal returns despite the perpetuity of yearning as well as the hybridity of Afro-Atlantic identities.

The innumerable series of flights taken by Black Americans toward Africa are necessarily bound up with speculative cultural production, which consists of fantastic works that often blur chronological time and portray interactions between real, ghostly, and imagined figures. As a genre, speculative fiction "gives authors the ability to ask relevant questions about our own society in a way that would prove provocative in more mainstream forms. . . . [I]t is a literature of freedom, freedom for the author to lose the chains of conventional thought, and freedom for the reader to lose themselves in discovery."[8] While recent Black speculative texts such as science fiction are often understood through the lens of Afrofuturism, I maintain that Afrofuturism is a subgenre of Afro-speculation of the twentieth and twenty-first century that is concerned with the artistic reimagining of the function of science and technology in the construction of utopic Black futures.[9] Afro-Atlantic speculative thought germinated in part as a corrective response to slavery, which the filmmaker Haile Gerima referred to in an interview with Pamela Woolford as "a scientific adventure, an attempt by an industrialized society to create a robotic or mindless human being, pure labor. . . . [T]he plantation school of thought believed [resistance and rebellion were] always provoked by outsiders, that Africans were not capable of having that human need."[10] Speculation became a subversive way of life for Black Americans, who were determined to self-actualize, forge communities, and experience pleasure on their own terms.[11] Afro-speculation as a modality for living is conjectural and conditional; the evidentiary matters not. Afro-speculation is an investment in the unseen and precarious; it is a gamble. It is the belief in the possibility of the establishment of new, utopic realities outside of dominant society despite the lack of proof that Black social life is conceivable. The humanistic qualities and liberatory nature of the genre renders speculative thought a fantastic, radical epistemological modality through which Afro-Atlantic identity can be lived across time and space.

The Afro-Atlantic speculative also relies on multilayered flights of the imagination. This is evident in mythmaking processes, which have long served as powerful tools by which many African-descended communities have sustained themselves. Centuries before the advent of today's technologies, Afro-Atlantic peoples and stories traveled, inspiring the establishment of transatlantic bonds that exceeded the borders of the Western imagination. The speculative fictions and acts addressed in this book, then, are synergistic and performative, traversing alternative spatial and temporal continuums. To be sure, the potential for Afro-Atlantic speculation as a genre and modality lends a sanguine quality to how one imagines the future. Yet, as I will demonstrate in the following chapters, Black American speculation regarding ancestral homelands can become divorced from its revolutionary potential if the imagination is hampered by myopic desires to reclaim precolonial Africa.

Freedom Dreams: Historical Flights and
Black American Migration

I held all beyond [the veil] in common contempt, and lived above it in a region
of blue sky and great wandering shadows.
—W. E. B. Du Bois, *The Souls of Black Folk*

Black Americans have been perpetual travelers enraptured by the promises of flight since the Middle Passage. Flight is transcendence over one's
reality—an escape predicated on imagination and the incessant longing to be free. On the slave plantation, resistance in the form of truancy
and fugitivity often relied on individual- and group-devised trickery and
silence to escape what Stephanie Camp refers to as the "geography of
containment," wherein coordinated forces inside and outside the borders
of the slave master's territory attempted to maintain control of enslaved
people's movement.[12] In cataloging his escape from the bonds of slavery,
Frederick Douglass stated that his "only chance at life was in flight."[13] By
utilizing the speculative, haunting language of flight to describe the radical nature of his successful fugitivity and the steps needed to ensure the
future ascension of other enslaved persons, Douglass prescribes a kind of
fugitive epistemology that centers on Black unity and requires the strategic implementation of silence to give pause to slave owners, imbuing
them with terror and increasing the possibility of a proper chance at a
liberated social existence:

> I would keep the merciless slaveholder profoundly ignorant of the
> means of flight adopted by the slave. I would leave him to imagine
> himself surrounded by myriads of invisible tormentors, ever ready to
> snatch from his infernal grasp his trembling prey. Let him be left to
> feel his way in the dark; let darkness commensurate with his crime
> hover over him; and let him feel that at every step he takes, in pursuit
> of the flying bondman, he is running the frightful risk of having his
> hot brains dashed out by an invisible agency. Let us render the tyrant
> no aid; let us not hold the light by which he can trace the footprints of
> our flying brother.[14]

Flights of the imagination, as physical movements or devices of cultural
production, reconstruct middle passages to reconceptualize the voyages as well as to lend a sense of revolutionary possibility to freedom

dreams.[15] Such movement is realized via countless modes of transport (by foot, boat, train, automobile, airplane, and so on) and remains important to Black Americans' enduring desire to move freely—to assert their corporeal and psychic liberty. The immediacy of doing away with the shackles of slavery led to the imagined promises of Black colonies, most notably the 1847 settlement of Liberia, which was led by the American Colonization Society and carried out by Black American freedmen. Black American settlers assigned Liberia the motto "the love of liberty brought us here," though their Christian uplift ideology almost immediately and perhaps unwittingly cast the West African nation into a pattern of tribal devastation that reverberates in the contemporary period and presages the problematic issues inherent in positing a literal return to Africa as the antidote to injustice and dispossession.[16] For those who remained in or returned to the United States after the early failures of Liberia, survival depended on their reactions to the reality of their continued oppression.

As Black Americans discovered during their years of bondage and just after the Emancipation Proclamation, the laws preserving the freedom of American citizens were intended for whites only, particularly for the protection of white men. Black American traveling culture ties freedom to mobility.[17] Mobility—a person's control over his or her place in the world—is central to subjectivity and to one's sense of self. Freedmen and runaways had continued their migrations, particularly to the North and West, where slavery was illegal and they assumed racism would be less intense.[18] In cities such as Boston and New York, Black American migrants competed with European immigrants for jobs and routinely were denied skilled labor positions, soon discovering that while discriminatory practices were not legislated, oppression and racism existed in the form of everyday practices and de facto segregation.[19] Whatever hopes Black Americans had held out for freedom after the Civil War withered away when Reconstruction failed in 1877.[20] Not only was the South still suffering from postbellum economic hardships, but also racial tensions were even more acute than in previous years, resulting in increased Black Code restrictions, lynchings, and white supremacist terror.

During the post-Emancipation moment, the goal for Black migrants was to carve out a homeland where they would be fully free and safe from domestic terror. Traveling culture in the first half of the twentieth century consisted of a range of relocations by ordinary people, mostly within the United States, to flee Jim Crow laws and/or to find jobs in the differently racist North, Midwest, and West. The cosmopolitanism of the Harlem Renaissance, which saw the international movements of Black American artists and intellectuals as well as their political engagements with their African diasporic counterparts, demonstrated the unique role that transnational flights would play in the Black social movement, though the vast majority of Black Americans would not realize that level of mobility.[21] Black Americans in the North were accustomed to a marginally greater sense of freedom than their Southern counterparts, yet both groups were struck by the sense of liberty that they experienced in European countries as exiles and during military service, particularly in France during World War I. When Black soldiers, in particular, returned to the United States emboldened by the generally benevolent treatment that they had received, the gracelessness with which many American white people received them was more than simply disheartening. Specifically, the Red Summer of 1919 was filled with race riots, lynchings, and an eruption of other massacres, all of which were prompted in part by a perception that Black men were behaving "above their station" by wearing their decorated uniforms in public and that they were generally not as passive as they had been before they served overseas. W. E. B. Du Bois, who notoriously had argued that Black Americans should participate willingly in the war to illustrate the community's loyalty to the United States and thus increase the possibility of Black Americans being welcomed into the nation as recognized citizens, lamented in the wake of continued lynching and disfranchisement after the men returned:

> [The United States] decrees that it shall not be possible in travel nor residence, work nor play, education nor institution for a black man to exist without tacit or open acknowledgement of his inferiority to the dirtiest white dog. . . . But by the God of Heaven, we are cowards and jackasses if now that that war is over, we do not marshal every ounce of our brain and brawn to fight a sterner, longer, more unbending battle against the forces of hell in our own land. We return. We return from fighting. We return fighting. Make way for Democracy! We saved it in France, and by the Great Jehovah, we will save it in the United States of America, or know the reason why.[22]

In the midst of Du Bois's increasing but measured agitation, which he expressed in his writings in the magazine *The Crisis* and through his activism in the courts with the NAACP's legal division, the revolutionary outlook of Jamaican-born Marcus Garvey began to pique the imaginations of hundreds of thousands of restless African-descended people through his international Pan-Africanist organization, the Universal Negro Improvement Association.[23] Garvey had immediate plans, though they went unrealized, to repatriate African diasporans to a settlement in Liberia. Restrictions on this international mass movement—both economic and imposed by the U.S. government—curbed the formation of the Black nation that Garvey imagined, but some Black Americans continued to migrate within the United States in response to the collapse of a range of proposed legislative acts that were intended to mitigate the lasting effects of Reconstruction's disappointments.

Most Black Americans in the South, though, were unable or unwilling to migrate. They demanded their freedom in the face of a range of hindrances including the Jim Crow segregation laws, which limited the rights Black Americans were able to exercise and, to a disturbing extent, reinstated the slave plantation–era geography of containment. The immediate response to Jim Crow and the danger of certain death was further flight: the Great Migration of roughly 1.6 million Black Americans from Southern states to the North, Midwest, and California between 1910 and 1930 to find jobs and escape intimidation and discriminatory practices. The Second Great Migration in the 1940s through the 1960s propelled 5 million Black Americans away from the increasingly treacherous conditions in the South, where church bombings and threats of physical violence were prominent and legal penalties for anti-Black domestic terrorism were virtually nonexistent.[24] The majority of Black Americans remained in the battleground that was the South, and it was these everyday people who organized and supported the social movements that gradually improved their communities.[25]

In addition to civil rights activism within the nation's borders, Mary Dudziak suggests that beginning in 1960, which is heralded widely as the Year of Africa, the U.S. government felt tremendous pressure to incorporate Black Americans fully into society, as officials feared the establishment of a Black fifth column: a radical, clandestine organization that would seek vengeance within the nation.[26] Generally, Black Americans were encouraged by successful African anticolonial movements, and civil rights leaders began traveling en masse to countries such as Ghana in the late 1950s, where they engaged with Pan-Africanism and socialist thought under the tutelage of Kwame Nkrumah and political exiles in the African diaspora, all of whom urged Black Americans to continue the fight back in the United States informed by a more radical philosophy.[27] The irony did not escape the U.S. government that sub-Saharan African countries were struggling for and gaining their freedom from colonization, while increasingly radical Black Americans, who lived in the supposed bastion of freedom, were still striving for basic liberty and looking to socialist nations for new methods to achieve that objective. During the civil rights movement of the 1950s and 1960s, violence grew worse in relation to the intensity of Black activism, but undeterred leaders emerged from local religious and social institutions to inspire and organize the movement. Captivated worldwide audiences watched in dismay as policemen violently brutalized peaceful demonstrators with high-pressure fire hoses and trained attack dogs. International newspaper and television images of the Black plight in the South provided evidence of U.S. hypocrisy regarding democracy, and the American government, which desired to possess more influence abroad, turned its attention to passing legislation that addressed civil rights disparities. Local strategists increased their protests through the establishment of boycotts, freedom rides, and sit-ins at white-only establishments, as well as the National March on Washington in 1963—all of which kept the international media's spotlight on their efforts and eventually helped accelerate the passage of the 1960s civil rights acts.

In line with the short-lived "days of hope" that had disappointed, oppressed, and disfranchised Black Americans since Reconstruction, the post–civil rights era is marked by a conservatism that has upturned the discourse of civil rights liberalism and "makes its arguments about racial conditions without endorsing racial inequality."[28] As a result, affirmative action and other programs that were developed beginning in the early 1960s to redress economic and social injustices and promote Black upward mobility remain political fodder and, consequently, are rolled back continuously, reinforcing high unemployment rates and keeping significant numbers of Black Americans living below the poverty line.[29] In his June 1965 commencement speech at Howard University in Washington, D.C., President

Lyndon Johnson gave a compelling rationale as to how affirmative action programs might address hundreds of years of systemic discrimination:

> Freedom is not enough. . . .
>
> You do not take a person who, for years, has been hobbled by chains and liberate him, bring him up to the starting line of a race and then say, "you are free to compete with all the others," and still justly believe that you have been completely fair. . . .
>
> This is the next and more profound stage of the battle for civil rights. We seek not just freedom but opportunity. We seek not just legal equity but human ability, not just equality as a right and a theory but equality as a fact and equality as a result.[30]

Johnson's speech presciently cautioned that the period after the passage of the civil rights acts would not be paradisiacal—that the 1970s and beyond would be a crucial, enduring phase of the journey toward the realization of civil rights for all Americans. By the 1980s, Manning Marable issued a call for a new Reconstruction after the promises of the 1960s civil rights legislation and affirmative action strategies had been met with extreme resistance from the American political right:

> The vision of a society freed from bigotry and hunger, freed from unemployment and racial violence, will be realized only through a Third Reconstruction which seeks the empowerment of the laboring classes, national minorities, and all of the oppressed. The "freedom" of capital must be restricted for the common good. A Third Reconstruction will arise in the not-too-distant future, to fulfill the lost promises of the first and second social movements. Its vision is quite clear. It is now only a question of power.[31]

Under contemporary neoliberalism, the negative effects of continued disfranchisement are framed as signs of Black pathology, a belief that requires a willful ignorance of how slavery redounds in the post–civil rights moment.

Freedom remains elusive as racism is persistently renovated. In response, mobility has been transformed further into a politics whereby Black Americans have desired increasingly to establish a sense of home elsewhere. Saidiya Hartman astutely notes about the state of Black social alienation and desire for living otherwise in the post–civil rights moment: "The transience of the slave's existence still leaves its traces in how black people imagine home as well as how we speak of it. . . . It's why we never tire of dreaming of a place that we can call home, a place better than here, wherever here might be."[32] Black Americans suffer from ever-evolving, intersectional forms of captivity—overrepresentation in the prison-industrial complex; race and gender discrimination and profiling; and unequal access to quality education and health care.[33] Dishonor and dispossession pose a perpetual predicament, but this is not to suggest that it is a position of absolute powerlessness, as evidenced in the centuries of Black American migration and cultural production during and since slavery and the range of radical social movements that have grown out of an acute rejection of domination and injustice—particularly the continued interest in establishing and improving relations between African peoples worldwide. Flights in the post–civil rights era illustrate that, as Nikhil Singh writes,

> one consistency of the black political imagination across its ideological and generational divides has been its combination of grassroots insurgency and global dreams. Perhaps it will only be by again inventing forms of politics, solidarity, and identification linking the local and global scales of human oppression that we will be able to address the increasingly obvious inadequacies of the modern nation-state as a vehicle of democratic transformation and egalitarian distribution for the world's peoples.[34]

From Diaspora to Neoteric Pan-Africanism: Moving toward Black Fantastic Thought

On the eve of the U.S. voyage into the new social realm produced by the end of the mid-twentieth-century civil rights era, Malcolm X offered a series of prescriptions about the significance of transnationalizing the U.S.-centered Black social movement. X had traveled throughout Africa in 1964, making a well-documented visit to Ghana, where a relatively large contingent of Black American exiles and expatriates had settled. The actress, singer, and author Maya Angelou recalls that Malcolm X advised her and other Black Americans to return to the United States to assist with the struggle for civil rights: "'The country needs you. . . . You have seen Africa, bring it home and teach our people about the homeland.'"[35]

In his autobiography, X recounts a speech that he made to a captivated audience in Ghana in which he did not outright reject the sense of diasporan loss that compels a desire for the motherland, but he refigured return as a recalibration of the collective mind-set, which he deemed necessary for the evolution of an efficacious, perdurable transnational Black radicalism: "I said that physically we Afro-Americans might remain in America, fighting for our Constitutional rights, but that philosophically and culturally we Afro-Americans badly needed to 'return' to Africa—and to develop a working unity in the framework of Pan-Africanism."[36] X's instruction to relegate Africa to the political and cultural imaginaries was an evocation of a proto-Black fantastic ideology, and it served as an early prediction of the unsustainability of diasporic-centered thought.

Scholars generally have maintained that peoples of the African diaspora possess the following attributes regarding their foreparents' dispersal: an imagined sense of an African homeland, alienation in the host country, a desire to return to Africa, and a "continuing development of a collective consciousness informed by the historical struggles for liberation and motivated by the shared sense of obligation to preserve the collective being, the ontological totality."[37] Of import here is Michael Echeruo's suggestion that it is the burden of return that is the condition of possibility for the diaspora:

> No person can claim to be part of a diaspora who cannot, however improbably, claim also to be traceable by descent to a lineage and (hence) to a place.... The power of the idea lies in the principle of it: that a return is possible forever, whenever, if ever. It is this possibility—this inalienable right to wish a return, to reclaim connections to a lineage, however fractured, that makes one individual a part of a diffuse and disparate collection of persons we call the diaspora.... The commitment to return is not an obligation. It is only a prophetic expectation to be realized in Never-time.[38]

This passage from Echeruo is fascinating in his assertion that the possibility of return sustains. For African diasporans, whose condition was produced by the transatlantic slave trade, there often exists a "rift of separation, 'the loss of identity,'" which can only "be healed when these forgotten connections are once more set in place."[39] Stuart Hall maintains that the reparation of that which is forgotten or fragmented does not hinge on return; return is not discounted wholly, but he finds that the formation of cultural identity is possible by thinking in terms of one shared culture, where an imagined Africa is the constant that brings and holds diasporic communities together, often resulting in the type of transnational social movement that Malcolm X envisioned. Regarding Africa, Hall surmises that it is "the great aporia, which lies at the centre of our cultural identity and gives it meaning," signifying that though Africa is invoked as an instrumental referent, it is impassable and inherently contradictory.[40] As such, a literal return to origins is rendered futile as an unyielding political strategy.

Given that the original Africa is no longer there and cannot be reclaimed, it is intriguing to analyze what Black Americans discover and create upon setting foot in Ghana, Brazil, and South Carolina as cultural roots tourists and "ex-patriots" or expatriates. Black American engagement with that which ceases to exist raises questions about what compels them to relocate permanently or return to that which is ethereal. Because the African portions of their histories were virtually erased during the Middle Passage and throughout their centuries of bondage in the New World, where multiply cultured, tongued, and historied peoples were strewn together, some African-descended peoples' attempt to recover the source—generations after the initial break—has depended on their ability to travel and imagine other possibilities for living. While the fact of diasporic longing attends to the emotive, this examination is concerned more with what follows yearning. The difficulties inherent to return projects prompt the movement of several people described herein toward the Africa in their imaginations, but the larger initial questions become: What can emerge from homelessness? What new worlds are imagined out of thin air? Unlike diasporicity as a political framework for understanding Black lives in the West, fantastic, speculative thought such as Pan-Africanism is not beholden to nor has it ever been concerned solely with conversations about territory or sovereignty. My aim, then, is not to discount diaspora wholly but to demonstrate that travels toward Africa can become problematic if they are clouded by an individualist concentration on homeland returns.

During her monologue, the embodied ghost child and titular character of Toni Morrison's *Beloved* recalls the Middle Passage, offering a sharp critique of the U.S. Reconstruction project as well as the attendant consequences of transatlantic slavery and racialized violence: "all of it is now . . . it is always now . . . there will never be a time when I am not crouching and watching others who are crouching too."[41] The very prescience of Beloved's rememory and, by extension, Morrison's authorial voice captures the political sentiment undergirding the movement toward the utilization of the speculative by Black Americans in the post-1965 era.[42] Morrison's tale of rememory and the establishment of Black American communities during the Reconstruction period reinforce the importance of effectively coming to terms with painful pasts to position oneself for the possibility of social life. As a political project, *Beloved* reconstructs the memory of the Middle Passage as symbol and symptom, asserting Morrison's position that that which happened in the traumatic past has an impact on the African-descended today.

Alternatively, Kamari Maxine Clarke argues against the centering of the Middle Passage in the understanding of Black life transnationally, cautioning that "unless African American diasporic cultural production is understood in relation to contemporary issues on the African continent, the signifier of Africa in the African Diaspora will remain an insignificant symbol of African realities, always present in its invocation of African Americanness, but absent in the continuing trajectories of plunder in postcolonial Africa."[43] Clarke understands such claims on Africa to be what Fred Moten refers to as an "externally imposed murderousness—an effect of the strange of nostalgia in diasporic civil society and neo-imperial rapaciousness."[44] Clarke's provocative statement calls for a particular kind of reverence that imposes on anyone who identifies as or assigns "African" as a self-descriptor the responsibility of acknowledging the more pressing issues in present-day Africa. This book responds to Clarke's critique by considering the performative aspects of this obligation and by reflecting on whether Clarke's charge operates in reverse. Are African governments, for example, responsible for recognizing and enlisting in the effort to better the welfare of diasporic Africans if and when they wield the language of kinship to usher "home" diasporic persons with the financial means to travel and buttress African development and investment strategies?

Related provocative arguments regarding the Black American utilization of speculative thought in cultural production and homeland travels often raise class concerns.[45] The ability to escape is indeed predicated on the possession of the wealth to move for most migrants, rendering the ability to fantasize in these ways a mark of the privileged. It should be noted, however, that imagining an alternative life does not always cost financially; oral myths, for instance, are often passed down generationally, remembered, and repeated, which suggests that financial upward mobility is not a prerequisite for spiritual ascents. The quest for social and psychic freedom, to be sure, hinges not on the taking of literal flights. What I seek to encourage here are more measured readings of those who elect to fly toward Africa, particularly more expressed empathy for those who fail in their attempts to take up what José E. Munoz refers to as "disidentification" survival strategies to escape marginalization in the contentious post-1965 moment in the United States by claiming their ancestral pasts through African self-identification (naming) and in representations generally.[46] This is especially vital when these imaginings are not coupled with what critics might imagine are the proper connections of travelers and cultural producers' diasporic plights to current affairs on the African continent. Clarke's usage of "insignificant" is compelling in that it reads as presentist, even in her sincere regard concerning eradicating the continued pillage of Africa by establishing humanitarian diasporas. While Black Americans are not the only diasporic people who claim, long for, or represent Africa in their nomenclature and cultural performances, they and others occasionally position Black Americans as the single people of the diaspora. And while it is the case that Black American voices are privileged at times to an alarming degree, it is unsettling that Black American cultural production, participation in cultural roots tourism, and histories of expatriation are sometimes dismissed and critiqued as effectively neocolonialist. Black Americans are now regarded by some scholars as exceptionalists who participate in the perpetual "scramble" for Africa, imposing their own individualistic narratives without regard for those of contemporary Africans. The idea that roots travelers and cultural producers absolutely arrest Africa in the distant past and take much more from the continent than they give has the potential to render Afro-Atlantic speculative acts, in general, as decidedly parasitic and ahistorical. The impasse that results from such distinctions is nearly impossible to overcome.

Yet, as I will show about Hartman's travel narrative, *Lose Your Mother*, which has been described by some critics as fretful and pessimistic,

Hartman actually frontloads her disappointment in her failure to integrate into Ghanaian society as a returned daughter rather than crafting a chronological narrative of lamentation. This move allows her to turn to speculative methods to fill in holes in slavery's archives and to imagine the interior lives of African slaves, rescuing from oblivion the stories of those traumatized by their kidnapping, sexual violence, and other Middle Passage horrors. Offering more generous readings of pilgrimage narratives allows for the exploration and delineation of the possibilities for Afro-Atlantic speculation as a means by which African societies and New World–based slave descendants might more fervently assert agency over what and who is remembered as well as find accord in their related, centuries-long experiences with empire. I argue throughout this book that the passage of time alone does not rectify slavery's sordid histories; for there to be any sort of unification and the implementation of a truly transnational political column to address the emotive and systematic ways in which Black people are socially alienated—what some may understand as an efficacious, indefatigable Pan-Africanism—continental and diasporic Africans must recognize the impact of transoceanic slavery and postcolonial histories on Black communities worldwide. Slavery does not belong to diasporans solely; it, too, is bound up inextricably with the postcolonial condition. Africans kidnapped and sold in the slave trade are as much the ancestors of diasporans as they are the foreparents of those who remain on the African continent. All should acknowledge the lost ones and relate to one another in sincerity, or else systemic breaches will continue to stunt any significant movement toward new spaces of linkage.

Each of the flights discussed in this book reveals the extent to which writers, travelers, the travel industry, and local and national governments operate in concert to produce return for diasporans and the temporal stakes inherent in such constructions. These moments are ripe with possibility and illustrate that an embracing of a neoteric Pan-Africanism—that is, new underground political expressions that are marked by fantastic modes of transnational Black social relations outside of normative politics—has substantially more potential for lasting reform than the economic elevation of an elite few. Derived from a movement of avant-garde Latin and Greek artists during the Hellenistic period that championed a new style of literature in rejection of the strictures of more traditional forms, *neo-*

teric is used here to signify newness in thought or to describe those who speculate about contemporary Black politics innovatively. In calling for a neoteric Pan-Africanism, then, I am suggesting the necessity of a break with an old order that has tended to allow the radical potential of Pan-African thought to be usurped by governmental entities with suspect and sometimes downright malevolent intentions. My formulation of *neoteric Pan-Africanism* is inspired in part by Richard Iton's "black fantastic," which he outlines as an "unsettling [of] governmentalities and the conventional notions of the political, the public sphere, and civil society that depend on the exclusion of blacks and other nonwhites from meaningful participation and their ongoing reconstitution as raw material for the naturalization of modern arrangements."[47] The speculative acts outlined throughout this book, to be sure, are not solely concerned with advancements toward idyllic Afro-futures. Each series of flight is imperfect yet instructive in locating what radical Black comportment might look like in the present moment. Neoteric Pan-Africanism is not synonymous with or even contingent upon literal returns. It is about determining how to live more freely in the present and how to fly resolutely into the future.

As an interdisciplinary endeavor, this book analyzes various forms of cultural production and employs their tropes as heuristics to reflect on the stories that I encountered in each imagined Africa. Important here are the converging threads, which consist of the major myths about slavery and Africa that circulate at each site; tour guide and governmental narratives geared to Black Americans and other African diasporan visitors; tourist reactions to the landscapes of each site; specific stories about how people chose to move from the United States and what that movement entailed; how Black Americans renarrativize local histories; and tourists' transitions to expatriates in the Africa of their imaginations. This book also draws from my interviews with and observations of expatriates, frequent travelers, roots tourists, tour guides, and local and state officials from 2005 to 2014. I attended and participated in a number of cultural events, including Candomblé ceremonies, *samba de rodas*, Door of Return ceremonies at slave castle–dungeons, slavery reenactments, orisha festivals, several Ghana@50 events, and the official closing ceremony of U.S. President Barack Obama's historic first visit to Ghana in 2009. At each location, I also acted as a participant-observer of several tours that were designed for African diasporan travelers.

Afro-Atlantic Flight's framework and analyses of real and imagined flights are distinct and complement a growing body of scholarship that critiques diasporan imaginings and mythmaking about slavery and Africa as developed in post–civil rights Black American fiction. The narrative politics that undergird such cultural productions, which center on protagonists who are dealing with loss and complex spiritual burdens, offer tools with which to examine whether and how the dispossession experienced by Black Americans is assuaged by literal fantastic movements across temporalities vis-à-vis engagements with rememory, remnants of transatlantic slavery, and imagined Africas.[48] By focusing on everyday travelers in the post-1965 era rather than a few eminent figures as well as by centering on the duplicitous scripts utilized by government officials and cultural roots tourism industries to promote particular kinds of Africas for diasporic consumption, this book also broadens discussions about the relationship between Africa and its transatlantic slavery diaspora. Competing agendas such as development, Pan-Africanist activism, and repatriation often complicate the promise of neat homeland returns to Africa. Guided by earlier anthropological, historical, and literary analyses, this book evaluates and reframes return as a sustainable Afro-Atlantic political strategy.[49] *Afro-Atlantic Flight* engages with the performative aspects of the speculative—that is, how the African-descended constantly reimagine Africa through exchanges between similarly dispossessed Afro-Atlantic peoples. The vestiges in these imagined Africas are bound up with memories, longings, and series of mythmaking that have sustained these Afro-Atlantic peoples as they forged communities in the Americas. The continued embracing and commemoration of these essences also operate in the contemporary moment as impetuses for roots tourism and permanent migrations.[50]

Chapter 1 examines the turn to speculative literary and filmic texts about slavery and Africa during the post-1965 era by analyzing how writers have applied the trope of flight in cultural production about Black Americans. As a literary and filmic device, flight offers the space for protagonists to come to terms with their complicated transnational identities by allowing—often forcing—them to experience their ancestral pasts as a restorative measure. Through the examination of a range of travel memoirs, novels, and films, including Haile Gerima's *Sankofa*, Saidiya Hartman's *Lose Your Mother*, Thomas Allen Harris's *É Minha Cara/That's*

My Face, and Reginald McKnight's *I Get on the Bus*, I argue that such productions of slavery and Africa have helped structure and advance the Afro-Atlantic imaginaries that are examined in subsequent chapters.

While chapters 2 and 3 expressly demonstrate how the formal and informal heritage tourism industries in Ghana and Bahia, respectively, perform Africa to ascend into Western modernity, chapter 2 considers the post–civil rights migration of expatriates to Ghana, a nation that has a storied history of welcoming Black Americans (mostly well-known political figures and professionals) "home" since Nkrumah led the nation to its independence from the British in 1957. There has not been another government-sponsored effort to attract Black Americans to return to the country as permanent residents since the 1966 coup that deposed Nkrumah. However, there have been recent, extensive tourism and diasporan investment pushes that rely heavily on the Nkrumah triumphalist narrative and the promotion of vestiges from the era of the transatlantic slave trade. Homeland myths and Pan-Africanist rhetoric draw in Black Americans, initially satiating their longings for kin recognition and the sense of freedom that are attached to geographic returns. This Afro-Atlantic exchange sets up a critical conversation about the uses of speculation and the possibilities for establishing a neoteric Pan-Africanism. I explore what ordinary Black Americans seek when they flee the United States and locate the significance of the breaches they encounter when they arrive in the imagined homeland as produced and performed for them in Ghana.

Chapter 3 focuses on what it means when the movement toward Africa takes place within the diaspora by focusing on the narratives produced by Black American emigrants and travelers who maintain residences in and split their time between the United States and Bahia. Black American travel to Brazil began in earnest in the early twentieth century, when the nation promoted itself as and was widely believed to be a racial paradise—a model for positive race relations and a site of capitalistic possibility. Black Americans traveled to Brazil during the 1920s through the 1940s with hopes of experiencing life without color-line limitations but quickly realized that while racial categories in Brazil were not the same as those in the United States, a problematic bias remained, which drastically reduced Black American interest in the country. By the 1970s, Black Americans cast their sights on the northeastern state,

Bahia, which is often described as the most important spiritual center of the country because 80 percent of its population is African-descended and because of its attendant cultures. Today, Bahia's tourism market attracts a large contingent of Black American tourists to its festivals and Candomblé strongholds in Salvador and Cachoeira, as there is the impression that Afro-Brazilians have been able to retain Africa in ways that Black Americans have not, and many have identified Bahia as the place to achieve happiness and the American Dream. This reading of Bahia is based largely on the myths that Afro-Bahians themselves propagate about their relationship to their nation and Africa. Such narratives and the ensuing performances of Africa are, in part, indicative of Afro-Bahians' attempts to assuage their *saudade* for freedom and the motherland. This chapter examines how the variegated act of longing occurs as Black Americans and Afro-Brazilians grapple with their diasporan positions and collectively produce and sustain Africa in Bahia. I also explore the stories that are imparted to Black Americans regarding liberty, race, and nation in Brazil and chart what occurs when bodies that are Black and therefore other in the local (the United States) attempt to identify with and live among a presumed sameness on an intradiasporic scale.

Chapter 4 investigates how Black American cultural producers in the U.S. South have applied speculative thought to challenge and renarrativize persistent Southern myths that venerate the antebellum period, forcing narratives of supposed pastoral pasts to confront slavery and racism in a public fashion. It then considers the post-1965 Black return migration to the U.S. South and how expatriates within the United States have invented their African selves in South Carolina as well as the crafting of this selfhood in the purview of Africa as it is enacted by the nearby Gullah sea island culture. Further, this chapter offers a reading of Black separatist schemes centered in the South and concludes with an examination of how the African Oyotunji Village in Sheldon, South Carolina, has redefined homeland returns by literalizing the development of an African nation in the Lowcountry. As one approaches the entrance to the Oyotunji Village, one is greeted by a sign that reads: "Welcome to Oyotunji Village. You are now leaving the United States of America." Founded in 1970, Oyotunji is a Yoruba-based revivalist community that has fashioned its culture after village traditions practiced in precolonial Nigeria. Unlike other manifestations of Yoruba spirituality in the diaspora, the *òrìsà voodoo* practiced at Oyotunji is strictly Black nationalist and rejects syncretism with Western faiths. The Oyotunji people's understanding, representations, and performances of Africa are steeped in a mimetic form of the Yoruba faith, which they utilize to authenticate their post-modern, separatist nation to tourists. The Oyotunji maintain their village financially by organizing Yoruba-inspired festivals throughout the year, providing spiritual readings to guests for a fee, and initiating those interested in becoming Yoruba priests and priestesses. Through physical movements shaped by flights of the imagination, these Black Americans alleviate a degree of the pain caused by the initial break, and, in the face of the Lowcountry's geography of silence about slavery, reclaim connections with their ancestors, the spiritual realm, and Africa.

The conclusion of *Afro-Atlantic Flight* reflects on the limitations of and possibilities for the collaborative cultural productions that are outlined throughout the book and ponders the turns that Afro-Atlantic speculation and return might take given the advancement of speculative, scientific technologies, such as DNA testing, which purport to detect and establish ancestral linkages between dislocated Afro-Atlantic test takers and peoples in specific African countries.

◆ ◆ ◆

This book underscores, then, that to imagine the potential for Black social life in the midst of imminent death requires faith in the immanence of speculative Afro-Atlantic flights, whose radicalness can be understood in concert with what Grace Hong has conceptualized as the "leap" in her discussions about Black feminism. Hong describes the leap as an action that

> defies the real—the demands of physics, of gravity—in order to be impossibly airborne, even if for a moment. The "clear leap" implies a work of imagination, the ability to believe that a different future might be possible, despite the seeming inevitability of a crushing present. It does not concede the future to the present, but imagines it as something still in the balance, something that can be fought over, "in order to blast a specific era out of the homogeneous course of history."[51]

For a growing number of Black Americans, life in the United States feels hopeless; the constant, futile search for belongingness in quasi-promised lands within the borders of the nation has exhausted them.[52] It is through the implementation of return flights toward the Africa in their imaginations that Black American authors, filmmakers, laypersons, and travelers attend to dispossession by emphasizing the significance of Africa to Afro-Atlantic identity, renarrativizing master accounts, and creating and representing new worlds and alternative existences.

CHAPTER 1

Fantastic Flights

THE SEARCH FOR ANCESTRAL TRACES IN
BLACK SPECULATIVE NARRATIVES

Thomas Allen Harris's documentary *É Minha Cara/That's My Face* traces a formative period of the Black American filmmaker's early life during which he is haunted in his dreams by spirits and a hovering, red-faced female figure that his Christian grandmother suggests is Satan but that a Cuban family friend conversely identifies as a mystical being representing a messenger from the Yoruba pantheon. Harris, frightened and intrigued by the insistence of these visions, seeks answers to their recurrences throughout his life, eventually expressing a longing for psychic unification with the ancestors across time and space. The narrative composition of Harris's film consists of interviews with his family members about their religious beliefs and Africa and how they intersect with or part from the journey that Harris initiated just before his eighth birthday, when he became aware of his double vision. "My left eye," Harris explains in a voice-over, "sees completely normal, but my right eye never, ever focuses—it's as if it sees not the object but its essence . . . its aura. . . . Now I find myself with this double vision, looking for a place where I can be at peace as myself searching for my own Africa."[1] Harris's grandfather's reported unrealized desire to discover his distant ancestral roots and failure to secure a sense of freedom from American racism that only Africa could offer piqued Harris's mother's interest in ancestral homelands as well. This generational fascination with moving toward Africa in rejection of social and cultural isolation within the United States propels Harris's own journeys in northeastern Brazil.

The documentary is, in essence, an exercise of generational speculation about Africa, which is carried out by the youngest descendant's intradiasporic travel. The soundtrack—music, interviews, narrator's script—is fused deftly with old family pictures and Super 8 silent film footage shot by Harris, his grandfather, and his stepfather from the 1960s to the 1990s in the United States; Tanzania; and Bahia, Brazil. Images dissolve into one another throughout the film and serve as an indication to the audience that Harris's past and present are intertwined. Evocative refrains, too, occur—particularly in the aural insistence of a disembodied female voice, perhaps Harris's version of a ghost or deity, chanting for him to "Go to Brazil, find the orixas there," which is juxtaposed with the repetition of a recording of his grandmother's persistence, "You need to believe in the Lord Jesus Christ. You need to serve Him." This time travel to recoup family lore and images sets the audience up for Harris's impending journey to Bahia. Africa, as Harris had experienced it on the continent proper in Tanzania as a child, had not sated his desire for identity completion. He is led to Bahia in search of spiritual salvation, contact with ancestors, and clarity. In a startling voice-over directed at the haunting presence of his avidly Christian, long-deceased grandmother, Harris explains his pending spiritual exploration: "All my life, I've felt the presence of a power beyond me, but your God is not mine. Your Christ is not the face I see in my dreams. Where do I find that face? My face?"

Taking its cue from Harris's quest for recognition in *É Minha Cara*, this chapter examines the trope of travel as it is utilized in cultural production by and about Black Americans as a means of allaying dispossession via time travel back to the era of slavery, intradiasporic movements, and traversals of the African continent. In literary and filmic texts, various modes of travel offer spaces for authors and their protagonists to come to terms with their complicated diasporan positionalities by allowing— often forcing—them to experience their ancestral pasts and Africa as potentially restorative, redemptive measures. It is as if the travelers in these texts are haunted by a ghostly imperative to seek out the faces—the literal visages, cultures, and traditions—of their ancestors. In what follows, I will analyze several neo-slave narratives and travel accounts concerning travel toward Africa to illustrate how speculative flights work to provide a twentieth- or twenty-first-century response, if not always an antidote or an answer, to the radical violence of and dispossession caused by eighteenth- and nineteenth-century transatlantic slavery. In these diverse contemporary texts, including Maya Angelou's *All God's Children Need Traveling Shoes*, Octavia Butler's *Kindred*, Haile Gerima's *Sankofa*, Eddy Harris's *Native Stranger*, Paule Marshall's *Praisesong for the Widow*, and Reginald McKnight's *I Get on the Bus*, the inherited mark of slavery is not necessarily healed but, at least, is palliated by the travel that these protagonists undertake. Potentially restorative travels are not only made by the fictional characters that I will discuss but also by actual persons who head back to sites of slavery for healing. While scholars heretofore have tended to think about the neo-slave genre as that which illustrates how the past informs the present and future, I argue that it also works in the reverse—using trips back to repossess imagined origins. Fantastic flights are vexed propositions, as they allow protagonists to attend to the wounds and ruptures caused by slavery. Yet, as will be explored in the nonfiction travel accounts covered throughout this book, speculative acts often lead dispossessed travelers on perpetual return journeys to recover what they imagine has been lost.

Lived Experience: The Fantastic, Neo-Slave Narratives, and Shame

This perplexing emotion is also passed from each generation to the next; the transfer is mediated directly by critical scenes of shame which become internalized through imagery but which then are reactive and reenacted with others.

—Gershen Kaufman and Lev Raphael, *Coming out of Shame*

Throughout the speculative texts explored in this chapter, there is a necessity for the Black American protagonists, who are always already travelers and always already socially alienated, to re-create, revive, become one with, and/or convene with the physically dead and thus repatriated though ever-present ancestors. The realization of such desires often hinges on the employment of the fantastic, whose themes in literature typically involve the following: "harried souls in search of peace, asking for specific actions"; "ghosts condemned to endless travels"; "personified death walking among the living"; "inversions of dream and reality"; and the "repetition of time sequences."[2] As a literary mode, the fantastic reveals "forgotten Middle Passages between Africa and America . . . [and] 'indicates a rupture in recognized order, the irruption of the inadmissible in the midst of the unalterable everyday legality,' like a crack in the spatial time continuum that serves as a framework to ordinary experience."[3] This fantastic is not science fiction or fantasy in the way we might imagine it traditionally, but a new understanding that includes communing with those who have gone before. Readers often see this temporal dynamic portrayed in texts in which elders from the U.S. South, for instance, serve as griots whose repetitive storytelling and warning to their migrating families to "never forget" their ancestors inscribes a rootedness and regard for the past as prologue. In addition to nonfiction narratives that chronicle the diasporan's travel to the African continent, several authors employ the fantastic to explore alternatives to Black American *natal alienation* and genealogical isolation.[4] The impulse that undergirds these literary and filmic narratives has helped structure a more popular imaginary that propels much of the cultural roots tourism and expatriation that I explore in subsequent chapters. The cultural texts examined herein approach Black American flights in the following ways: time travel to the past in which the protagonist assumes an active role on a slave plantation; dreamscapes and hallucinations about the protagonist's ancestors and her African pasts and futures; and the author-protagonist's physical return to the African continent or other symbolic Africas as described in fiction and nonfiction texts. I show how instability throughout each narrative drives the protagonists to a crisis point, forcing them to grapple with questions of diasporan identity with which they may not have dealt previously—particularly not to the degree that temporal displacement, madness, and trauma proffer.

The production of post–civil rights era neo-slave narratives and historical fiction has been crucial to Black American cultural identity and to the engagement with master narratives, which often marginalize the African descended from the nation. Neo-slave narratives, Ashraf Rushdy explains, "assume the form, adopt the conventions, and take on the first-person voice of the antebellum slave narrative" in service of intervening in contemporary debates to which they offer a historical situation.[5] The production of these texts also illumines the desire of authors to return to the literary form through which Black Americans originally had asserted their "political subjectivity in order to mark the moment of a newly emergent black political subject."[6] In these speculative texts, Black American authors respond to the linking of Black social alienation with what Ron Eyerman refers to as "cultural trauma" among Black Americans and other diasporans. Cultural trauma, Eyerman maintains, is "mediated through various forms of representation and linked to the reformation of collective identity and the rewording of collective memory. As opposed to psychological or physical trauma, which involves a wound and the experience of great emotional anguish by an individual, cultural trauma refers to a dramatic loss of identity and meaning, a tear in the social fabric, affecting a group of people that has achieved some degree of cohesion."[7]

While the trauma need not have been experienced directly by all, this dispossession or natal alienation, "the loss of ties of birth in both ascending and descending generations,"[8] is endemic to Black Americans and other diasporans, who historically have responded by attempting to construct a triumphalist narrative through the collective memory in which "the past becomes present through symbolic interactions, through narrative and discourse, with memory itself being a product of both, 'called upon to legitimate identity, to construct and reconstruct it.'"[9] The cultural trauma catalyzed by the Middle Passage and slavery may be sutured by the exercise of what Sara Clarke Kaplan has described as "diasporan melancholia," an "embodied individual and collective psychic practice with the political potential to transform grief into the articulation of grievances that traverse continents and cross time.... As a political practice, diasporic melancholia can thus be understood as ... the refusal to declare the past resolved."[10] According to Kaplan, melancholia is practiced through a range of engagements with the past, including religious ceremonies and spiritual possession. It is crucial that we understand that this phenomenon—the practice of a kind of intentional melancholia— occurs not only in literary and filmic texts, some of which I will examine herein, but also in real lives. To be sure, this study brings into focus such a cultural logic as it appears in both cultural production and lived tourism and expatriation.

Engagements with the traumatic and unspeakable are also enacted in Black American traveling culture whereby physical movements across the Afro-Atlantic (including Africa) and flights of the fictive literary and filmic imaginations propel the traveling protagonist toward the past to engage with historical realities, which arm her with the necessary understanding of the prior events and institutions and perhaps even improve her and other Black Americans' chance at realizing social life in the present. The idea of a palimpsest is critical here, as it demands a rejection of quasi-progressive thought in the post–civil rights moment that posits that the United States has moved into a postracial moment and that the sins of the past have been reconciled sufficiently. The present, in fact, is "always written against a background where the past is erased but still legible."[11] In the neo-slave narratives discussed in this chapter, each author employs time travel by figuring the temporal as horizontal and chaotic, while Western time is conceived as movement from an origin point through cyclical periods of rest and conflict—it thrives off progress. The African diasporan sense of the temporal is synonymous with Sheila Smith McKoy's concept of "limbo time," which is "located in West African belief in the cycle of time. Tradition bonds African culture across space and time to the extent that the living are responsible for answering to their ancestors for their behavior. In essence, tradition binds Diaspora cultures to their African roots across space and time in that the ancestor—the mythical and spiritual embodiment of another time—maintains a constant relationship with the living. In effect, there exists a living transcendental pact that is grounded in another temporal space."[12]

In my examination of these speculative texts, I maintain that the ancestral past is deemed by each author as critical to her protagonist's (immediate) future, and that, concerning the larger context of the Black American imaginary, neo-slave narratives highlight the traveler's understanding that to satiate her longing for origins, she should visit sites from which her inherited dispossession commenced to grapple with her plight and shame and to move closer to Africa culturally and politically. While the original narrative form of the written Black American travel narrative—that which was written by freedmen and freedwomen about their fugitivity to promote an abolitionist agenda—focused mainly on the liberty offered by the future and distance away from the reality of the plantation, a brief reading of Butler's novel *Kindred* reveals a compelling trend in post-1965 speculative texts about slavery and Africa that points strategically to the importance of remembering the past to critique and manage one's positionality in the present. The novel also signals why the

U.S. South is emerging as an alternative site of homecoming and ancestral memorialization for diasporan travelers.

Kindred is set in the midst of the U.S. bicentennial year of 1976, a year that was highly anticipated and rife with extravagant events across the country to commemorate the nation's independence from British colonial rule. The novel is a fantastic exploration in which Dana Franklin, the protagonist, involuntarily travels into and out of her family's life in antebellum Maryland beginning in 1819, maintaining the memories of both of her lives on either temporal side.[13] In a 1991 interview with Randall Kenan, Butler revealed that *Kindred* manifested as a "reaction to some of the things going on during the sixties when people were feeling ashamed of, or more strongly, angry with their parents for not having improved things faster, and I wanted to take a person from today and send that person back to slavery."[14] Butler sought to develop a narrative to challenge a faction of young Black nationalists who naively postured as if the revolution began when they became politically conscious. She accomplishes this literary critique by forcing Dana to endure the physical and emotional trauma of slavery, including ruthless violence, though Dana reappears in the 1976 moment each time she meets the threat of certain death. Through Butler's frustrating, capricious time travel methodology, Dana interacts with her ancestors and experiences slavery directly, and identifies the foremost purpose of her flight to be the saving of the rambunctious Rufus Weylin, a young boy whose family owns her enslaved forebears. In fact, when Dana is summoned to the past for the first time, she is going about her everyday life in Los Angeles, unpacking books in her and her husband's new home when suddenly she feels ill, her vision blurs, and she falls to her knees, only to become conscious in the same position but in the grass nearby a river, where she sees a small boy floating face down. She rushes to save his life, not yet realizing that she does so to ensure her own.

Dana, who has some knowledge of her family's history, quickly pieces together from her interactions with people on the plantation that the child she has saved from drowning, Rufus, is her white great-great-grandfather. Interestingly, Butler positions Dana as a potential savior of her family's legacy, and because Dana is endowed with some knowledge of her genealogy and snippets of the family's slave pasts, she utilizes her arbitrary returns home to Los Angeles to pack bags (which she straps to herself) with twentieth-century medicines and small weapons with which to defend herself from imminent white terror. Butler confuses Dana's sense of time by allowing her to remain in the nineteenth century for weeks or even years, but when Dana returns to the contemporary moment, she realizes that she has merely been away for minutes. Another compelling aspect of this novel is that Dana's husband, Kevin, who is a white American, also gains the ability to travel in time after Dana's initial call back to the past. His role during their travels is to protect Dana by pretending to be her master, which saves her from harm on numerous occasions, but this new power dynamic also triggers tension between the couple. A pointed conflict emerges, for instance, when Kevin observes that the period is not as violent as he had gleaned from historical narratives: "One [whipping] is too many, yes, but still, this place isn't what I would have imagined. No overseer. No more work than the people can manage" (100). Dana interrupts emphatically: "No decent housing . . . no rights and the possibility of being mistreated or sold away from their families for any reason—or no reason. Kevin, you don't have to beat people to treat them brutally. . . . I never realized how easily people could be trained to accept slavery" (100). While Kevin goes on to qualify his statement to make it clear that he does not intend to downplay the brutality of the era, this interaction can be read as a moment of racial disjuncture in which Kevin does not realize fully his privileged positionality as a white man in that era, as well as a person armed with knowledge from the future; he, essentially, is able to traverse both of his temporalities in a freer way than Dana. Dana recognizes that "Kevin and I had fitted so easily into this time [because] we weren't really in. . . . We were watching history happen around us. And we were actors. While we waited to go home, we humored the people around us by pretending to be like them. But we were poor actors. We never really got into our roles. We never forgot that we were acting. . . . Now and then . . . I can't maintain the distance" (98–101). Though their early experiences in the past certainly demand that Dana and Kevin posture in ways to protect themselves from harm, the larger gesture that Butler makes here and in Dana's gradual acceptance of and into the Black community on the Weylin Plantation, underscores the power of covert resistance, moving strategically, silence, and the benefit of suspending one's pride for the betterment of a united front.

In this way, the narrative offers a genealogy of Black American resistance and champions a nonjudgmental stance regarding the measured response that many enslaved persons embraced to survive the cruelty of the era.

Along with Butler's expressed desire to write against the ahistorical Black nationalists' desire for swift progress, Butler aimed to provide a counternarrative to the bicentennial celebrations by centering slavery as the condition that led to the possibility of American independence. Butler accomplishes this by having Dana slowly lose control of her bearings while she comes to understand through personal experience that the slave plantation's geography of containment was sustained by the very real threat of corporeal injury. Dana observes that "slavery was a long, slow process of dulling" (183), and it is through this dawdling progression toward emancipation that she eventually ceases the performance and accepts her traveling fate. Butler constructs slavery and a sense of being closer to Africa temporally as a felt reality for Dana rather than an abstraction by forcing her into her family's past six times. Dana and Kevin may have felt as though things were becoming normalized or that they were assimilating in some ways to deal with their dislocation, but I want to emphasize that they retain the privilege of knowing what a free existence (though limited by myriad forms of social persecution) feels like in the twentieth century. Notably, Dana and Kevin have no inclination as to when their travel will end, but rarely do they express fears that they will somehow die in the past. Dana understands that for her to protect the survival of her matrilineal lines and to ensure her own birth in the future, she must help Rufus escape deadly threats such as the potential harm that the enslaved man Isaac poses, even though it would ensure Rufus's continued raping of Isaac's wife, Alice—a reality that most certainly tests Dana's ability to be an actor in history as she had mentioned previously. Timothy Spaulding clarifies the complex function of ancestral connections in *Kindred*: "If Rufus represents the 'patriarchal pull of the linear' that sends Dana into the past as critic Lucie Armitt suggests, then Alice represents the matriarchal pull of the circular that connects Dana's present identity with her spiritual and blood ancestor of the past."[15] It is this latter "pull" that drags Dana into the historical past, destabilizing her physical movement, as the threat of violence heightens her desire to comprehend the events that occur around her. But what might have happened if Dana had decentered her focus on the *grandfather paradox* and more fully and speculatively embraced her enslaved present moment with her Black kin?

Midway through the novel, Rufus and Dana develop an unlikely and unstable relationship as confidantes based on a growing mutual affection and curiosity, though the power dynamic and the mysticism of Dana's various reappearances in Rufus's life render it such that they cannot truly trust one another. In a moment that sharply solidifies the ideology of the era of plantation, Rufus rummages through Dana's possessions and opens a twentieth-century historical text about slavery that she brought with her across time in hopes of more successfully contending with the social demands of plantation slavery. Rufus immediately refers to the material as "abolitionist trash," and when Dana responds that the book actually was published a century after slavery ended, he snidely questions, "Then why the hell are they still complaining about it?" (140), presaging some fifty years before slavery was abolished, the perpetual utilization of an ahistorical, persistent refrain that champions notions of progress and the importance of moving forward regardless of whether social realities match the rhetoric in the post–civil rights moment. To ensure that Dana is not inspired to lead an insurrection or other form of slave revolt, Rufus convinces her to jettison the book into the fireplace in exchange for his promise to mail Dana's letter to Kevin, who has been separated from her and effectively has disappeared into time for the equivalent of five nineteenth-century years, though he has often written letters to the Weylins with the hope of locating Dana.

Dana's final return to her Los Angeles home is made possible by her ultimate act of killing Rufus, whose alcohol-fueled, violent temper over the course of his life had made him impossibly manipulative and violent. At the time of their final physical struggle, which is prompted by Rufus's attempted sexual assault on Dana, Rufus has already fathered Dana's matrilineal line through the birth of Hagar, his daughter with Alice. Butler fashions an unidentified presence that controls Dana's travel, then, to orchestrate this movement across generations and show that the past and present are connected eternally. Dana saves Rufus from death numerous times only to slay him herself. She had reflected about her travel some time before this event: "Once—God knows how long ago—I had worried that I was keeping too much distance between myself and this alien time. Now, there was no distance at all. When had I stopped acting? Why had I stopped?" (220). Dana's narrative of temporal, physical, and psychic loss parallels that of her ancestors, though her steadfast allegiance to Rufus and her own survival throughout the novel rather than to her Black kin remain controversial aspects of the narrative. Dana had stopped performing a role because her time travel was indeed real life, and she had reached a crucial point at which she realized that her movement across time was an opportunity to allay the wounds of her inherited dispossession. Rufus's last grasp at Dana's body results in the slamming of one of her arms through a plaster wall, which left the rest of her body in the present moment. A permanent reminder of Dana's family's and the nation's legacy, the literal dismemberment also serves as Butler's political corrective for Dana's belated engagement in a physical action that allowed her to triumph over and challenge slavery's legacy with its "direct and insidious violence, the namelessness and invisibility, the endless personal violation, and the chronic inalienable dishonor."[16] Butler issues a significant warning against Dana's refusal to commit fully to living speculatively. To be sure, Dana accepts the fact of her time travel, but she refuses to consistently and therefore radically identify with her Black kin to subvert their containment. Butler advances the notion that speculation must be understood as a literary tool *and* as a collective, revolutionary modality through which Black life under (neo-)slavery should be lived. Interestingly, Dana is freed from the forced time travel on Independence Day, and her physical wound underscores the great national injury that made the U.S. celebration of the bicentennial possible. Dana, as a representative of transatlantic slavery's diaspora, will forever "bear the mark"—and the loss—of her kindred.[17]

The Sankofic Corrective

The word *sankofa* is a Ghanaian Akan term that literally means to go back and take, and it is translated often as "to move forward, you must go back and retrieve your history." Gerima's film *Sankofa* embraces the speculative in a comparable fashion to Butler's novel, only Gerima displaces the modern-day, Black American protagonist from her role as a visitor at a Ghanaian slave castle through a "metaphoric Middle Passage between the nineteenth and twentieth centuries" and eventually relegates her to a plantation in the U.S. South, reinforcing the significance of slavery and the imagined homeland to the construction of Black American identity.[18] The film begins with a thundering male voice calling upon ancestral spirits to perform an intervention. A montage of images flashes across the screen, including plantation fields; a Black woman's face; and a male drummer, who is outfitted in seemingly traditional African garb and white body paint. The powerful male voice simultaneously commands the audience and the spiritual realm to "listen!" followed by an extended ancestral summons: "Ancestral spirits arise! Lingering spirit of the dead, rise up and possess your bird of passage. Those stolen Africans step out of the ocean from the wombs of the ships and claim your story. Spirit of the dead, rise up! Lingering spirit of the dead, rise up and possess your vessel."[19]

Here, the audience is alerted that ancestral spirits will embody a "vessel" through which to renarrativize the transatlantic slave trade and plantation slavery. The first action shot commences at a slave castle in Elmina, Ghana, and moves through the Middle Passage to a plantation and a maroon community, where the protagonist, Mona, learns historical lessons and undergoes intense physical trauma on her journey to embrace her ancestral past. Crucial to this discussion are how and why Mona is forced to travel as well as her eventual reappearance in the present. As the next scene commences, a bird of prey is shown perched in a tree as it watches the fishermen below in Ghana's Elmina community, a sight that Sylvie Kandé and Joe Karaganis suggest symbolizes "the souls of those deported Africans who sought a way back to Guinea and [alludes] to those birds that followed the bloody wakes of the slave ships."[20] The camera's gaze suddenly focuses on Mona, a Black American model, who wades through the Atlantic Ocean toward the shore. Once back on land, Mona begins a provocative photo shoot on the slave castle grounds. As she gyrates and poses for the photographer, the shot cuts between Mona and an older gentleman in white ceremonial body paint as he beats his drums and sings emphatically. Sonically, the drumming intensifies in relation to Mona's increasingly lewd performance, which is heightened by her animal print costuming. In the next portion of the photo session, Mona is outfitted in a modest Ghanaian garment made from kente fabric; her now elegant, reserved manner stands in stark juxtaposition to the demeanor that she asserted earlier.

Though Mona has toned down her actions in this latter shoot, an elderly man with an Adrinkra-designed sankofa staff approaches her and the photographer and stares at them angrily. Contextually, the viewer gathers that the Ghanaian elder is displeased by the pair's sexually suggestive and otherwise indecent behavior in a place that demands reverence. The elder again moves toward a startled Mona and gives her a fervent order in a local language—"Back to your past. Return to your source."—before rehearsing an elegy about the cruelty of slavery which stated in part: "They disgraced us, put us to shame. Go back. It is special ground."[21] A security officer abruptly ushers the elder off the premises after this confrontation, and a guide nearby nonchalantly explains to his white tour group members that the spectacle is one created by "Sankofa—a self-appointed guardian of the castle who claims to communicate to the ancestors through his drums." After Sankofa's charged reprimand to Mona, which is very much Gerima's insistence on the recuperation of a Pan-African politics as well as a renovation of Mona's individualistic mind-set, a curious Mona ventures tentatively into a slave dungeon, and what sounds like a voice-over providing a historical situation for the film's audience turns out to be a tour guide lecturing a group well ahead of Mona. As the final tourist turns the corner and slips from Mona's and the audience's sight, the light in the dungeon immediately diminishes, and a fire ignites to illumine the faces of shackled African men and boys who stare at Mona, prompting her to scream in horror and run toward what she believes to be an exit.

Mona's cries for help go unheard; the captives move slowly toward her as she pounds her fists desperately on a door until it opens, revealing a white slaver and his men who drag a resistant Mona, who had taken a few steps outside, back into the dungeon. She attempts to reason with them by disavowing her ancestral legacy: "You're making a mistake. Stop. I'm not an African . . . don't you recognize me? I'm Mona. I'm an American." The men ignore her protests, strip off her shirt and brand her back with a hot iron rod, indicating that she is not only an African in their eyes, but that she is also their property, human cargo to be loaded onto a ship and sent into the unknown. As Mona screams in horror, her pained voice becomes a piercing accompaniment to a recording of Aretha Franklin wailing a powerful rendition of the hymn "Precious Lord, Take My Hand," whose words plead for guidance from a higher power and parallel and intersect with Mona's Sonic distress. Mona then faints and is lifted up by the shackled men. In crafting Mona's rejection of her ties to Africa in such a sensory-driven fashion, Gerima emphasizes the necessity of maintaining a reverential posture on hallowed ground as well as demonstrates the shame and disconnection that some dispossessed descendants of slaves feel about the peculiar institution. In an interview about *Sankofa*, Gerima expressed his anguish regarding the seeming onslaught of negative critiques of post–civil rights Black American cultural production that explores the significance of Africa to Black lives:

> Why is society always running for cover when Africans in this country want to make linkage with Africa? . . . Eighty-nine percent of African-American men and women writers are dealing with Africa now. Are they trying to exorcise something out of their system? Is this a memory trying to gash out of their bodies? And why is it underestimated? It's been discouraged for years. . . . Being [an Ethiopian], I have always been amazed that whites panic when a Black person tries to link with Africa. . . . So, there is this continued tendency to belittle Black people's obsession, belittle Black people's fantasy. . . . Blacks have to create monuments, healing symbols, Nat Turners: they have to convey their variety and the truth of their history: they were nice; they also fought; they were lynched. This presentation of history shouldn't be shy; they shouldn't be afraid.[22]

Gerima's stance indicates that the creation of speculative cultural production, indeed, along with literal travels, remains a radical, self-reflexive way by which Black Americans reimagine history; engage with the imagined fantastic, spiritual memories within; and elide the borders of the American master narrative from which Black Americans and other people of color have been excluded. Thus, in the next scene, Gerima—bold and undeterred by those who dismiss engagements with Black speculative thought—mystically transitions Mona into the nineteenth-century house slave, Shola, on the Lafayette Plantation in an unnamed location in the U.S. South.

This sudden time travel is an unexplained feature of the film, but it harkens to a sense of cyclical time in which all that has happened in the past and all that will happen in the future is interrelated. The film's temporal upheaval allows Gerima to write against slavery, an institution that thrived on the dehumanization of Black people by attempting to modify them into machinelike, mindless beings. By way of Shola's harrowing experiences on the plantation, the audience discerns that Mona's psyche will become reconditioned with knowledge of her ancestral past and the sacrifices made to secure her freedom. The Mona/Shola embodiment can be read in two interrelated ways: the time travel serves as a corrective measure to equip Mona with a sense of the sacrifices made and brutality endured by her foreparents; and Mona and Shola are separate people on a diasporic temporal continuum whose past, present, and future are one. Because the extent of what the audience knows about Mona's life is limited to her modeling career and ignorance of the slave castle's sacredness, it is Shola's history—intertwined with Mona's—that composes the whole individual who is chronicled for the majority of the film.

Sankofa contains extended, graphic montages between scenes of a naked Shola being ogled, beaten, and/or raped by white men. These visceral images are intended to evoke a sense of shock and discomfort in the viewer and to force a particular emotional reaction to the film from its key intended audience—African diasporans. A notable example from the film occurs during a rebellion, when a group of enslaved persons burn acres of sugarcane and fight off their white enemies before the overseer and his men overwhelm them. Without identifying the actual culprits, the white men select a group of slaves of whom to make examples— whether they are guilty of arson matters not. As a warning to other slaves who may be considering running away or resisting in another manner, the overseer and his men hang up these ill-fated chosen slaves in wooden cages in the trees and starve them to death, leaving their bodies suspended to be picked apart by vultures. After observing this horrific scene, Shola attempts to flee to the safety of the hills, where escaped slaves had created a liberated community reminiscent of maroon and *quilombo* communities in the Caribbean and Brazil, respectively, but she is caught and dragged back to the Lafayette Plantation. At varying intervals in the narrative, brief flashbacks cut to explicit scenes of Shola being raped by her master, and it becomes evident that a combination of terrorizing experiences had prompted her flight. When the next scene opens, Shola is being prepared for her punishment; she is stripped naked with her hands tied above her head, and her owner whips her mercilessly as a priest performs an exorcism, demanding that Shola proclaim her allegiance to

Jesus Christ. Shola's love interest, Shango, named after the Yoruba warrior god, remains helpless outside.

Apart from its portrayal of the sexualized nature of religious violence, this scene captures a moment in which an enslaved woman's sonic distress is actively listened to by a male counterpart who, if he desires to live, is unable to intervene due to the strictures of the geography of containment. Gerima offers an interesting reimagining of a primal scene of violence on a Black woman who dared to take control of her own body, recalling a moment in Frederick Douglass's autobiographical fugitive slave narrative in which Douglass observed his Aunt Hester stripped and beaten by Captain Anthony for meeting with her lover.[23] At the outset of *Scenes of Subjection*, Saidiya Hartman refers to the brutal beating of Douglass's Aunt Hester—a definitive act that reveals to Douglass how slavery produces slaves, contains Black bodies, and emasculates Black men—but Hartman refuses to quote directly from that particular moment of brutality so as to not reproduce the violence.[24] Indeed, several authors have differed on how they imagine the function and necessity of including such violent episodes. Hartman's monograph instead offers a remarkable examination of the violence inherent in moments of quotidian slave life and considers "those scenes in which terror can hardly be discerned—slaves dancing in the quarters, the outrageous darky antics of the minstrel stage, the constitution of humanity in slave law, and the fashioning of the self-possessed individual."[25] Hartman's refusal and ultimate decision to look "elsewhere" ultimately causes her to "[run] right back to" that which is refused.[26] It seems to follow, then, that it would have been a futile exercise for Gerima to craft his representations in *Sankofa* with solely subtle references to the sadistic beatings heaped on slavery-era Black bodies through dialogue between characters, for example, as the institution of slavery was maintained through and would likely have been impossible to carry out without physical force and the wholesale restriction of Black mobility. Objections could, of course, be raised about whether Gerima is gratuitous in his creative decision to include several instances of extreme violence, but such complaints tend to be a matter of viewer preference (and perhaps varying levels of spectator discomfort) as opposed to a critical flaw in Gerima's speculative narrative or in the reasoning behind his radical call to diasporans.

Shola's punishment for attempting to take control over her body also recalls a critical moment in the early pages of *Kindred*, when Dana recounts observing white patrollers humiliating a married couple who had to covertly visit each other. After kicking down the cabin door, vigilante night riders wrench the husband and wife from their beds, physically and verbally assaulting their naked bodies. Dana, who was in search of her relatives when she encounters the patrollers, is in a precarious situation since she, like the husband, is a truant from the plantation. Dana lies quietly in a cluster of bushes nearby and is forced to witness the repercussions for one taking license over his body as a fugitive. Dana recounts her reaction to the family's patriarch being tied to a tree and whipped in front of his wife and child:

> I could literally smell his sweat, hear every ragged breath, every cry, every cut of the whip. I could see his body jerking, convulsing, straining against the rope as his screaming went on and on. My stomach heaved, and I had to force myself to stay where I was and keep quiet. Why didn't they stop! . . . I had seen people beaten on television and in the movies. I had seen too-red blood substitute streaked across their backs and heard their well-rehearsed screams. But I hadn't lain nearby and smelled their sweat or heard them pleading and praying, shamed before their families and themselves. I was probably less prepared for the reality than the child crying not far from me. (36)

Historically, it was often the case that enslaved persons were forced to observe the spectacle of public whippings as the overseer's means of maintaining an atmosphere of fear and curbing instances of truancy and attempts at permanent flight. Most striking here is the way in which the sight and the immediacy of physical harm paralyze Dana. She is not forced to look because the vigilantes do not know that she is there, but she is compelled by the scene; lived experience of the dehumanization and humiliation that maintained slavery allows her to access the root of how shame became associated with the institution. In several neo-slave narratives, indignities are suspended at various junctures in the story line and occasionally by the end of the film or text, particularly when the enslaved population revolts or triumphs over the oppressor in some way. Chronic dishonor is why—in other forms of travel, especially in the cultural roots tourism analyzed herein—Black Americans are attracted to such triumphalist narratives as Ghana's independence story as well as to the spiritual persistence of Africa as it is thought to exist throughout the diaspora. When there is shame, there is often silence and the desire to be separate or to detach oneself from what is perceived as docility or weakness in the face of bodily injury. Shame is sometimes a trait of the slave and his descendant; Black American authors writing in the post-1965 period have traveled back fantastically to the era of the slave trade to attend to and write against that sentiment.

Gerima's narrative logic and political project, then, are manifold. As Kara Keeling posits, on the one hand, "Mona is decolonized, sent to experience the violence of slavery so that she can be reborn as an African"; on the other hand, "the [African-descended] spectators must be made to experience Mona's experience of slavery in such a way that the colonial models occupying the spectators' optic nerves can be extricated so that their minds can be returned to their supposedly original African state."[27] Unlike the other texts examined here thus far, the ideology that guides the sankofic process very much extends from individualistic concerns to the development of a more Pan-Africanist sensibility, while also ensuring that audience members of other ethnicities are endowed with a better appreciation of the humanity of African-descended peoples. After her brutal exorcism, Shola readily participates in communal life with the other slaves, including their various acts of resistance and rebellion as well as their engagements with traditional African religiosity, which she had only hesitantly expressed interest in previously—the guilt from her Catholic upbringing had haunted and thereby confused her path to radicalism.

Concomitant to the commencement of the major slave insurrection in *Sankofa*, a flash-forward depicts a naked Mona exiting the dungeon and Shola in the field fending off sexual advances from the slave master. A defiant Shola uses a machete to stab her owner repeatedly before she takes flight on foot to escape the slave catchers who attempt to track her down with bloodhounds and gunfire. In a voice-over, she narrates that disembodied voices encouraged her to keep moving although she grew tired: "'Keep on running, sister! Run, run, run.' This big buzzard was flying next to me; he spread his wings and swooped me up and up and up—just like what Shango said." The camera angle shifts to a God's-eye position, with the buzzard hoisting Shola (and the viewer) over the ocean as fade-ins appear of Sankofa performing an intense incantation while beating his drums fervently. Shola's flight here alludes to the Flying Africans myth in that it serves as an extraordinary display of a rejection of enslavement, demonstrates a desire to return home to Africa, and signals that Mona's metamorphosis is complete. In the next scene, Mona/Shola reappears in the filmic present moment, naked and crying through the slave dungeon door and into the arms of an older woman who tells her, "My child, welcome back. Embrace me." In theatrical fashion, Mona shouts "Mama" and falls into the woman's arms for comfort. This melodramatic moment is symbolic of a rebirth through the canal as Mona exits the dungeon and cries uncontrollably until she is consoled by the Mother Africa figure and covered with a piece of cloth. *Sankofa* thus ends with a born-again Mona, walking past her photographer as if she does not know him—an act that serves as a rejection of the West and a sign that she has gone through a transformation, though the viewer does not have enough information to determine the extent of her change or whether the original Mona/Shola embodiment had perished as a result of the overseer's gunfire to make way for the new descendant who emerges from the dungeon.

What is clear from Gerima's narrative logic is that returns to the past have the potential to render the dispossessed African whole; that is, "the film presents slavery as that which must be exorcised in order for the African to continue the process of his historical progress, which was interrupted by slavery."[28] Near the end of the film, Mona joins a group of Black tourists seated next to the griot, Sankofa, on the expanse of the slave castle dungeon. Mona approaches Sankofa and gazes at him reverently, then takes her place among the visitors. The final glance is important here: when the newly reborn Mona/Shola looks over her shoulder, she recognizes a woman who appears to be Nunu, a former slave of Ghanaian descent from the Lafayette Plantation, who had died in the past. A tear trickles down Nunu's face as she nods affirmatively when she sees Mona/Shola, who may or may not have crossed into the spirit realm during her final flight away from slave catchers. This quiet recognition ends the film on a hopeful note that cyclical histories ensure the omnipresence of the ancestors. To the imaginary that actuates cultural roots tourism and expatriation, neo-slave narratives such as *Kindred* and *Sankofa* confirm that lived experience can bring one closer to repossessing one's imagined origins and perhaps even render one African.

Ghostly Interventions: Dreamscapes, Ceremony, and Rebirth

As sedimented traces of the memory of slavery and the Middle Passage, the ancestors and spirits are multiply-located. They wait across the ocean, in Guinée, where the souls of the displaced and dispersed living return upon their death. They rest under the waters of the Atlantic, where captive Africans drowned themselves in an ultimate rejection of the conditions of social death. They reside in the *hounfo, candomblé, and ilé,* whose allegiance they are owed, and in the minds and bodies of their people, whom they mount.
—Sara Kaplan, "Souls at the Crossroads, Africans on the Water"

Ancestors in the Black American literary tradition typically are developed as haunting figures whose coetaneous presence and absence "stand for that which cannot be disappeared but remains, sedimented in the bodies of the living and the dead, in communities and in nations, producing a spatial memory of a past that is not over and must be confronted."[29] In Marshall's *Praisesong for the Widow,* the protagonist, Avey Johnson, begins a spiritual transformation during a drawn-out physical fight with her deceased great-great-aunt Cuney, with whom she had spent her childhood summers learning stories about her family's history on the sea islands of South Carolina.[30] The narrative conflict commences with Avey's physical struggle with this recent ancestor that occurs as part of a recurring dream that is interspersed with flashbacks from her childhood, during which she and her Aunt Cuney shared in the retelling of family stories. A significant tale in Avey's family's exercise of rememory is the story of the Ibo Africans, who, upon landing on the shores of the fictional Tatem, South Carolina, to begin their new lives as slaves, made an immediate, radical decision to walk across the Atlantic Ocean back to their homelands. As she ages, Avey begins to question the validity of the family myth and asks, "but how come they didn't drown?," a query that casts disappointment and grief upon her Aunt Cuney, whose own grandmother had witnessed the Ibos' rejection of slavery and "took off after 'em. In her mind. Her body she always usta say might be in Tatem. But her mind, her mind was long gone with the Ibos" (39). As an adult, Avey ignores her Aunt Cuney's instruction to return "home" by adjusting her mind-set to align with the Ibo ideology. During Avey's terrifying dream sequences, Aunt Cuney becomes physical, grabbing Avey by the wrist and dragging her toward the landing on the sea islands. The increasing intensity of this recurring dream and Avey's severe bodily pain upon waking, combined with food poisoning and bouts of paranoia and hallucinations, eventually drive Avey to abandon her friends on their Caribbean cruise for the comforts of her extravagant New York home. The narrator explains Avey's resistance to her Aunt Cuney's pleas: "in instilling the story of the Ibos in her child's mind, the old woman [Aunt Cuney] had entrusted her with a mission she couldn't even name yet had felt duty-bound to fulfill. It had taken years to rid herself of the notion" (42). If ancestral spirits had sent Mona to the plantation for her disregard of and detachment from the memory of slavery in *Sankofa*, it is Avey's shame and willing disavowal of a known ancestral past through her full assimilation into Western culture, which is marked by its emphasis on the individual's accumulation of material wealth, that catapults her journey throughout *Praisesong for the Widow*. Barbara Christian finds that Avey's psychic compass is calibrated initially such that her conscious movements drift away from rather than toward an African sensibility, though her "unconscious run for freedom takes her south, physically South to Caribbean, psychically South to Tatem, South Carolina, while consciously she believes her promised land to be North, her safe comfortable home in North White Plains."[31]

I have illustrated thus far that dispossession has the potential to cause a sense of spiritual fragmentation. However, such an unsettled existence can be attended to by embracing rememory and invention, the piecing together of histories in service of resisting cultural bankruptcy, emptiness, wayward movement, and longing. *Praisesong for the Widow* and Harris's *É Minha Cara*, with which I opened this chapter, attend to fragmentation through the rejection of the materiality of the West and the sacred intervention of ancestors and deities as experienced through intradiasporic travel. Initially through force, physically disturbing dreams and hallucinations, and psychically haunting presences, the protagonists—Avey and Harris, respectively—come to understand that lying prostrate before the ancestors and religious deities enables a kind of rebirth, though this deference and movement closer to imagined Africas does not wholly undo diasporic loss.

The majority of *Praisesong for the Widow* focuses on Avey's attempts to escape what she suspects is a mental breakdown by fleeing her Grenadian vacation, which she is not able to accomplish until she submits to a period of spiritual restoration and ritual. In the process outlined by the narrative, she transitions from recreational to cultural roots tourist through a complicated conflation of further dream sequences, including the liberation of her unconscious and the attendance of and participation in ceremonies. Hobbled by six pieces of luggage, Avey is well into her trek to the airport when she discovers that the town has virtually shut down for the day, save a growing line of people waiting to board a set of dilapidated boats. She is recognized by a few of the travelers as someone who belongs in their queue, but a taken-aback Avey, whose focus is on returning to New York as soon as possible, eventually finds a taxi and discovers in her conversation with the driver that the people she encountered on the dock were out-islanders who had chosen to live and work on the mainland but return en masse to their Carriacou roots each year to pay homage to their ancestors and culture. The section that follows, titled "Sleeper's Wake," consists of a dream sequence that occurs as Avey rests at a hotel overnight before her flight home. Avey's deceased husband, Jay, who had ridiculed Tatem as primitive and backward and encouraged Avey's rejection of Black culture as they ascended to an upper-middle-class lifestyle in White Plains, is the central figure with whom she grapples throughout the sequence. By the time she has revisited the entirety of their marital relationship in this dreamscape, she awakens and literally strips herself naked of the fancy accouterments that represent the materialism for which she had sacrificed her heritage. This fitful, forced rememory in which Avey's "mind [is] in one place while her body is in another" forces her to deal with the guilt that she has long repressed.[32]

To rid herself of the memories conjured by the previous night's dreams, Avey takes a walk on the beach until the landscape transitions into undeveloped territory outside of the tourism border, where she meets the nonagenarian Lebert Joseph, a barkeep who is preparing to leave for an excursion. Avey confides to Lebert that she has been experiencing horrific, realistic visions about her Aunt Cuney, and the elderly gentleman knowingly explains that ancestors will "turn your life around in a minute, you know. All of a sudden everything gon' wrong and you don' know the reason. . . . Is the Old Parents, oui. They's vex with you over something. Oh, they can be disagreeable, you see them there. Is their age, oui, and the lot of suffering they had to put up with in their day. We has to understand and try our best to please them" (165). Avey, Lebert explains, would need to participate in the excursion that he and the out-islanders she had seen the day before would be attending, as it would provide a way to assuage her ancestor's haunting persistence. Lebert's advice is prompted in large part by Avey's answer to his query, "And what you is? What is your nation?" (166–67), which highlights Avey's sense of failure at not passing down what she knows of her family's heritage and also a further degree of shame, as she possesses no knowledge of her ancestral nation or familial origins like Lebert does. The Beg Pardon portion of the pilgrimage served as a sacramental rite of forgiveness for wrongs as well as a dance during which community members and the out-islanders take turns performing the dances of their respective tribe. Based on her status as a natally alienated diasporan with no knowledge of her ancestral nation, Avey is informed that she would not be able to participate until the creole dance, in which anyone could participate. Avey expresses grief about her rootlessness, to which Lebert responds, "You's not the only one, oui. . . . That's why when you see me down on my knees at the Big Drum singing the Beg Pardon, I don't be singing just for me. Oh, no! Is for *tout moun'* . . ." (174–75). At the moment Avey accepts Lebert's invitation, he transitions into an intermediary between Avey and the old souls, and it is through what began as a chance meeting that Avey reconciles with her past.

One of the significant threads that this encounter with Lebert unveils about Black American travel toward Africa is that loss and shame are heightened by the belief that diasporic counterparts located closer to the Africa in their imaginations have been able to maintain a pristine or more authentic cultural sense than the travelers have. As will be explored in subsequent chapters centered in Bahia and Ghana, rituals such as those found in *Praisesong*'s Carriacou include visits to spiritual houses of Afro-Brazilian Candomblé as well as through Ghanaian naming ceremonies and offerings to the ancestors. These complex, cross-cultural engagements are contingent upon what Joseph Roach calls the "kinesthetic imagination," wherein memory is transmitted through multiple forms of movement and "inhabits the realm of the virtual. Its truth is the truth of simulation, of fantasy, or of daydreams, but its effect on human action may have material consequences of the most tangible sorts and of the widest scope. This faculty, which flourishes in that mental space where imagination and memory converge, is a way of thinking through movements—at once remembered and reinvented—the otherwise unthinkable, just as dance is often said to be a way of expressing the unspeakable."[33] It is through the fantastic convergence of the imagination and longing that Avey's mind/body cleansing progresses as she endures a series of movements leading to the voyage to Carriacou. During her rest upon the antiquated water craft, Avey dreams of her childhood church in Tatem, a memory elicited by a group of women who sat near Avey and Lebert on the boat; the women, who remind her of elder women from that church, immediately gather that Avey is not feeling well and organically take responsibility for watching over her. In her dream, Avey has a recollection of an Easter Sunday service in which the pastor admonishes those who have embraced the "shameful stone of false values" and have "done buried your spirit, your heart, your minds, shutting you off from the precious light of salvation" (200). Taking on the physical being of her child self who sat in church feeling a gradual sickness from overindulgence in Easter chocolates, (young) Avey attempts to fend off the urge to vomit as the pastor's voice thunders and the call and response from the congregation shakes the church. Senior Avey, who soon realizes that the contents of her dreamscape are affected by the rough boat ride, awakens and vomits uncontrollably before shocking herself further by relieving her bowels. Symbolically, she is ridding her old self of the Christian "stones" that were blocking the transition through which the ancestors were taking her via the spiritual liaison, Lebert. When the purging ceases, the group of elder women assists Lebert in moving the barely conscious Avey to a bunk in the small deckhouse so that she can properly rest for the remainder of the journey. As Avey regains consciousness, she imagines that she is aboard a slave ship during the Middle Passage, as she is confused and incapacitated by a physically restricting area, experiences grave discomfort, and the stench that she has helped create further nauseates her. The sensory excess of the space heightens Avey's imagination and connects her sonically to the lamentations of slaves crossing the Middle Passage: "Their moans, rising and falling with each rise and plunge of the schooner, enlarged upon the one filling her head. Their suffering—the depth of it, the weight of it in the cramped space—made hers of no consequence" (209).

In *É Minha Cara*, Harris also seeks out diasporan spiritual religiosity, but in a more intentional manner than Avey does. Harris spent his childhood mostly in the Bronx, New York, but he moved with his mother and brother to Dar es Salaam, Tanzania, where his mother taught for two years as a professor. His mother explains this temporary expatriation: "We thought of Africa as home because we knew that America didn't want us. Although we lived here, we fought for our rights here. . . . We thought of Africa as some place that would love us as we loved her." Instead of enrolling in a private international school, Harris elected to attend public school with Tanzanian children, and this direct, everyday contact brought a sacred connection to the surface, which eventually made him feel "something other than American," perhaps an "American African." When Harris and his family returned to the United States, his mother married a South African freedom fighter, and their lives were immersed in Pan-African activism. A sense that Africa offered emancipating, unifying, and regenerative possibilities, then, remained in his familial consciousness.

As mentioned above, Harris had for some time questioned his childhood religious worship of a white Jesus Christ in the African Methodist Episcopal church, and when his faith does not offer him sufficient answers about the existence of the ghostly presences that haunt his dreams, he begins a journey of discovery. An acquaintance assists Harris on his quest for a more authentic spiritual identity by analyzing his dreams through the lens of the syncretic religion Candomblé, a mixture of religious beliefs that slaves brought from Africa and the Catholic beliefs of the European slave master. After he receives the Candomblé-inspired interpretation of his dreams, Harris concludes: "My mission was clear. To find what I was looking for, I had to go to Brazil. I have to follow the path where the spirit takes me." Notable about this mythopoetic documentary is that he is able to articulate his grandparents' and mother's histories and understanding of their dispossession through interviews, family pictures, and omnipresent voice-overs (typically spoken by Harris), which provide the narration, but the composition of each scene is also intriguing and haunting.

THE HEALING

The denouements of *Praisesong for the Widow* and *É Minha Cara* place the protagonists at ceremonial sites in which ancestral, ghostly presences are summoned. Lebert's daughter bathes a recovering Avey in a symbolic rebirth that prepares Avey for participation in the evening's Beg Pardon, while Harris travels to the northeastern Brazilian state of Bahia to convene with the Candomblé deities first by attending a ceremony during Carnival and later by placing offerings to the orixas during the Festa de Yemanjá, a reverent celebration of the orixa who controls all bodies of water and is syncretized with the Virgin Mary. What Avey witnesses in the kinesthetic imaginations of the out-islanders is life changing, though she recognizes the improvisation and the firm grip with which the dispossessed hold on to and even create their "remembered" pasts:

> All that was left were a few names of what they called nations which they could no longer even pronounce properly, the fragments of a dozen or so songs, the shadowy forms of long-ago dances and rum kegs for drums. The bare bones. The burnt-out ends. And they clung to them with a tenacity she suddenly loved in them and longed for in herself. Thoughts—new thoughts—vague and half-formed slowly beginning to fill the emptiness. . . . The theme of separation and loss the note embodied, the unacknowledged longing it conveyed summed up feelings that were beyond words, feelings and a host of subliminal memories that over the years had proven more durable and trustworthy than the history with its trauma and pain out of which they had come. (240–45)

Certainly, not every dispossessed traveler experiences spiritual fulfillment as quickly as Avey, if ever. This is in part because Avey's evolution is a kind of spiritual repossession: a process that includes forced rememory and a recovery of Avey's Gullah usable past, rather than a case in which the diasporan has absolutely no access to or known connection with historical remnants of her ancestors and attempts to reclaim traces from the imagined source. This journey also, as Abena Busia deftly observes, "reverses the location of the promised land, which now, rather than being in the United States as represented in the prosperity of the plantations or, today, the Fulton street of [her husband's] success, becomes Africa as represented by Carriacou."[34] The Black American travel narrative toward Africa indeed depends on these moments of identification in which a known or perhaps a "long forgotten fragment [drifts] up to imprint itself" on the traveler's imagination (225).

As Harris prepares for his quest for recognition in Bahia, he reveals that he feels as if his "body had been on ice since [he] left Tanzania" as a child—that he could not express openly his Africanized identity without ridicule because his childhood peers in the United States were ashamed of their African roots and believed in the negative, primitive images created for them in various forms of popular media. It is in the orixas and their duality—syncretized spiritual gods with ties to African religions and Catholic saints—that Harris sees himself. Avey, by contrast, found a significant moment of recognition vis-à-vis the continuity in the creole dance at the Beg Pardon, where the shuffling feet of the creole-identified peoples reminded her of the ring shout practiced in Tatem. In a gesture to suggest that Avey had come full circle with her ancestors, Marshall describes Avey's performance as one steeped in cultural memory that prompts her to dance as if "the ground under her was really water" (248). This, of course, is emblematic of her reclamation of Africa and demonstrates her alignment with her family's version of the Ibo Flying African myth, which inspired and informed the spiritual and cultural paths embraced by her more recent foremothers.

For Harris, it is spirituality that "soothes [his] aching heart" early in his visit; as he journeys throughout northeast Brazil, Harris identifies unifying elements (despite diasporan cultural differences) that suggest that he has found Africa in a way that he can understand. In the bare-bone "voices of the drums" during the Brazilian Carnival, Harris narrates, "I felt the orixas touching me and I wanted to reach out and touch them back, but which orixa holds the key to my salvation?" Jorge, an Afro-Brazilian, becomes Harris's guide to Bahia's spiritual world, though Jorge remains skeptical of Harris's motives: "Is that all you're looking for? Aren't you really searching for a connection to a world that no longer exists—like all the other Black Americans who come to Bahia in search of their roots?" Harris does not answer Jorge's question regarding his rather apparent desire to move closer to a primeval African homeland, but he tacitly addresses the query throughout the remainder of the film, as his journey is not complete until Jorge educates him about Blackness in Brazil, accompanies him to ceremonies, and guides him on a boat ride to Praia Grande, where he states that one can see the real "African face of Brazil." During his trip to Praia Grande, a *mãe-de-santo* (or Candomblé priestess) reads her cowrie shells to determine which orixas protect Harris. She reveals that Yemanjá is the presence that had been visiting Harris in his dreams since he was a child and Xangô, the orixa of justice, was the orixa who had opened his paths, dictating Harris's travels and presenting him with surrogate guides along the way. Perhaps the most poignant moment of the documentary occurs after the priestess reveals that Oxalá, the deity of creation and king of the orixas who is syncretized with Jesus Christ, is Harris's guardian. At this point of the film, the still shot of the mãe-de-santo dissolves into an image of Harris's aging grandmother, whose fair complexion and narrow facial features happen to resemble those of the Bahian priestess, concretizing that Candomblé offers a way for him to reconcile his Christian roots and the pull of the African spiritual realm through the gods of duality in the Yoruba religious pantheon.

É Minha Cara concludes in a manner that indicates the potential healing, liberating powers of intradiasporic ritual experiences, carefully treading the line to ensure that it is clear that there are limits to the possibilities of return travels. The reclamation and generational repetition of familial stories and ancient spirituality, as shown by Marshall and Harris, arms dispossessed individuals with a foundation that allows them the possibility to endure despite social alienation. At the conclusion of his documentary, Harris articulates his belief that "for us children of the diaspora, the terrible rupture of slavery continually opens up new possibilities. Could we not begin by returning to the ancient gods?" In this question, there is a sense of optimism that the diasporan might be able to begin healing the wounds associated with the original dispersal through African spiritual restoration. And the last line of the film—"One kid points to my face and says 'É minha cara.' He looks like me."—solidifies Bahia as the source of the necessary recognition and sustenance.

Evidence of the African past is attractive for tourists who are intent on making connections outright as well as for those who have unintended cathartic moments. These literal diasporan treks are not necessarily about traversing a particular physical geography, contemporary realities, or a temporal moment that is long past. Movements toward "a world that is no longer there," as Jorge presumed about Harris's desire for possessing Africa in Bahia, are about the locating and gathering of fragments—it is the positioning of oneself to witness, receive, and perhaps embody the essence of the long dead with hopes of recovering a portion of that which (before forced flight) had been deemed lost permanently. In significant moments of coalescence between texts, the sound reverberating from drums summons the ancestors in *Sankofa*; at the Beg Pardon in *Praisesong*, the rhythms emanating from the keg drums stand in for Africa, articulating through a dark, "plangent note" the innermost desires, aurally speaking the "separation . . . unacknowledged longing" with sounds intimating the "distillation of a thousand sorrow songs" (245). The pitch of the Bahian Carnival drum corps's cadence, too, resonates—it mediates the intensity of the physical exchange that has been occurring between Harris and the deities for years. Actively mourning and denouncing the rendering of the past as resolved politicizes these flights of the imagination, as suggested in Marshall's description of the unnamed actor driving the percussive rhythm of the Beg Pardon: "After centuries of forgetfulness and even denial, they refused to go away. The note was a lamentation that could hardly have come from the rum keg of a drum. Its source had to be the heart, the bruised still-bleeding innermost chamber of the collective heart" (245). Marshall's usage of "they" is indicative of the ancestors' persistent presence and the worshippers' insistent dedication to their rememory as they dance reverently in the textual present; as separate entities, the participants and ancestors reembody each other, marking the circuitousness of African diasporic time. Avey's and Harris's dreamscapes occur within the diaspora, where identifications are possible and rituals provide them clarity. In the case of actual movements within the African continent, misrecognitions can be staggering.[35]

Homeland Returns: Misrecognitions and the Native Stranger

Post-1965 Black American nonfiction cultural production has tended to reimagine the plantation and other major sites of the peculiar institution, refiguring slavery in an effort to democratize master narratives regarding American progress and freedom.[36] While these movements are connected to and create a sort of speculative coupling with homeland returns, the latter are rendered fantastic in the returnees' utilization of travel to reclaim and engage with slavery's past as well as through the employment of their imagination in their yearning for and actualization of contact with the ghostly. Returns to the imagined beginning are radical in their rejection of the reality that has been constructed for Afro-Atlantic peoples, as "there is no future in the New World . . . death is the only future."[37] Death in this sense denotes the condition of literal lifelessness, social exclusion, constant fear of violence, and unwarranted retributions for simply being Black that render the possibility of social life nearly unfeasible.

In her conceptualization of rememory, Toni Morrison expresses, through the voice of the protagonist, Sethe, perhaps the most significant explanation of how life, death, memory, and haunting function in Afro-Atlantic speculative epistemologies: "Places, places are still there. If a house burns down, it's gone, but the place—the picture of it—stays, and not just in my rememory, but out there, in the world. What I remember is a picture floating around out there outside my head. I mean, even if I don't think it, even if I die, the picture of what I did, or knew, or saw is still out there. Right in the place where it happened." [38] The Afro-Atlantic ideas of return and rememory strike me as substantial exercises of Afro-Atlantic speculation whereby travel, escape, and mourning are taken up as forms of resistance against the narrative of progress and the supposed healing properties of the passage of time, of forgetting; they are not backward-looking weaknesses or pathologies. The declaration that all that has happened before remains where it occurred lends credence to the act of making speculative flights in service of reuniting with ancestral foreparents. Inasmuch as dispossession is about the loss of ties to ancestry, return is often figured in cultural production as a means by which to attend to the dishonor experienced as a result of the inherited, if only residual, slave condition. Speculative flights have been crucial to Black Americans precisely because "for the slave [descendant], freedom begins with the consciousness that real life comes with the negation of his social death."[39]

To address and thereby reverse social alienation—a condition that suggests permanence in the Western sense of finite temporal beginnings and endings—post–civil rights Black American literature about homeland returns has trended in two principal ways: didactic texts that stress reverence for and interactions with the ancestors as necessary to the protagonist's identity formation; and experimental texts whose methodology relies on fragmentation and uncertainty to portray the diasporan condition, which prefigures the problematic border at which diaspora and Pan-African politics fracture. What is most striking in the more contemporary texts is the intent of the traveler, in the present moment, to go back in time to reckon with a heritage thought to be long lost but retrievable. The tension in many pilgrimage accounts lies in the desire for what once was, when the imagined origin point has not been simply frozen in time. The time-travel methods described above attest to the difficulty of the diasporan's quest to remember the past by going back. In fact, even the fiction writer depends on the supernatural and/or overt mental debilitation to allow characters to wrestle with their imagined loss. Real-life travelers have no such powers, though many describe spiritual moments in which the ancestor is felt, which compel them to traverse the imagined homeland full of hopes for catharsis.

Black American nonfiction travel writers are criticized often for being too idealistic about the centrality of returning to Africa. Perhaps overly concerned about the importance of objectivity in travel accounts, John Gruesser, for instance, argues that these narratives tend to fall into one of two extreme categories—dream or nightmare—depending on whether the traveler's expectations are met or disappointed. He surmises that some of these authors resort to an Africanist rhetoric which, once tested on the ground, results in their imitating the colonial mentality of many European narratives about travel in Africa, only he finds that Black Americans bring "a romanticized preconception of the continent; when Africa refuses to live up to their expectations, these writers become disillusioned with it and alienated from it."[40] While Gruesser is correct in his observation that misconceptions occur during homeland journeys, my analysis seeks to move beyond the debates about gauging whether what the travel writer presents is objective and if what she feels is authentic. The critique of literary homeland returns is perhaps emblematic of the nature of the genre and expectations that readers and scholars endow Black American authors with, in general. The strictures of travel writing and self-reflexivity pose the risk of debilitation for diasporan authors whose personal engagements and expectations certainly color the framing of their narratives. As a canon, Black American literature generally has been expected to be as solidly political and instructive as it is entertaining to its audience. Travels toward geographic and imagined Africas, however, often prompt more questions and confusion than firm proclamations.

To engage with one of Gruesser's examples and illustrate the transition made in texts about migrations initiated during the post-1965 period, I will briefly discuss Angelou's autobiographical *All God's Children Need Traveling Shoes*, which chronicles the author's expatriation to Ghana in the early 1960s, a turbulent yet crucial period during the civil rights struggle in the United States and an era of newly won freedom for numerous sub-Saharan African nations. Postindependence Ghana experienced a hopeful moment rife with radical activity that was instructive and inspiring to the movement in the United States. Though published some twenty years after Angelou's two-year exile, *All God's Children* portends the significance that Pan-African unification would have after civil rights legislation had been passed. While assisting her son in his relocation to Accra, Angelou becomes enraptured by the peoples and cultures of Ghana, but she is soon struck by the one-sided recognition. In her haste to realize a sense of homecoming, Angelou makes the mistake of reading Ghanaians as kin because of their skin color, while most Ghanaians read her as simply a foreigner. She and many other Black American expatriates attempted to repossess Africa, though most Ghanaians did not welcome them or consider their respective quests for liberty related. Angelou laments this impasse: "At least we wanted someone to embrace us and maybe congratulate us because we had survived. If they felt the urge, they could thank us for having returned."[41] She explains that she and the other migrants rarely discussed their hurt at not being acknowledged as returnees by most Ghanaians; the émigrés, she confessed, simply "create[d] real places or even illusory places, befitting our imagination. . . . Since we were descendants of African slaves torn from the land, we reasoned we wouldn't be so arrogant as to take anything for granted. We would work and produce, then snuggle down into Africa as a baby nuzzles in a mother's arms" (19). This admission, romantic in its longing and tragic in its unrequitedness, occurs at the beginning of the text, setting the tone for the book—which is marked by Angelou's desire for recognition as well as her intent to illustrate how she came to the realization that she, like the Ghanaians who dismissed her kinship gestures, needed to acknowledge her ancestral past in a more concrete manner. For instance, as determined as Angelou is to connect with Ghanaians on the basis of possible distant linkages, she avoids the slave castle-dungeons along the coastline for the first year of her expatriation, as their presence unsettles her: "What did they think and feel, my grandfathers, caught on those green Savannahs, under the baobab trees? How long did their families search for them? Did the dungeon wall feel chilly and its slickness strange to my grandmothers who were used to the rush of air against bamboo huts and the sound of birds rattling their grass roofs? I had to pull off the road. Just passing near Cape Coast Castle had plunged me back into the eternal melodrama" (97). Angelou ponders the fate of her ancestors, descending into a spate of emotional unraveling. When she questions whether families had searched for their missing kin, she locates what is perhaps the source of a legacy of familial longing and underscores the intensity of her disappointment in having to create illusory Africas. Many of the exiles embraced the fantastic Pan-African ideal of working and producing together in Ghana to show their sincerity in returning; yet constant, dramatic refrains regarding reminders of slavery's past occur, illustrating the precariousness of homeland migrations and forecasting imminent issues with unification. On two subsequent occasions, however, Angelou is recognized during her travels throughout Ghana, which heartens her and sates her yearning for acceptance.

While traveling alone by car to Dunkwa, the hometown of an acquaintance, Angelou realizes that she is nearly out of fuel and that there is no hotel in the vicinity. She informs an unnamed woman about her predicament and is welcomed into the woman's village, where several people observe Angelou's manner and physical features and conclude that she is a member of the Bambara tribe from Liberia. Angelou does not bother to correct their assertion, admitting: "At that moment I didn't want to remember that I was an American. For the first time since my arrival, I was very nearly home. Not a Ghanaian, but at least accepted as an African. The sensation was worth a lie" (102). The second incident occurs as Angelou visits the Keta region. Several women in the community express their grief when Angelou arrives, placing their hands atop their heads in distress and keening at the sight of the familiar stranger. Angelou's friend explains that the women believe that Angelou is a descendant of their ancestors who had been forced into slavery. He interprets the women's grief by offering a history of slavery's impact on the village:

At one point every inhabitant was either killed or taken. The only escapees were the children who ran away and hid in the bush. Many of them watched from their hiding places as their parents were beaten and put into chains. They saw the slaves set fire to the village. They saw mothers and fathers take infants by their feet and bash their heads against tree trunks rather than see them sold into slavery. What they saw they remembered and all that they remembered they told over and over. . . . That is why they mourn. Not for you but for their lost people. (206)

These two instances of recognition, based on unprovable truths that are steeped in mutual yearning, assist Angelou in further historicizing the diaspora and understanding that the peoples and cultures of the African continent are changing constantly and not suspended in time waiting for long-lost kin to return. Important here is not just that she reminds the women of their ancestors visually, but also that their ancestral stories are remembered and retold. The cathartic moment at Keta, which Angelou describes as somber and pleasurable, occurs in their belated moment of communal mourning of the infanticides, murders, and kidnappings that nearly destroyed the village (206). As descendants of the orphans who successfully hid from the slave catchers, the Keta women weep for their literally stolen foreparents and, as her friend points out, "not for [Angelou]." This distinction is important in the admission that though Angelou's appearance prompts the mourners' tears, they are concerned with a specific past event and dead kin, while Angelou and other diasporans travel to sites of mourning burdened and affected by that very history of turmoil and strife in the present moment. *All God's Children* ends in a somewhat pat manner, which is common in this narrative form: the returnee goes back and experiences some deterrents, but his or her presence in the imagined homeland is in some fashion such that the traveler is redeemed by the conclusion and returns to the United States or remains in Africa better for having traveled. Most nonfiction narratives in the post–civil rights era, however, tend to focus more narrowly on ruptures in their explorations of the role of Africa in the returnee's sense of self.

Nonfiction travel writers have begun to complicate return narratives by openly discussing their journeys even when their stances are in flux and they question the viability of their diasporic visions concerning return.[42] Rather than structure their accounts as if the action is taking place in the present, these authors sometimes utilize a mixed narrative strategy in which the protagonist's voice offers the action in present tense, following up selected episodes with commentary based in part on what she had learned on the trip to the homeland. This analyzing reads as a form of self-correction ("How could I ever have been so romantic and mistaken about Africa?"), though these moments also can be enlightening about the linkages that the protagonist makes between an incident that occurs while on the pilgrimage and how she was raised or a particular pathology that she feels plagues the Black American community. Some of these authors battle a range of uncertainties while attempting to claim their ancestral homeland both spiritually and physically, often contradicting themselves in their sincere searches for more meaningful, tangible connections to the past. In her analysis of Black American tourism to the remnants of slave castle-dungeons in West Africa, Hartman gets to the crux of contemporary engagements with the legacy of slavery, particularly the ways in which temporal realities and the exercise of mourning shape the diasporan traveler's understanding of her movement: "Tears and disappointment create an opening for counterhistory, a story written against the narrative of progress. Tears reveal that the time of slavery persists in this interminable awaiting—that is, awaiting freedom and longing for a way of undoing the past. The abrasive and incommensurate temporalities of the 'no longer' and the 'not yet' can be glimpsed in these tears."[43] When diasporan travelers mourn at the various sites from which their ancestors were ripped, then, they participate in an iteration of the practice of diasporic melancholia in Africa, where the traveling protagonist much more actively seeks to produce evidence to counter the idea that slavery and African origins are and should be disconnected from how one speculates about present and future possibilities for Black social life.

Throughout his 1989 travel narrative *Native Stranger*, Eddy Harris's ambivalence is palpable through the contradictions and qualifications he expresses about his relationship to Africa.[44] While explaining his reasons for taking the year-long trip to several nations, Harris historicizes the pending journey as one for which Black Americans long because "the specter of Africa looms like the shadow of a genie, dormant but not altogether harmless, always there, heard about since childhood as some magnificent faraway world, a place of magic and wonder" (13). He further characterizes the journey as one that he hopes will help him define himself and find, in a fine moment of resonance with Thomas Harris in *É Minha Cara*, "the face of God, perhaps even [his] own face" (27). Eddy Harris no doubt desires to experience a mystical transformation that he purports lies solely in a pilgrimage to the continent, yet he disavows Africa at the same time by forcefully separating himself based on presumed cultural divergences. He frequently echoes variations of the refrain "I am not African" throughout his travelogue. To be a native stranger for Harris, then, is to have a sense of being from a place but not of that place. It is the state of being an outsider within, someone in limbo, a constant wanderer. This distinction is fascinating because it gets at the heart of a diasporan dilemma found in the texts discussed thus far. Typically, narratives romanticize return before the protagonist arrives in the homeland and perhaps arrive at midjourney or conclude with some of the contradictions Harris sets out as an introduction to his travels:

> So how does a Blackamerican [sic] travel to Africa? Certainly not as an African, for that I am not. Nor as a cultural European, for I am more than merely that. And more, too, than hybrid. Another race, perhaps, newborn and distinct, forged in the blast furnace of slavery, tempered and tested in the foundry of survival. We are an African people and perhaps we see the world and react to it differently. Perhaps we have different ideas about style and love, language and religion, and about the earth. At the same time we are an American people, products of new culture and defined by it. And we see the world through American eyes. I felt like Jekyll and Hyde. (28–29)

In his quest to "be African for a while," Harris sets off on an S-shaped trek across Africa where he chronicles in a journalistic manner the passing relationships that he forges with locals, run-ins with crooked policemen, and his reactions to poverty and cultural differences (35). Harris does not follow through with the goal of being African—there are no recollections of his participating in any ritual or ceremony, for instance—and he merely goes about life as a tourist who, at chance meetings, takes the opportunity to critically analyze Africa as it exists around him. This is not to say that Harris fails to cue the reader in on moments when he feels spiritual connections, however. Notably, he has an affinity for sound, collecting recordings of various African people singing as they go about their everyday lives with the hope that he will be able to "carry away a little piece of [their] soul" (113). In a rare moment in Senegal, he writes that he feels particularly linked to the place: "In bed I listened for the hypnotic rush of the sea and fell asleep. Suddenly, deep in the night, I woke up dancing. I was sitting up straight and I was bouncing, sleep-dancing in my dreams, to music I could not hear, to rhythms I could only feel.

Africa" (114). Just as he experiences this moment of belonging, there is also a sense of disconnection. When he calls a friend to tell him about his psychic awakening, Harris is informed about a recent case of brutal violence that resulted in the slaughter of a group of Senegalese people. Instantly, the spell of Africa, which had entranced him just hours before, lifts, and his prose takes on an unemotional tone that serves as a way to separate him from the continent.[45]

In the narrative immediately preceding his sleep-dance, Harris had opined that the "chains of slavery" caused an acute sense of loss—the lack of known names, history, ancestral linkages, dignity—that led to a sense of shame and self-hatred among a faction of the Black American community (107). With the so-called hardship of Africa "in his blood," he at once revels in the fact that it is no crime to be Black in Africa and in the almost certain possibility that someone exists on the continent who resembles him and that "when I find him, our hearts will shake hands" (36). For Harris, being African becomes less about longing for an origin or unification and more about the freedom of mobility that he possesses as an individual on the continent. A series of encounters with undesirable people along with societal disparities continues to cloud Harris's already tentative desire to belong, causing him to redefine perpetually his relationship to Africa:

> I could not go home again yet here I was. Africa was so long ago the land of my ancestors that it held for me only a symbolic significance. Yet there was enough to remind me that what I carry as a human being has come in part from Africa. I did not feel African, but was beginning to feel not wholly American anymore either. I felt like an orphan, a waif without a home. . . . The thought of running into someone who looked like a relative terrified me, for that would have been too concrete, too much proof. . . . I hardly knew what I was looking for, except perhaps to know where home once was, to know how much of being black has been carried out in Africa. . . . Africa is not easy. I love this place and resent it at the same time, and Africa reciprocates, trapped as we both are in this middle ground somewhere between black and white, past and future. (138–286)

Perhaps Harris's failed attempts to make what he deemed to be an expected connection are in part consequences of his insistence on remaining

intensely protective of his pride in the face of an endeavor rife with uncertainty. A striking aspect of this memoir is that Harris's journey to engage with his ancestors does not include an effusive meditation on the
slave castle-dungeon at Gorée Island in Senegal. In fact, the three pages
that Harris devotes to the most substantial symbol of his return—one
of the most significant sites that legitimizes the word *native* in this text's
title—offer a historical situation that highlights the importance of the
structure to the transatlantic slave trade in a detached manner. Compellingly, there is a tinge of disappointment in Harris's concluding thought
about the edifice: "Amid all the color, the old slave cells are somber now,
monuments to a history long forgotten in the never-ending onslaught of
life" (125). The island was surrounded by a river of blood and tears, Harris
maintained, and those who remained seemed to move on with their lives,
rendering the structure an irrelevant relic in the contemporary moment.
Was the symbol worthless without some sort of formal acknowledgment from those who remained at the site of origin? Hartman suggests
about such diasporan interactions with the imagined homeland that "it
was one thing to be a stranger in a strange land, and an entirely worse
state to be a stranger to yourself."[46] Indeed. Harris's text concludes am-
biguously, though his concentration on humanity, flight, and corporeal
liberty is remarkable:

> Africa is the birth[place] of mankind. Africa is the land of my ances-
> tors. But Africa is not home. I hardly know this place at all. . . . The
> sweetness lingers, leaving me with a desire to return here, to taste
> still more. . . . I do not feel a part of this place, it's true, nor a part of
> these people simply because of an accident of birth. I am not one of
> them. . . . I will go home to my world . . . no one will ask me for my
> identity papers. And the roads will be good. When I am tired of driv-
> ing, an airplane will be waiting to fly me somewhere else. I am lucky
> to live where I do. . . . But now when I do these things there will be
> second thoughts—I hope—for although I am not one of them, I really
> am one of them, the Arab and the Berber, the Bassar and the Bantu,
> and the Boer. There is a connection now, a real one—a racial one, to be
> sure, but more important, a human one. (314)

In the post-1965 era, authors and creators of cultural production have
also attempted to elide temporal boundaries and the impasses high-

lighted in Angelou's and Harris's travel memoirs to access deeper levels of contact with the past that connect it to the present and imagined futuristic moments—levels disallowed by the strictures of nonfiction and realism.

A return to the motherland proper, Senegal in particular, was necessary for the Black American author McKnight to feel as if he could begin re-creating himself at his imagined site of origin: "Here I was at sort of the pregenerative site of everything my ancestors, my forebears came from. I was in a place that really made me look at myself as a self that was individually unique, but also part of this enormous historical process."[47] Early in his academic exchange, McKnight became ill and was taken care of by the host couple with whom he lived. As he struggled with severe headaches and body pains, the wife nurtured him often by telling him stories in French and Wolof, which McKnight perceived to be folkloric myths, though he did not speak either language well enough to know for certain. During his illness, McKnight wrote through his discomfort, and the result became *I Get on the Bus*, a self-reflexive, fantastic novel that is inspired by his everyday experiences in Senegal as well as the stories that he imagines his caretaker imparted to him.[48] The manner in which McKnight describes his malady and his many trips aboard buses throughout Senegal is constructed in the novel as a metaphor for the persistent longing, pain, dislocation, and multifariousness of the diasporan condition. McKnight recalled about his illness, "You're kinda in a fever dream; you're in and out of consciousness all the time."[49] The fictionalizing of his real-life experiences allows McKnight to reimagine the possibilities in locating the cause of his seemingly diaspora-exacerbated psychosis. Through his experiences in Senegal, McKnight determines that for the diasporan, "the point [of traveling to Africa] is not to be there for your comfort, but for your growth."[50] McKnight, fictionalized as the protagonist, Evan Norris, and the reader travel through a speculative exploration of the psychic, compellingly lending clarity to the mind-set of displaced persons who attempt to return to their imagined ancestral beginnings.

I Get on the Bus opens with the protagonist's corporeal incapacitation and severe mental instability: "I am not here. I am missing. I would scream, but I have no language for screaming. There is too much to see. I am blind. I am deaf. I cannot breathe. I cannot breathe. I cannot breathe. My head hurts. The bus stops. I get off. I walk. How odd that I can walk" (7). As Evan's positionality slowly is uncovered, we learn that he is suffocating under the intensity of his relocation to Senegal, though he has been in the country for three months. His new surroundings present a physical and psychological attack on his being such that he is unable to adjust. Evan had become ill with what is probably cerebral malaria, but throughout the text, he refuses treatment, preferring to struggle with painful headaches, bouts of dizziness, and hallucinations. Oddly, Evan revels in the discomfort: "There is something enriching about this pain. There is something very, very intriguing about it. It is doing something to me. And I will not take my medicine until I find out precisely what it is. I will not leave Africa until I know what it is. I will keep ambling down to Dakar until I know what it is" (15). Evan had traveled to Senegal on a Peace Corps assignment that was not going well. A few months into his job, Evan found his position as an English instructor so unsatisfying that he regularly skipped classes and half-heartedly taught when he showed up because he felt that the students and administrators were not truly concerned about whether or how he instructed his classes. Evan finds himself on "the bus" at various times throughout the text—which in certain circumstances is an actual means of transport but at other times is a symbol of his constant travel toward clarity as well as the unstable nature of his Afro-Atlantic identity. This confusion manifests itself through his experiences with extended, hypervivid hallucinations in which "the world spills into [him]" (6).

Evan remains in Senegal on a sort of self-discovery mission, though for readers his first-person narration is unreliable, and we are drawn into the task of determining what is real versus hallucinated as Evan attempts to figure this out simultaneously. Initially, he had been determined to earn an assignment in South America, but his psychiatrist-turned-girlfriend, Wanda, convinced him to "do something for Us" by moving to an African country instead (163). What at first blush appears to be a push for Pan-African solidarity—take care of your own people first—is later exposed to also be a point of contention between Evan and Wanda, who were raised in the upper-middle class in Denver and Chicago, respectively, but who hold disparate understandings of how one should perform Blackness. Wanda had grown up surrounded by what she describes as a "proud" Black community, while Evan recalls his upbringing as one in which he and his siblings knew more about Black music than Black people; the few Black friends that Evan had were nervous about and ashamed of their race and desperately used bleaches and scouring pads in an attempt to achieve lighter skin and clothespins to try to narrow their noses (162). He admits to being intimidated by Wanda's brand of racial awareness and resents her for debasing his friendships with white people: "It has only been in more recent years that I have questioned my own blackness, questioned whether my thoughtlessness and indifference to things that tore others apart did not really indicate my emotional barrenness. If anyone is to blame for these questions . . . it is Wanda" (162).

Evan is in a state of perpetual movement throughout the text, traversing Senegal in search of a sense of family and a new job, and attempting to escape horrific, unexplained visions often involving death and murder. To negotiate this instability, he seeks understanding through the advice of the familiar (other Black American expatriates) and the cultural integration proffered by the unfamiliar (the Senegalese Gueye family that lives in N'Gor). The Black Americans that Evan encounter present varying outlooks on their relationship to Africa, all of which are antithetical to what Wanda described about her trip to Kenya, where the world bloomed "like a black rose" in a way that never made her "[feel] so wired for living" (165). It is unclear how long Wanda spent in Kenya to gather her impressions, but Evan's Black American expatriate informants candidly suggest how he should negotiate life in Senegal. Calvin Whitaker, the administrator at the American Cultural Center, asks if Evan has come to Senegal with hopes of reclaiming his African heritage and becoming African by living with a local family; Evan expresses confusion and never answers directly. Whitaker explains to Evan about Black American roots seekers in Senegal:

> You know, those space cadets who come out here thinking they're
> gonna get reunited with their long-lost kin and all that bullshit. Got a
> lot of that type coming out here after *Roots* came out. They try to come
> out here and be what they can't be. But let me tell you something,
> brother. The majority of these niggers out here don't give a walking
> fuck for you or me or any other black American. Shit, most of the

ancestors of them niggers in N'Gor, Ouakam, Yoff, and so forth, the better-off ones anyway, made a great deal of their money selling folks into slavery. Think about it man. You might be shacking with some family that got fat off selling your great-great grands to some European slavers. Can you relate to that? . . . I've lived here twelve years and have never even set foot in a village. Nothing but a bunch of trifling fools out there. I can't tell you what to do, man, but if I were you, I'd get my ass out of N'Gor. (57–58)

Alternatively, Africa Mamadou Ford, an expatriate who makes a living by selling American T-shirts in marketplaces and exploiting the resources of local women, encourages Evan to assimilate into the native population. Ford was not yet aware that Evan had already begun immersing himself in the culture by living with the Gueye family and falling in love with their American-educated elder daughter, Aminata. Ford advises Evan:

You gots to force yourself on 'em. Make 'em feed you. Make 'em take care of you. It ain't about getting over, it's about getting African. It's the only way. Man, don't be like them folks who come out here and soak their lettuce in Clorox and drink bottled water. What you gotta do, see, is walk through these villages out here. Get with the real folks. . . . They think it's a honor to feed strangers, man. A honor. . . . One thing you gotta understand about being an American out here, homeboy: you number one amongst these niggers. (92–93)

A host of other Black Americans tells Evan how he should behave in Senegal, and their disillusionment further causes him to suffer a crisis of disconnection, while he actively attempts to address his thoughtlessness, indifference, and perceived emotional barrenness. Just as he felt like an outsider in the United States, he is a stranger in Senegal, too, not only because he is an American but also because he does not possess adequate linguistic skills to be able to communicate effectively. Further, Evan adds a psychedelic edge to an inherently unpredictable homeland journey by refusing to take his quinine pills and failing to seek medical assistance, preferring to see where the pain will take him. The pain results, in fact, in Evan's traversal of multiple consciousnesses, which only amplifies his confusion. By settling in with the Gueye family, Evan is nursed back to relatively stable physical health, though he unwittingly places trust in a family whose patriarch, a respected *marabou* (or faith healer), dislikes him and spends a great deal of time (if we are to trust our psychologically incapacitated narrator) leading his family in their psychological warfare against Evan. The relationship is further complicated by Evan's infatuation with Aminata, whose allegiance remains with her family as she attempts to convince Evan that a jinn (evil spirit) is following him and that he must kill Ford—who, it turns out, has a sordid history with the Gueye family. In his psychosis, Evan tries to assuage his sense of diasporan loss and unstable sense of Black identity by attempting to assimilate into the Senegalese culture through the adoption of local religious beliefs, which, again, further confuses his sense of himself:

> How could I not have ignored what people said to me? How could I have believed any of it? And how could it not have affected all that I do and see here? There are just too many ways to read a book.... This is not where I want to be. This is not the kind of person I want to be. Since I have been here people have called me "spacey." I am not. People have called me weird. I am not, really. People have said, or implied, that I am not black enough. That disturbs me. I do not know whether this is true. Perhaps I am rootless, but does this mean I am not black? (130–61)

Cerebral malaria is not Evan's sole problem, and his identity crisis did not begin when he set foot on Senegalese soil. The madness prompted by the malaria is, in an odd way, an elucidation agent, pinpointing dispossession as the cause for Evan's aloofness. Rolland Murray finds that this text inverts "the traditional topos of return, refiguring the journey not as a consolidation of identity but as an undoing of it,"[51] which is nowhere more evident than in McKnight's portrayal of Evan's reaction to the slave castle at Gorée Island:

> Each time I go there I can smell taste touch the very fibers of slavery. The old holding-pen walls, the pebbles on the strand, the air, all vibrate with atoms of dried blood, evaporated sweat, desiccated vomit.... It is the perfect place for self-pity. There is pain there, but it is not my pain. It is like a chorus for my solo. Perhaps too many years have passed since what, for lack of a better term, I could call my ancestral leave-taking. Perhaps I am no longer African, or African only

in the vestigial sense. . . . I go there not because of some overpowering emotion that takes hold of me but because the ancient emotion does not overwhelm my own. (84–85)

Evan's complicated reactions at Gorée are reminiscent of Eddy Harris's in *Native Stranger*. Both men downplay the centrality of the slave castle to their sense of identity loss, which ironically catalyzed their travel back to Africa. Evan's engagement at the site of origin concretizes for him the idea that his pain is the ultimate injury and that his ancestors' suffering is somehow detached from his. Evan does not pretend to understand the agony of slavery, but he expresses a connection to the slave castle even in his ahistorical disavowal by seeking out the site on multiple occasions ("each time I go there") to mourn his personal identity crisis. On one particular visit, a homeless man whom he had encountered elsewhere begs for alms and, in a sudden movement, "[the man] bends over as if looking for something on the ground, throws his arms forward, and dives off the cliff" in a Flying African–like moment that is absent of the triumphalism repeated in Afro-Atlantic cultural productions (87). The blind man's suicidal flight mesmerizes Evan to the extent that he also feels "weightless, as though I, myself, am careening through the air. I hear him hit the water" (87). As Murray gathers in a beautiful reading of this scene, "through the blind man's suicide (whether real or imagined), the text positions slavery as part of the historical unconscious, a repressed stranger always working to disrupt the integrity of the self's enunciation."[52] McKnight's resistance to the Flying African myth, too, rejects the romanticism inherent in imaginary flights, as Evan hears the moment at which the man lands in the water, whereas most narratives avow that those ancestors who took flight during slavery disappeared from view and out of earshot as they glided beyond the horizon.

I Get on the Bus emphasizes the continued contestations at sites of slavery and remembrance as well as the current debate regarding whether and how to merge Pan-African and diasporan politics—particularly in places such as Ghana, where the cultural tourism industry thrives, as thousands of diasporan tourists visit each year. McKnight's narrative suggests that diasporans are always moving; they are seeking identity completion, and in some cases, returns to geographical Africa are but "one pole in an improvisatory dialogue between the *individual* and his *com-*

munal history (emphasis added)."[53] Evan's instability does not necessarily negate the redemption that symbolic returns offer to other diasporans, but it simply suggests that the psychic transition is never easy nor does it evolve in the same manner for everyone. Near the end of the novel, Evan concludes about his sense of identity:

> I bleed my way from Africa to America. In time I will no longer be able to hold each particle together. The slow boil of the ocean will break me down, atom by atom. . . . My consciousness will rise up like vapor, will steam and roll, half-invisible, far into the sky, get caught up in the clouds, choke them till they can hold no more of me. The clouds will cast me down in a silent dry rain. I will hang in the air, between sky and soil, sky and sea, floating in disjointed voiceless madness for all eternity. The wind will rise and push these fragments around the circuits of the world. (220–21)

The merger of histories between those who have been violently separated for centuries—those whose cultures and intricacies of behavior are so fixed to places thousands of miles apart—would only indicate that return, regardless of the tourism productions enacted to welcome cultural roots seekers home, is not a given. Evan, like all dispossessed Africans, is on the bus eternally.

Coda: To What Ends? Searching for Evidence of Long-Dead Strangers

In her travel narrative, *Lose Your Mother*, Hartman maps her travels to Ghana to locate somehow the traces of strangers—ancestors who had languished in the slave castle-dungeons along the coast of Ghana.[54] This text is guided by Hartman's pronounced agenda to engage fantastically across temporalities. She describes her mission as one centered on the search for those Africans who were marked as expendable: "I had not come to marvel at the wonders of African civilization or to be made proud by the royal court of Asante, or to admire the great states that harvested captives and sold them as slaves. I was not wistful for aristocratic origins. Instead I would seek the commoners, the unwilling and coerced migrants who created a new culture in the hostile world of the Americas and who fashioned themselves again, making possibility of dispossession" (7). Perhaps Hartman's pinpointing of the forgotten ancestor is due to a sense of incomplete fulfillment during her previous travel to Ghana. She had arrived this time to confront the shame associated with her inherited slave status by attempting to align with the disgraced and forgotten. This desire to feel something more at the dungeon echoes the wishes of Angelou, Evan, and Eddy Harris, only Hartman surmises that she can be sated solely at the site of injury not through engagements with contemporary peoples, participation in ceremonies, or investment in tourism lures. Her understanding is that those sold into slavery were individuals who more than likely had no ties to royalty, though tourism scripts and diasporan revisionist histories tend to rely on such redemptive narratives as a way to heal divestment and to offer a sense of pride to the dispossessed. Hartman's journey is an unmediated sankofic exercise in the sense that it is self-created, rather than organized by a cultural roots entity to produce an anticipated, cathartic response. On one level, Hartman's inability to "reach through" and somehow commiserate with those who had passed through the sites centuries earlier makes little sense practically, but on another, spiritual level, her disconnection is real, felt, and interminable (119).

Throughout *Lose Your Mother*, Hartman interweaves autobiographical material with a historical disquisition on slavery and poses theoretical questions about diaspora, the conceivability of return, home, and misrecognitions. She looks back for the ancestor to place her family's recollection of their slave past alongside her feelings at the port of displacement. When she arrives in the slave dungeon, she immediately finds that her goal is not realizable: "I traced the perimeter of the cell disappointed. I stepped over the gutters traversing the floor. My hand glided over the walls, as though the rough surfaces were a script that I could read through my dull fingers. But the brush of my hands against the stone offered no hint or clue. What I wanted was to feel something other than bricks and lime. What I wanted was to reach through time and touch the prisoners" (119). Hartman acknowledges through conversations with other Black Americans, particularly expatriates, and Ghanaians that she does not desire permanent return as it is typically understood. During her fieldwork, she not only witnesses that misrecognitions occur to such a degree that diasporans have great difficulty adjusting, but she also considers herself "nonreturnable goods"—a member of the tribe of strangers who wishes to bear witness to her possible ancestral histories but not attempt to repair it with "fictive kinship [which] was too close to the heart of slavery's violence for [her] comfort" (199). When the chief at the Salaga slave market in northern Ghana inquires whether Hartman and the other Black American tourists with whom she is traveling had realized their desires during their pilgrimage in Ghana, they fall silent, though they each want to respond negatively: "Had we possessed the words, we might have said that it was not as if we expected to find something that could make history hurt less or fill the hole inside us, because it was not the kind of hole that could be filled and then would go away. Coming here was simply a way to acknowledge it. There was no turning back the clock. But it didn't feel like it was moving forward either" (199). Hartman's recollection underscores that the transatlantic slave trade was an irreparable loss whose aftereffects reverberate perpetually in the present and will in the future, though travel to and the reimagining and observing of vestiges from the great injury remain significant to many Afro-Atlantic peoples.

She indicates that her first trip to Ghana had been paradisiacal, but on her subsequent visit, she convincingly critiques the formal and informal Ghanaian (slavery) tourism industry's marketing of an insincere narrative that draws in the diasporan through kinship markers such as "my sister/my brother", belongingness in phrases like "welcome home", and the presentation of relics from the era of the slave trade. Yet Hartman does not maintain this hard line. Versed in issues regarding transatlantic slavery and diasporan identity, she ends the text with more optimism than she began. During the last stop on her tour of one of Ghana's slave routes, Hartman is observing a group of girls singing while jumping rope, when a young man walks over to her and offers a translation of their song for her: "'Sister' was the first word out of his mouth. As soon as I heard it, I readied myself for what I was sure would follow. It was the lure and I waited for him to reel me in. . . . 'The girls are singing about those taken from Gwolu and sold into slavery in the Americas. They are singing about the diaspora.' Here it was—my song, the song of the lost tribe. I closed my eyes and I listened" (235). Hartman's reaction to this performance is significant in its unveiling of her ambivalence, particularly because she ends her text with this willing suspension of disbelief. Her search for strangers, which she identifies as fruitless early in her recollection of her journey, suggests that the entirety of the text is a meditation on her yearning to locate sincere evidence to suggest that the ancestors have not been forgotten—that they have not been marked wholly as dishonored, "expendable and defeated" persons (7). Hartman identifies the young man's explanation of the children's song as a "lure," raising doubts about his translation but relishing nonetheless this fleeting moment of recognition. The final scene of Hartman's narrative evokes a moment in *Praisesong for the Widow* during Avey's trip to Carriacou, when Avey allows herself to be drawn into the Beg Pardon though she feels a "momentary twinge of disappointment" initially at the sight of the dilapidated boats, ramshackle setup of the ceremonial space, and obviously improvised nature of the out-islanders' worship (240). Such moments often occur in homeland journeys, as travelers suspend their disbelief to feel as though they have truly taken flight and are a part of something authentically African. As will be explored in the following chapters, instances of apperception, feigned or sincere, catapult flights toward rootedness.

Post-1965 speculative cultural production, as demonstrated in the wide range of literary and filmic narratives that I have examined throughout this chapter, influences the imaginary that sustains and provides a number of tropes with which to examine the arcs of real-life migrations and other acts of renarrativation that occur in Ghana, Bahia, and the U.S. South. Shame and ignorance of the collective slave and ancestral pasts are characteristics of dispossession, but the practice of return through travel toward Africa has the potential to slake these sentiments. In their fantastic quests to rise out of their social alienation, Black American travelers, like the protagonists of post–civil rights cultural production, engage in alternative forms of time travel as they move literally and figuratively closer to Africa. In their search for felt connections with the past, these travelers hope that they will be imbued with contentment, a sense of purpose, and the space to experience social life. Memories and rememories are articulated via lived experience: engagements with the ancestor in traditional "African" religious ceremonies and solemn visitations of vestiges that remain at various sites of injury can assuage, though breaches occur often as the native/stranger binary impedes an all-encompassing embrace and travelers are left to question what it truly means to fly home. In the examinations that follow, I posit that while attending to cultural loss is viewed by the people whose stories are recounted as pertinent to the construction of their Afro-Atlantic identities, a sense of responsibility must be assumed, as it is only through the coupling of the recalling and recuperation of the past with sincere engagements with contemporary Africa and Africans that dispossessed cultural roots tourists and expatriates can ascend to the realization of the Black fantastic.

CHAPTER 2

The Production of Homeland Returns

MISRECOGNITIONS AND THE UNSTEADY PATH
TOWARD THE BLACK FANTASTIC IN GHANA

Bats have taken up residence at the slave castle in Elmina, Ghana. Reminiscent of a foreboding gothic scene, the winged creatures traverse the dank, gloomy interior of one of the edifice's upper rooms, adding a sense of active haunting to the centuries-old site of human atrocity. One certainly feels as if she has wandered into a time machine that transports her into an atmosphere that is concentrated to the extent that the horrors of the past are rendered palpable. As a UNESCO World Heritage site, Elmina Castle has undergone several measures to preserve it for historical and tourism purposes since 1979, including a continued effort to whitewash the outside of the castle periodically to mask its gradual disintegration. Each year, thousands of roots tourists of African descent file through the dungeons, cells, tradesmen's quarters, and church in the edifice, with hopes of making connections with their long-lost ancestors. Ghana, known as the Gold Coast during the period of the transatlantic slave trade, is but one country from which slaves were stripped and forced as commodities across the Atlantic. Yet its castles at Elmina and Cape Coast represent the few known, accessible slave vestiges that remain in West Africa today.

Under the intense heat of the Ghana sun, I traveled with Ghanaian and Black American friends to the Central Region via Ghana's Intercity STC bus service to tour once again these well-known vestiges of the slave

2.1 Elmina Castle. © iStock by Getty Images.

trade and attend the Pan-African Historical Theatre Festival (PANAF-EST).[1] As we paid our entrance fees at the slave castle, we discussed the fee schedule, which was such that non-Ghanaians paid approximately ten times more to enter, a fact that has resulted in consternation among many African diasporan visitors who feel as though their ancestors have already paid the ultimate price for what James Baldwin refers to as "the ticket."[2] Before we could more formally question the stark discrepancy, we were quickly ushered along to join a group of mostly white international visitors, who were waiting for the tour to begin. As we commenced our journey into the dungeons, our guide warned that the floors would be slippery as we descended. The idea of falling onto the grimy surface terrified me each time I entered a slave dungeon. I attempted to maintain control of my footing, but my typically too-large researcher's shoulder bag—filled with a book, notebook, voice recorder, camera, antiseptic gel, and hand wipes—made keeping my balance a chore as we negotiated the cavernous pits. Though the descent into the lower portion of the castle allowed relief from the glare of the sun, the air inside was humid and putrid; the bowels of the slave castle are dank and dark, save for a window, which was more of a small hole near the top of the wall and which served more as a futile light source than a means by which to breathe. I slipped a couple of times as the angle of decline in the men's dungeon became severe and the traction of my sandals began to fail me. I had visited the slave castle several times before, but those previous experiences did little to still my current discomfort. I grew uneasy as my ears were attacked by the scramble of words straightforwardly emitted by the guide: *kidnapped, bodily waste flowed freely, dead bodies slumped, women were raped, thrown into cells for misconduct, beaten, chained, women and men were packed tightly into each dungeon, disease, very little food, some refused to eat and died, they could barely breathe, they couldn't breathe*. Each utterance inflicted pain on our newly formed, transnational group psyche and heightened our existing heat-related distress. In the background to our guide's script, the other tourists' queries, and the collective gasps and disbelief at what we were witnessing in the now empty corpse of the immense structure, the ocean thundered. It seemed irate.

On the upper decks, some of the tourists expressed their surprise at the luxury of the slave dungeon officials' living spaces, with their prime views of the Atlantic, as well as the existence of a church in the structure. The ease with which we walked through this portion of the edifice and our ability to breathe freely contrasted sharply with the terror and fright that we had, minutes before, experienced and imagined in the dungeons below. A persistent thought flooded my mind: *in the underbelly is where you would have been centuries ago—this is what your people suffered*. A lump grew in my throat, and I wanted to weep. It was all too much. I calmed down as we exited the castle, and I stood in the vast courtyard near a series of cannons. I gazed out at the direction to which they pointed— toward the expanse of the Atlantic. It was the beginning of my fascination with the dirge bellowed by the ocean as it crashes against the shores in Ghana and across the Atlantic in Bahia and South Carolina. Each of the times that I toured Cape Coast and Elmina Castles, I looked out over the expanse of the sea and listened.

During a trip to Elmina two years earlier, I had ventured from Accra alone, staying at the nearby Black American–owned One Africa Hotel. I spoke with the co-owner, Seestah Imahküs Robinson about her nearly twenty-year stay in Elmina, and she informed me that she and her husband had chosen their plot of land because they could see the slave castle

2.2 A woman looks into the Atlantic Ocean. © Victoria Okoye/African Urbanism

from there and that they felt as if they had been called by the ancestors to serve as protectors and guides for diasporan visitors. During that visit to Elmina Castle, I was invited to join a group composed of white Europeans, but I resisted because tourism scripts for groups of diasporans are not always the same as that which is performed for "mixed" company. In fact, tour guides often utilize a matter-of-fact tone and historical framing for mostly white audiences, while they employ a more graphic, emotional, and deliberately spoken narrative for diasporan tourists. I was determined to observe how the narrative might change further during a personal tour. Visibly annoyed by my request to not join the large group, the Ghanaian guide escorted me around the structure, gradually becoming tolerant of my queries about the slave trade. He later insisted that I become an actor in his scripted performance. The tour guide urged me to feel what slavery was like by prodding me to enter one of the tiny cells in which captives were confined as they awaited whippings or perhaps even death. Fear of the unknown prompted me to say no several times, until my curiosity and his persistence led me to relent. It is compelling the ways in which visitors to the dungeons "re-enact in some small measure an aspect of the captive experiences," whether it is when they walk single

2.3 A tour group at the slave castle in Elmina, Ghana, stops at a cell marked with a skull and crossbones. Photo by author.

file through the low-visibility dungeons and out of the Door of No Return or when they are encouraged to perform a task as clouded with disgrace, shame, and terror as fashioning shackles upon their arms or entering a holding corral as I had been.[3] Though a sense of unease gripped me, I desired to get a sense of the restrictions of the space and acknowledge the torment that the captives had endured, only I did not expect the guide to close the door once I entered. I felt suffocated immediately and demanded that the guide, who stood laughing riotously on the other side of the bars, release me. Even in the postslavery moment, a pronounced sense of fear and the ongoing renovations of slavery and colonization make it feel as though it could happen again. I had traveled to the dungeon with a critical eye, but nonetheless I was struck by trepidation and feelings of despair. The guide's calculated performance had succeeded in producing the cathartic reaction.

Catharsis, a liberatory act of purging, marks the moment of contact with the past and with the ancestor—it is the most anticipated moment in flights toward imagined Africas and a central force that compels diasporan returns. Throughout this chapter, my analyses of the currents of Black Americans who move toward Africa and the intentions behind how return and Africa are produced in Ghana employ a mixed methodology that utilizes stories from my experiences as a participant-observer of numerous Black American roots tours at sites of slavery in Ghana as well as events such as the country's Ghana at Fifty anniversary celebrations and U.S. President Barack Obama's historic first official visit to sub-Saharan Africa in 2009; interviews that I conducted with selected travelers and expatriates over an eight-year period; and literary analyses of Black American travel narratives by Maya Angelou, Saidiya Hartman, and Seestah Imahküs Robinson. Fiercely warning against romantic longings for and the feasibility of expatriation to Africa proper, critics of such cultural roots seekers' yearnings often argue that one cannot go home again because the people there, along with the protracted years of physical and cultural separation, will not allow it to happen.[4] And while I concede that any impulse to arrest Africa in the precolonial past to experience actual engagements with its ancient peoples and traditions is indeed futile, I will demonstrate that the labor of teasing out the intricacies of how diaspora and the related, problematic project of promulgating the possibility for Black uplift through capitalism remain vital.

Pan-Africanism and the Ghanaian Triumphalist Narratives

An oft-repeated story recalls a compelling moment in 1957 when Vice President Richard Nixon led a U.S. delegation to Ghana's independence festivities, which were attended by international heads of state and members of the British royal family. At one point during his visit in Accra, Nixon approached a group of Black men and asked them, "How does it feel to be free?" The men replied, "We wouldn't know. We're from Alabama."[5] This brief exchange is clearly a charged confrontation, though there is no historical account of what happened after the men corrected Nixon's assumption. The Black American men undoubtedly recognized Nixon and seized the opportunity to emphasize the hypocrisy expressed by the vice president's attendance and boast, in the face of the political oppressor, the fact of their mobility. The American government's nonchalance regarding the astounding second-class treatment of Black Americans and other ethnic groups, particularly in the terror-inducing South, did not align with what Nixon's presence was intended to emanate. His celebration of a Black country's freedom from colonization was an indirect acknowledgment that Black people are worthy of liberation—that they are, in fact, capable of running their own lives and building their own country. The conversation also illustrates why Black Americans in the 1950s began looking to Ghana as a model of Black triumph over white supremacy; perhaps the men from Alabama were catalyzed to engage more politically if and when they returned to the United States.

Kwame Nkrumah and his Convention People's Party (CPP) had organized in 1949 to mobilize the Gold Coast masses rather than rely simply on elite intellectuals to "[adopt] all legal and constitutional means by which . . . to attack the forces of imperialism."[6] Gradually, Nkrumah and the CPP gained political influence in the Gold Coast, and by June 1954, they had a majority of the assembly seats available in Parliament, turning the direction of all future votes and battles over legislation in their party's favor. Just after midnight on March 6, 1957, Nkrumah stood at the podium in Accra's Independence Square and declared to the citizens of the new Republic of Ghana: "At long last, the battle has ended! And thus Ghana, your beloved country is free forever!"[7] Nkrumah's legacy as a hero of the Ghanaian independence struggle was a major tool by which the fledgling government aligned itself with other African nations and the people of its diaspora in Europe and the Americas.[8] As the first sub-Saharan African country to achieve sovereignty, Ghana's successful struggle influenced the freedom dreams of other colonies throughout Africa as well as the ongoing civil rights movement in the United States. Nkrumah held a Pan-Africanist outlook that also championed the rise of what he called the New African, maintaining that Ghana's "independence is meaningless unless it is linked up with the total liberation of the African continent."[9] After 1957, Black political figures and creative artists from various countries poured into Ghana as students of Nkrumah's socialist vision. Pan-Africanist sympathizers who had heeded Nkrumah's desire for their assistance in helping him build up his nation also visited and/or relocated there.

In tracing the roots of Pan-Africanism, the Ethiopian writer Ato Kifle Wodajo found that "in Africa itself the seeds of Pan-Africanism were implanted the moment the first alien coloniser set foot on her soil."[10] However, it was a later, more intellectualized and organized ideology, which was very much steeped in the nineteenth-century focus on transnational Black uplift, that rallied the Ghanaian populace behind Nkrumah. The Trinidadian Henry Sylvester Williams is credited with establishing the

African Association in 1897, which became the Pan-African Association in 1900, in response to the scramble for Africa that began in 1882.[11] Delegates from across the globe attended the Pan-African Congress in London in 1900 to strategize on behalf of Africans on the continent and in the diaspora, setting forth the following objectives, which were drafted by W. E. B. Du Bois and distributed throughout sovereign countries: "To secure civil and political rights for Africans and their descendants throughout the world; to encourage friendly relations between the Caucasian and African races; to encourage African peoples everywhere in educational, industrial, and commercial enterprise; to approach Governments and influence legislation in the interests of the black races; to ameliorate the condition of the oppressed Negro in Africa, America, the British empire, and other parts of the world."[12] Pan-Africanism remained the most prominent method of unification for African-descended peoples during the twentieth century. In 1945, the Manchester Congress saw the leadership and strategy transition from that mostly conceived by and concerned with the issues put forth by Black Americans. The Pan-African movement now had representation from throughout the West and Africa and was influenced significantly by the socialist ideology of the Gold Coast's Nkrumah and Trinidad's George Padmore.

Pan-Africanism itself, then, should be considered a speculative philosophy because it is faith in change that is massive and revolutionary in its quest for the freedom and elevation of African-descended peoples. After 1957, Nkrumah became the Pan-African movement's foremost leader largely because he had successfully countered colonialism. James Meriwether explains the Black American response to Ghana's liberation as recorded in the Black American press: "As Africans overthrew colonial rule and took their place on the world stage, they overturned old stereotypes about African 'primitiveness' and backwardness. Feelings of indifference, ambivalence, or even superiority toward Africans decreased in black America; racial pride in Africa increased."[13] While focused mainly on his nation-building project and the establishment of a United States of Africa, Nkrumah positioned several Black American professionals as well as other diasporans in his cabinet as advisors. It is in this moment of Pan-African embrace and socialist radicalism that Black Americans began—as they continue to do—to view Ghana as a potential refuge and site for redemption.[14]

To address those who might read Black American homeland migration as tragically romantic—what some scholars suggest is indicative of a general imposition of the desires of privileged, insincere Black Americans onto the national fabric of postcolonial African nations such as Ghana as well as in their representations of Blackness in cultural production—I invoke Richard Iton's astute suggestion that we engage Black American cultural production with critical caution rather than outright categorize these producers as suspect and rapacious even as they operate as the unintentional reproducers of American global hegemony in their attempts at flight:

> Nevertheless, the claim that the integration of cultural actors into the framework of black politics legitimizes exceptionalist understandings of African American inclinations overlooks the possibility that being exceptional in relation to the standard practices and norms prevailing in American life need not necessarily be a bad thing; naturalizes a national frame that deserves troubling; and arguably misses the point. Hyperactivity on the cultural front usually occurs as a response to some sort of marginalization from the processes of decision-making or exercising control over one's own circumstances; what might appear to be an overinvestment in the cultural realm is rarely a freely chosen strategy. American blacks are not "different" [from other African-descended peoples] in this respect because they have chosen to be but because of the exclusionary and often violent practices that have historically defined black citizenship and public sphere participation as problematic and because of the recognition that the cultural realm is always in play and already politically significant terrain.[15]

Black Americans, particularly cultural producers and those with the financial means to travel, are exceptional indeed and, in certain instances throughout history, have benefited from and been implicated in and/or directly responsible for reproducing the very forms of empire that have oppressed them. Rather than risking the dismissal of the interminability of anti-Blackness and the effects of empire on Black Americans by insinuating that they somehow categorically wield a level of power that they frankly do not possess, I advance here the undertaking of a more generous reading of what is occurring in these moments of interaction between Black Americans, other members of the African diaspora, and

Africans more recently from the continent that stresses the pressing need for the articulation of a transnational politics of return. I maintain throughout this chapter that speculative epistemologies have shaped and continue to shape the contours of Afro-Atlantic life, sometimes assuaging longing and shame, but most often revealing complicated relations between African-descended peoples as they attempt to participate in what might be identified loosely as Pan-African activity. The popularity of Ghana as a place for diasporans to attend to their sense of loss is tied to the existence and deliberate preservation of sites of slavery at which to mourn as well as to the triumphalist Pan-African narrative that was established as Nkrumah led the Gold Coast to freedom. The manner in which Pan-African ideologies developed and changed over time and how the governments that followed Nkrumah's co-opted the language of Pan-African unity in service of encouraging the development of kinship ruses to attract diasporan tourism and investment demonstrate that a contemporary revisiting of the ideology via a neoteric outlook might stem the misrecognitions and distrust that impede the possibilities for a global realization of the Black fantastic.[16]

In calling for a neoteric, or a new, formulation of Pan-Africanism as a codicil to Black fantastic thought, I am not suggesting a re-creation of the wheel but a pivot—a recentering of what has long been referred to in Ghana as Pan-African politics, but one that acknowledges that worldwide iterations of Black social alienation are indeed connected despite their individual particularities. As Iton argues, African-descended people are "outside the state but within empire" and are impacted by diaspora and the "cluster of disturbances that trouble not only the physically dispersed but those moved without traveling."[17] Malcolm X encouraged the Black American expatriates and exiles that he met in Ghana in 1964 to return psychically to symbolic Africas as a political act and advised them to resume their activism back in the United States, indicating that the establishment of a truly transnational African column would depend on the transformation of their consciousnesses.[18] As illustrated in what follows, literal returns to Africa, as cathartic and significant as they are to the cultural identities of those who are able to travel, are not trivial or useless, but they do prove themselves unsustainable as the sole alternatives for the African-descended masses who remain unable to move and are subjugated in the aftermath of colonization and transatlantic slavery. To be sure, the development of a sustainable political imaginary that acknowledges difference across various African-descended groups and rejects the involvement of acquisitive European and African political and corporate elites will actuate flight toward the Black fantastic.

Catharsis: Spiritual Pulls and Performances of Africa at Ghanaian Sites of Slavery

To these descendants, coming back to Africa through the slave forts is a necessary act of self realization; a recapturing of the "Lost Soul of Black Folk." It is
like lying on the psychiatrist's couch and getting rid of a great burden which
has been borne for centuries.
—Robert E. Lee, an expatriate, quoted in Bayo Holsey, *Routes of Remembrance*

Angelou's expressions of loss and grappling with her diasporan identity, as described in the previous chapter, did not involve her physical contact with Ghana's slave dungeons until a year into her exile. As she explains in *All God's Children Need Traveling Shoes*, she attempted to avoid the slave dungeons due to her acute dread about the emotional reaction they might induce and the daunting reports from her expatriate friends who had described being haunted by the cries of captives when they visited.[19] While traveling through Cape Coast on her way to Dunkwa, Angelou is forced somehow to deal with the horror she had intended to escape, and she comes to the realization that "there would be no purging, I knew, unless I asked all the questions. Only then would the spirits understand what I was feeding them. It was a crumb, but it was all I had."[20] While parked on the roadside, Angelou finally allows her imagination to venture into the past by envisioning what it must have been like to be a captive among the exhausted—defeated, dead to feeling and protest, sold by the greedy, and ultimately betrayed by history.[21] The act of witnessing the slave dungeon makes it possible for tourists to engage critically with bygone eras, as their mourning (not just that which is overtly dramatic) offers a "counter-narrative to the exclusions of U.S. national history and a personal seizure and appropriation of the narrative resources made available by tourism."[22] As a participant-observer at the slave castles, my interest was in the relationship between the ancestral pulls that compel tourists to sites of memory; the performances enacted in the dungeon of each structure; and the spiritual haunting that was so powerful that the ancestral realm seized visitors such as Angelou, who had not even set foot on the site but who had, in fact, actively resisted its presence.

On flights into Accra's Kotoko International Airport, it is quite common for one to witness the organic creation of Afro-Atlantic soundscapes. Members of diasporan tour groups have a storied history of expressing their joy during in-flight celebrations by clapping and shouting "hallelujah" and "amen" when their plane touches down. In 2007, a tour group from Atlanta sang celebratory songs at various points during their flight, enraging some travelers, who had hoped for a more subdued flight experience, but entertaining others who looked on encouragingly. Most notable was the group's rendition of the unofficial Black American national anthem "Lift Ev'ry Voice and Sing." During the last stanza, the group's voices soared through the cabin:

> God of our weary years, God of our silent tears,
> Thou who has brought us thus far on the way;
> Thou who has by Thy might, led us into the light,
> Keep us forever in the path, we pray.
> Lest our feet stray from the places, our God, where we met Thee;
> Lest, our hearts drunk with the wine of the world, we forget Thee;
> Shadowed beneath Thy hand, may we forever stand,
> True to our God, true to our native land.[23]

At the close of the song, a lone male voice thundered throughout the cabin, "Africa!" While their ancestors were distributed through the Middle Passage and into a life of slave coffles and auction blocks, forced labor, and dehumanization, the tour group members ensured that their trip to Africa would be on their own terms, regardless of the disapproval and discomfort that they might have caused other travelers. They had journeyed to Ghana, along with numerous other tour groups and individuals from across the globe, to applaud the country on its golden anniversary; to participate in scheduled trips to remnants of the slave trade; and, more generally, to connect with their imagined native land. In the sixty years since the Ghanaian government began welcoming Black Americans to the country as returning kin, many have found that flights toward home have alleviated the severity of their plight, offering a sense of freedom that eludes them in the United States.

Of great significance to most Black American expatriates' eventual migration are the experiences that they have at the slave castle-dungeons. The UNESCO World Tourist Organization's cultural tourism program on the slave route was charged with assisting Ghana in developing its tourism industry by strategizing with the country to establish a roots tourism sector geared toward dispossessed Africans, particularly Black Americans.[24] Of the sixty castles, forts, and lodges that once sat along the Ghanaian coastline, the most prominent are the slave dungeons at Elmina and Cape Coast. At these imagined sites of origin, tourists satiate their curiosity as well as reckon with their dislocation. An estimated ten thousand Black Americans answer such a summons each year, holding fast to the hope that images of what happened before the commencement of the slave trade have somehow remained. Generally, tour guides at the slave dungeons intersperse historical information with gruesome tales of how the captives were treated. As I described earlier, tourists file into each dimly lit dungeon, and the guide describes the overpacked conditions of the male and female holding cells where enslaved people were forced to live (and die) miserably in filth as they waited for a ship to carry them off into the unknown. Tourists are overwhelmed by the stench rising from the centuries-old building and often report smelling rotting flesh in the mildewing structure. When the guide moves into the narrative recounting stories of women being taken upstairs to the well-appointed quarters of variously titled European officials and soldiers to be sexually abused and tortured, and then points to the room that served as the castle's church, tourists become vocal in their disgust and anger at the violent hypocrisy that sustained the peculiar institution. Seestah Imahküs writes about her life-altering encounter at Elmina Castle: "As the Guide continued to describe the horrors of these pits of hell I began to shake violently; I needed to get out of there. I was being smothered. I turned and ran up the steep incline of the tunnel, to the castle courtyard, the winds from the sea whipping my face, bringing me back to the present. I couldn't believe what I had just experienced."[25] She recalls that some of the other tourists had remained silent with solemn faces as the horrific details were listed, while others wept softly. Seestah Imahküs rejoined the group as they exited the male dungeon and entered the women's cell, where she remained until the embodied spirits that she encountered vanished:

I dropped to my knees, trembling and crying even harder.... As I rocked back and forth on the dirt floor, I could hear weeping and wailing ... anguished screams coming from the distance. Suddenly the room was packed with women ... some naked, some with babies, some sick and lying in the dirt, while others stood against the walls around the dungeon's walls, terror filled their faces.... Cold terror gripped my body, tears blinded me and the screams wouldn't stop. As I sat there violently weeping I began to feel a sense of warmth, many hands were touching my body, caressing me, soothing me as a calmness began to come over me. I began to feel almost safe as voices whispered in my ears assuring me that everything was all right. "Don't cry," they said, "You've come home. You've returned to your homeland, to re-open the door of No Return." ... After years of wandering and searching, I had finally found home. And one day, I wouldn't be leaving again.[26]

According to Seestah Imahküs, the ancestral women were made manifest fantastically. As she processed the tour guide's narration and her reactions to the place, she lost physical control and was transported to the era of the slave trade, whose sights and sounds terrified her. In this transformative cathartic moment, the imagined foremothers lovingly calmed Seestah Imahküs, arming her with a place to call home and a purpose to realize—she was charged with reopening the Door of No Return.

When visitors near the end of their tour of the slave castle-dungeons, they are told that the final doorway facing the ocean is considered the Door of No Return. As diasporan tourists solemnly exit through the path that their ancestors took, the tour guide raises their spirits by congratulating them on having returned to redeem their forbears' cruel destiny. Shortly thereafter, the guide will typically encourage visitors to turn around and ceremoniously walk back through the doorway, which, aptly, has been fashioned with a sign that reads "Door of Return," to crystallize their homecoming. Along with the opportunity to confront slavery at its source, roots tourism is most effective when what is imagined and expected beforehand is met and exceeded. Recognition that diasporans have "returned" and that there is some regret on the Ghanaian side for slavery begins upon their landing at the airport when customs officials and porters greet tourists with *Akwaaba ...* welcome back!" and con-

IN EVERLASTING MEMORY

OF THE ANGUISH OF OUR ANCESTORS

MAY THOSE WHO DIED REST IN PEACE

MAY THOSE WHO RETURN FIND THEIR ROOTS

MAY HUMANITY NEVER AGAIN PERPETRATE

SUCH INJUSTICE AGAINST HUMANITY

WE, THE LIVING, VOW TO UPHOLD THIS

2.4 A plaque posted at Cape Coast Castle expresses regret for the transatlantic slave trade. Photo by author.

tinues as street vendors peddle goods to their "sisters" and "brothers." Occasionally, a group of small children will interrupt these acknowledgments by waving to and giggling intently at tourists while yelling what many tourists understand as a derogatory designation: *obroni*! Obroni—an Akan word meaning stranger, foreigner, and, by extension, a white person—is a shock for many Black American tourists whose presence in the imagined homeland, until that breach, typically is nothing short of enthralling. Such moments can disrupt temporarily the celebratory spirit that surrounds these groups, leading tour guides to dismiss quickly the description of the tourists as white as children's folly resulting from a lack of education about slavery. Direct verbal misrecognitions typically are brief encounters during tourism experiences, as the industry and less formal economies produced by laypersons have engineered several machinations to overcome such moments by appealing to the psychic desires of diasporan travelers through kinship narratives.

For example, during her initial visit to Ghana with a Hebrew Israelite tour group, Seestah Imahküs and her fellow travelers experienced an unexpected call to return as they walked around Cape Coast, while the townspeople prepared for the Fetu Afayhe harvest festival. Several members of her group were snatched away by unknown men in a small space of time. Fierce struggles ensued as the tourists attempted to escape, but it was soon revealed that the "kidnappings" were actually good-natured elements of the festival's tradition to claim new tribal members and to initiate some as chiefs of their villages in the Oguaa traditional area.[27] This unplanned interaction and kinship formation as well as the goals set by Ghana's Ministry for Tourism not only involve reckonings by roots tourists ("I belong here in Ghana") and recognition by Ghanaians ("Yes, you do. Akwaaba!"), but they also conflate responsibility for Ghana with return, increasing the likelihood of repeat tourism; expatriation; and, more compellingly, direct financial support to local villages and the country's economy.

After their tours throughout Ghana, Seestah Imahküs and her husband, Nana, decided to relocate to Ghana despite her family's protestations and her elderly mother's unwillingness to take the leap with them. To return permanently to one's imagined homeland often requires the severing of familial bonds that had otherwise sustained dispossessed Africans in the New World. In her travel narrative, Seestah Imahküs recalls her mother's emotional outburst as she and Nana prepared to leave: "Go on back to Africa, since that's more important to you than me! I ain't lost nothing in Africa. Y'all go on to your so-called 'roots' in Africa. Right here in the United States is my roots, thank you!"[28] At the moment of her mother's disavowal of Africa, Seestah Imahküs experienced a transition that solidified for her that a sense of motherland loss exceeds more recent natal ties: "As we pulled away from the house I saw tears running down her round, brown cheeks, her full lips in a big pout. I almost turned back, starting to cry and feeling a little hurt inside because she wasn't happy about our decision and I'd wished I could have left on a better note. But the pull to come home was stronger and more gripping than biological, if you can understand what I mean. It was spiritual: it was the ancestor calling."[29] It should be noted that not every tourist experiences a literal, personal call for return like Seestah Imahküs did, but what persists in the Black American tourist's imagination after their initial travels often is powerful enough to catalyze some to uproot their lives. The speculative act of traveling toward the past is radical in its refutation of the future-lessness promised by life in the United States, but what the post-1965 texts that I analyzed in the previous chapter—Reginald McKnight's *I Get on the Bus*, in particular—foreshadowed is that the speculative desire to recoup ancestral Africa by simply making a flight to the continent will be met with unrelenting resistance. As Seestah Imahküs, Nana, and the literary subjects and interviewees whose stories follow found, temporal disconnections will forever create breaches between those who understand the imagined ends of return in distinct ways.

Return, Responsibility, and the Breach

In *Lose Your Mother*, Hartman searches for the "expendable and the defeated"—remnants of the strangers who had been kidnapped from Ghana and strewn into the transatlantic slave trade, but what she locates are divisions between Ghanaians and Black American expatriates in contemporary Africa:

> I realized too late that the breach of the Atlantic could not be remedied by a name [change] and that the routes traveled by strangers were as close to a *mother country* as I would come. Images of kin trampled underfoot and lost along the way, abandoned dwellings repossessed by the earth, and towns vanished from sight and banished from memory were all that I could ever hope to claim. And I set out on the slave route, which was both an existent territory with objective coordinates and the figurative realm of an imagined past, determined to do exactly this.[30]

Along the routes of this research-motivated yet deeply personal task, Hartman meets John and Mary Ellen, who had lived in Ghana for twenty years and who—unlike Seestah Imahküs and Nana—felt trapped in Ghana and expressed few positive aspects about their lives there. The details of John and Mary Ellen's transition are not provided entirely, but drawing from the text, their travel was based on the assumption that they would be welcomed home. When the kinship embrace did not happen, they became disheartened and bitter because of how much they had been victimized, cheated, and targeted as outsiders, though they had given up everything in the United States to return. Hartman commiserates with the couple about their initial expectations and the ensuing misrecognitions that they experienced:

> HARTMAN: Last summer [Ghana] seemed like paradise. But living here it feels more like hell.
>
> MARY ELLEN: It just may be, my dear.
>
> JOHN: Mercenaries, thieves, refugees, prostitutes, broke soldiers, corrupt policemen, and the desperate hard-pressed enough to try anything are out there. . . . Remember that. . . . Keep your eyes open.
>
> MARY ELLEN: Welcome to the motherland. This is what it means to be a black American in Africa.
>
> JOHN: Not all of it—
>
> MARY ELLEN: I'm sick of it. John, he doesn't care. He wants to die here.
>
> JOHN: Where else can I go, Mary Ellen? Where else? You tell me.
>
> MARY ELLEN: We can go to Cuba.
>
> JOHN: I'm too old to try a new country.
>
> MARY ELLEN: I won't die here, John. Not in a place where people will spit on my grave. You know they hate us, or haven't you figured that out yet?[31]

Migrating in search of another homeland, as evidenced by Hartman's conversation with the couple, is unlikely John and Mary Ellen. They realize that their life in Ghana is more fulfilling than what they knew in the States, but John is keen to warn Black Americans that they must release their romantic notions about Ghana: "I can't stand watching folks from the States come here and lose the sense they were born with. The Ghanaians will take your head. . . . We have to stop bullshitting about Africa. The naïveté that allows folks to believe they are returning home or entering paradise when they come here has to be destroyed."[32] John highlights the gap between the imagined and real Africa that Hartman interrogates in her narrative, but his passion is misdirected. He is upset with himself for believing in the production of what he experienced as utopian—return—during the visits that culminated in his and Mary Ellen's permanent flight from the United States. The ways in which their imaginations were catalyzed by the seeming embrace of the people on their cultural roots tours and during other personal interactions has been rendered inauthentic or, at least, not representative of the disregard they now feel from the Ghanaian masses. Interestingly, Mary Ellen has not given up on the idea of continued movements for fear of age as John has; moving toward freedom—Africa or Cuba—remains an option for her, as she adamantly rejects the thought of being subjected to continued social alienation and eventually passing away in Ghana. Such a dishonored existence would reinstate the lowly status that their travel was intended to negate. The manners in which expatriates traverse imagined Africas as well as their reasons for migrating vary greatly, as do their reactions upon settling in. Yet nearly all are forced to confront the limitations of crafting transnational, Pan-African identities, as the touristic ruses that fuel the production of return eventually disentangle.

Timothy, an expatriate based in Accra, became active in Black radical organizations while in college in the United States, and he sought out linkages to Africa to reckon fully with his evolving identity. Bothered by how little he knew about the African continent, Timothy compiled a substantial list of books with the help of a radical organization's leader and read them in a semester's time, figuring that period as the point at which he was "born into consciousness."[33] In 1981, Timothy became a member of the All-African People's Revolutionary Party (A-APRP), which was founded in 1968 by Nkrumah and led at the time by Stokely Carmichael. A staunchly Pan-Africanist organization, A-APRP championed a united Africa, the establishment of a military arm to fight against settler colonialism and capitalism, and the eventual return of diasporans to the homeland. Timothy noted that once he joined Pan-Africanist organizations, he would go overboard in his rhetoric and posture, seemingly mentioning Africa "every two words" until one day a skeptic inquired about Timothy's previous travels to Africa, which he, incidentally, had not yet made.

In 1986, Timothy took his first trip to Upper Volta (now Burkina Faso) with two other university students at the invitation of Thomas Sankara, Upper Volta's revolutionary anti-imperialist president, who had traveled to the United States on a speaking tour and encouraged like-minded Pan-Africanists to visit. Timothy met with officials and leaders of women's organizations in Upper Volta, participated in festivals and ceremonies, and volunteered throughout the country, which "had a tremendous impact on me—coming to Africa for the first time and then being in a revolutionary society run by a young brother who was close to my age. That was very impressive. A young brother running an African country! And here we in the U.S. just recently got the right to have a cup of coffee in the same restaurant as white folks. I always kept in mind that I wanted to come back to Africa." This initial visit solidified Timothy's commitment to the ongoing, worldwide struggle to improve the lives of African-descended people, and by the mid-1980s, he was focusing mainly on community organizing through Black nationalist and anti-apartheid activism on college campuses in San Diego, California, feeling a "responsibility and duty to pass it on to the next generation." Holding firm to the importance of travel to Africa as a part of his Pan-Africanist sensibility, Timothy traveled to Ghana for the first time in 1991, rooming with a friend's family who he felt had treated him as if he were kin. Outside of his Pan-African ideology, being a part of that family dynamic and observing how Ghanaian people functioned day to day was important to his decision to relocate. Not only was this further confirmation of the sort of African family reunion ideal that he experienced in Upper Volta, but also a spiritual presence there enraptured him: "That's when I fell in love with Africa. I knew this was the place I belonged and this is where my ancestors came from. I just felt that when I came—something just grabbed me." After that sensory impression in Ghana, when the imagined manifested into reality, Timothy began to travel to Ghana at least every two years and later married a Ghanaian woman.

Timothy relocated permanently in 2002 and now has two sons whom he refuses to raise in America, where he believes they may be burdened with an inferiority complex—what Frantz Fanon describes as "the outcome of a double process: primarily, economic; subsequently, the internalization—or better, the epidermalization—of this inferiority."[34] Timothy explained the U.S. hindrance of repatriation movements such as Marcus Garvey's attempt to relocate a Black contingent to Liberia in the early twentieth century:

> Here's a racist country . . . they say that we're inferior, they discriminate against us, they don't like us moving up in their system. And they won't let us leave. What is that telling you? What does that tell you about the white folks in that country over there? There's a kind of psychopathic mentality that exists that says, "I don't want you around me, but I don't want you to go. Accept my superiority over you and you should accept your inferiority." This is maniacal. That was one of the

main reasons why I left because I didn't want my children raised in a society that was [run] by psychopathic killers, murderers, and rapists. And that's exactly what they are; we have examples throughout the history of the whole United States.

Timothy maintains a Fanonian outlook in his analysis of the phenomenon whereby the formerly enslaved and colonized begin to internalize their oppression and view themselves as inferior and powerless by virtue of their race. Through his expatriation, he takes control over his legacy by preventing that debilitating mentality from being transmitted to future generations.[35] Timothy's speculative flight in his repatriation and political thought, then, renders impotent the direct "psychopathic" behavior that caused and maintains the dehumanization of the African-descended.

Timothy's rationale also echoes Orlando Patterson's formulation about slavery and freedom in his discussion of how the United States has at several points halted mass emigration, including the U.S. government's rejection of Du Bois's travel to Ghana in 1957 for the independence celebrations, as the government was fearful of the transnational spread of socialism and the development of a Black fifth column. Patterson argues convincingly that the relationship between the formerly enslaved and the slaveholder is parasitic and that, therefore, "the dominator, in the process of dominating and making another individual dependent, also makes himself dependent."[36] Slaveholders and their descendants, to continue to consider themselves free and members of the dominating class, must delimit the mobility of the enslaved and their descendants. Before slavery, Patterson continues, there was no such thing as freedom: "Slaves were the first persons to find themselves in a situation where it was vital to refer to what they wanted in this way. And slaveholders, quick to recognize this new value, were the first class of parasitic oppressors to exploit it."[37] In the post–civil rights era, flight continues to serve as a form of resistance, and the notion of mass migration back to Africa intrigues Timothy. He established a Pan-African activist alliance in Accra, and he has become a well-known writer, giving book talks and speeches throughout Ghana, Europe, and the United States. Timothy remains critical of neocolonialism and encourages diasporans to repatriate to Africa proper to help various countries resist a relapse into foreign control.

To be sure, though their speculative movements from the United States are always already radical, other Black American expatriates do not necessarily arrive in Ghana armed with or with intentions of seeking out a Pan-African or humanistic political agenda that exceeds their individualistic desires. This observation reflects absolutely on their persons, but it also underscores the risks inherent in the utilization of the language of kinship to produce return for Afro-Atlantic travelers during their initial contact as tourists. For the following expatriates, leaving the United States in their retirement years has given them the opportunity to freely ruminate about their multiconsciousness, the possibility for life in Africa, and their responsibility to their imagined homeland.

> KATHERINE: Not all Black folks in America are African Americans [except] those of us who see Africa as a place worth remembering. As far as I'm concerned, I'm an African American. My ancestry comes from lots of different places. . . . My whole existence in the U.S. is defined by race, but to just say that I'm Black is limiting. I am African American.
>
> NATHANIEL: I feel blessed . . . that God has given me a gift. Ghana has offered me a new lease on life. I was in a rut.
>
> VICKI: I never felt secure [in America]. I always felt like something could be pulled from underneath me at any moment. When I came here, that feeling was gone. This is where my soul is. It's here in Africa. It's here in Ghana.
>
> MAMA LINDA: I really felt like I would die if I stayed in America. Our people talk, but they don't do anything. I got so tired of it. . . . The African American community does not have leadership. We are a people without a rudder, without a sail. We talk a lot of shit, but don't do nothing. I couldn't take it anymore.
>
> BABA: The U.S. is a powerful place to leave. You are not part of the United States. Here you can actually make a contribution. I appreciate the things that I have learned there, but they are for application here. I don't care how successful you are there, it don't mean nothing if you're not helping Africa . . . though I don't think Africa is concerned about me.[38]

In this series of responses, there are direct and implied observations that "living" in America, particularly without a sustained collective Black politics, is a state of death. Mama Linda identifies the complacency of some of the Black Americans who remain in the United States and refuse to rail against their social alienation as the inaction that propelled her toward Africa. Ghana offers these expatriates a sense of rebirth, which prompts each of them to stand firmly in Ghana regardless of whether "Africa is concerned" about them. Though they all mentioned moments of misrecognition, being cheated or robbed in some way by local entities, and other difficulties, their testimonies about Ghana belie the positions of their retired counterparts, John and Mary Ellen, in *Lose Your Mother*, as the couple's sentiments are steeped thoroughly in disillusionment and suggest that John and Mary Ellen are constrained by fear and distrust of undesirables who would "try anything" to exploit foreigners. To be a Black American in Ghana (John corrects Mary Ellen's assumption about the whole of Africa), according to their logic, is to be an unwelcomed, disgraced stranger whose outsider status rivals what they experienced in the United States. While it remains vital to acknowledge that homeland migrations do not assuage every returnee's longing for home, the more significant thread is the resiliency of the expatriate masses. Upward of five thousand Black Americans are believed to live in Ghana today.[39] While I do not intend to gloss over those who leave when Ghana does not live up to their expectations, this analysis is concerned with those who choose to stay—those whose imaginings of the possibilities for the establishment of an African home and sustainable politics are not defeated by moments of intervallic rejection.

Based on the reflections expressed in the transcript of my interviews, it is evident that there is fulfillment in finally locating a place that feels like home, though inconsistencies between what was experienced during visits to Ghana and reality affect expatriates years into their exile. Interestingly, much of the literature surrounding roots tourism in and expatriation to Ghana cites stories from Black American tourists to discuss how the authentic is fashioned and the realities experienced on the ground by those whose decisions to migrate were made in part because of the narratives and productions generated for them.[40] Often, scholars reflect solely on the breach—moments of *décalage* where the use of terms like *obroni* or the figuring of the returnee as an outsider are viewed as evidence that what was presented during tours at slave castles, villages, and other stops were fabricated and had somehow bamboozled those who returned permanently. As seen in the previous chapter on cultural production in the post–civil rights era, Africa and, by extension, freedom are imagined long before tours commence, and travelers usually are not unwitting victims of pretense. Tourists seek experiences with the authentic, which is staged by tour guides at sites of interest to produce "deep feelings and a sense of transformed identity because they mobilize familiar images, symbols, narratives and artifacts to stage events that could function as transformative personal 'experience.' "[41] These performances typify pilgrimage-like tours, as they are high-stakes products for journeys that often are emotional, once-in-a-lifetime visits. What concerns most critics is that the Ghanaian government has profited from the exploitation of diasporan desires by creating sites of mourning. While it is possible that some Black American tourists may be exercising a willing suspension of disbelief to engage with the imagined, a focus on the pretense that undergirds such ardent kinship gestures is crucial to understanding how disparate views regarding return thwart the realization of the Black fantastic.

AFRO-ATLANTIC INVESTMENTS

In the summer of 2009, the city of Accra prepared itself for a series of events that attracted international attention. Informally referred to by many Ghanaians as the "Obama Summer," the season began in July with President Obama's first trip and major address to sub-Saharan Africa and continued into August with PANAFEST, a celebration founded in 1991 by the Ghanaian playwright Efua Sutherland. The biennial festival has been a major tourism draw to Ghana's Central Region, as Black Americans and other diasporans are invited to "reconnect" with Ghanaians and enjoy arts and cultural activities. PANAFEST is also a site of Pan-African organizing, particularly the strategizing of ways in which to boost the development of Ghana. This festival as well as other, lesser-known events has been utilized as an occasion for reparation, as various chiefs throughout the country have conducted ceremonies to apologize to diasporans for their forebears' role in the slave trade. Such public declarations promote the healing of the imagined losses caused by the institution of slavery, while formal rituals and naming ceremonies during and outside of PANAFEST events also assuage the diasporan need for recognition and sustain the imaginings of Ghana as home by formalizing and adding a certain pomp and circumstance to these tourist arrivals. On a slightly smaller scale than Ghana's fiftieth anniversary celebration in 2007, the city's preparations for President Obama's visit were extensive. Buildings along the American leader's established routes throughout Ghana were updated with new coats of paint, and potholes were filled. Billboards featuring President John Evans Atta Mills of Ghana and President Obama and, sometimes, First Lady Michelle Obama were erected throughout the city. In marketplaces and at busy intersections, hawkers sold articles of clothing printed on "Obama"-stamped fabric that included images of the Obamas' faces and the Ghanaian and American flags. Hope was coming to Ghana.

When the Obama family arrived in Accra for their whirlwind twenty-four-hour stay, some newspaper headlines proclaimed, "Welcome Home." On the streets, this narrative of the Ghanaian family welcoming returning kin was repeated, especially regarding Michelle Obama, who was rumored to have at least one ancestor from the Cape Coast area.[42] The truth of the matter was that President Obama would not be seen in person by most, but he stated that his decision to broadcast his address from Accra was a nod to Ghana's successful democracy. In his address, which was telecast throughout Ghana and the world, President Obama walked a fine line between calling for a twenty-first-century Pan-Africanism grounded in self-sufficiency and a patriarchal chastising of African leaders for failing to stabilize their nations. Of course, expected objectivity and Obama's conservatism limited him from outright quoting from great Pan-Africanists, but his nod to socialist President Nkrumah's legacy was evident even as Obama wove into the speech his ongoing democratic themes of hope and possibility for the continent:

> In my country, African-Americans—including so many recent immigrants—have thrived in every sector of society. We have done so despite a difficult past, and we have drawn strength from our African heritage. . . . Fifty-two years ago, the eyes of the world were on Ghana. And a young preacher named Martin Luther King traveled here, to Accra, to watch the Union Jack come down and the Ghanaian flag go up. This was before the March on Washington or the success of the civil rights movement in my country. Dr. King was asked how he felt while watching the birth of a nation. And he said: "It renews my conviction in the ultimate triumph of justice." . . . [F]reedom is your inheritance. Now, it is your responsibility to build upon freedom's

2.5 A 2009 billboard of President John Mills of Ghana and President Barack Obama of the United States in Accra, Ghana. Photo by author.

foundation. And if you do, we will look back years from now to places like Accra and say this was the time when the promise was realized; this was the moment when prosperity was forged, pain was overcome, and a new era of progress began.[43]

The rhetoric espoused during the Obama Summer followed and indirectly buttressed what had been a massive effort by the John Kufuor administration (2001–9) to use a particular conceptualization of Pan-Africanism—in the government's rhetoric and strategy—to improve the nation's economic standing. For example, President Kufuor's plan for economic development included boosting the tourism industry and attracting diasporan investment in the country, a goal that saw its greatest strides in 2007, with Ghana celebrating its golden anniversary and the biennial PANAFEST celebration scheduled for that summer. While the government's plans to embrace diasporans appeared genuine on the surface, many members of the Black American expatriate collective vocalized their qualms regarding the seeming insincerity of the newly appointed Tourism and Diasporan Relations secretariat,

2.6 The Obama family stands outside of the Door of Return during a tour of the slave castle at Cape Coast, Ghana, in 2009. Photo by Saul Loeb © Getty Images.

which was more concerned about economic returns than the possibilities for radical returns.

During the 2007 Ghana@50 celebrations, Timothy complained: "The current call for African diasporans to come in and invest is really a bastardization of what Nkrumah was talking about. He was talking about people coming in and making a contribution to a society that was progressive and revolutionary. What they're talking about [now] is 'come in, give me your money and set up your business' and there's no citizenship . . . just 'bring me your money.'" By 2007, the rhetoric of the New Patriotic Party and the Kufuor administration consisted of what at first blush appeared to be a return to Nkrumahist thought. Timothy and the expatriate collective's cynicism in reaction to this move was catalyzed by the Ghanaian government's propagation of a precarious form of Black radicalism while under the tutelage of and increasing debt to the International Monetary Fund and the World Bank. The government conceived of the Ghana@50 initiative as a way not only to mark the nation's anniversary and subsequent successes but also to come to terms with its failures. Organizers invested $20 million to develop the fiftieth anniversary into a year-long series of activities complete with monthly themes that paid homage to Ghana's past, present, and future, including reconciliation with the African diaspora over Ghana's role in the transatlantic slave trade. The largest countrywide festivities occurred in the days just before and after Independence Day and included historical reenactments, fireworks, parades, theatrical and musical performances, and lectures.

Anyone in Accra during February and March 2007 would have noticed the regalia. Nearly everything—from government buildings and restaurants to light poles and tree trunks—seemed to be adorned in red, gold, green, and black, the colors of the Ghanaian flag. Some people even had attached large flags to the hoods and antennas of their automobiles. A palpable sense of pride and anxiety had gripped the country. Three weeks before Independence Day, the Ghanaian government continued its race to prepare the capital city for the foreign tourists, dignitaries, and Ghanaian returnees who would be visiting to share in its Golden Jubilee celebrations. Newspapers and radio stations spread the word that the government would be cracking down on unauthorized hawkers, who had been fixtures on major Accra roads as merchants of disparate items, often snarling traffic for miles. The biggest concern, however, was ridding the city's newly beautified landscape of the physically disabled street beggars who ducked and dodged between cars along busy, multiple-lane roads, imploring drivers for money.[44] Outright evidence of poverty and the national disregard of the disabled did not fit the modern, progressive image that the government wanted to portray to the world. It had worked diligently to create a particular environment that would foster repeat tourism and foreign investment.

Accra's W. E. B. Du Bois Centre hosted a "Press Conference/National Orientation" to articulate kinship ties between Ghanaians and the African diasporic visitors who would be attending the celebrations, to frame what would become a popular refrain concerning diasporic financial responsibility, and to highlight the upcoming, celebratory events planned throughout the country.[45] A Ghanaian-based dance troupe and an American neo-soul band provided entertainment between speeches by government officials and spokespersons for corporate sponsors of the Ghana@50 program. Nii Martey Kwao, the Black American chairman of Ghana's Golden Homecoming and 200th Anniversary of the Emancipation from the Slave Trade, spoke briefly about the historical linkages between the diaspora and Ghana, stating that "we are all black stars."[46] Kwao's kinship sentiment points to the nation's flag, whose bars of red, gold, and green form the backdrop for a lone five-pointed black star, whose inclusion was inspired in part by Marcus Garvey's Black Star Line's endeavors to repatriate Africans in the diaspora to Liberia. Pan-Africanist rhetoric set the tone for the entire press conference, with each speaker emphasizing the affinity that does or should exist between Ghanaians and Africans in the diaspora. The Golden Homecoming portion of the Ghana@50 activities consisted of concerts, an investment summit, a so-called diasporan family dinner, and visits to various slavery tourism sites. This sequence of events was designed to "officially welcome our brothers and sisters for joining us [in celebrating] our Golden Jubilee Anniversary and invite them to constantly visit Ghana and make here their home."[47]

The *Daily Graphic* newspaper reported that Accra's Independence Day parade was the largest in recent memory, with crowds that extended 100 meters (roughly 109 yards) around the city's stadium. By 7:00 a.m., the unreserved seats in the stadium had been packed with people for over an hour, after filling up during the previous night's president's party, which was a concert and fireworks display that stretched into the wee hours of the morning. Before the parade began at 10:00 a.m., thousands of Ghanaians and other revelers outside of Independence Square cheered, sang songs of triumph and freedom, and watched intently as dignitaries from around the world entered the grounds in shiny luxury vehicles newly purchased by the Ghanaian government. Tour groups from across the African diaspora, who had received official invitations that guaranteed them seats inside the square, made their way through the bustling crowd and took their respective places among other invited guests. Presidents and heads of state from more than twenty African nations; Britain's Prince Edward, Duke of Kent; World Bank president

Paul Wolfowitz; and a delegation from the U.S. Congressional Black Caucus also attended the parade.

Among the crowds surrounding the square were mimes whose bodies were painted in the colors of the Ghanaian flag, musical groups and drummers, and several people handing out free paper flags and boutonnieres crafted with greenery and ribbons. Hawkers, who gracefully balanced massive baskets of snacks and cool beverages on their heads, found thousands of willing customers, while police officers, some outfitted in dress uniforms and sitting atop horses, kept order in the sea of people. Most striking about this affair was the crowd's patriotic style, which ranged from Ghana shirts and flags tied as adornments on the body to clothing made from fabric with the Ghana@50 logo and elegant kente cloth outfits complete with golden accessories. The grandeur of the parade ceremony included music from military bands and a Scottish bagpipe and drums corps; dances performed by schoolchildren; and a speech by the guest of honor, Nigerian President Olusegun Obasanjo. Ghanaian President Kufuor's address began with an acknowledgment of political leaders and other unknown citizens who had assisted in the building of the nation before and after independence. He cited the "artificial boundaries imposed by the colonialists" as well as "political instability, tribal conflict, and economic mismanagement" as problems that impeded the continent's growth.[48] African leaders had learned lessons along the way, though, and Kufuor held that the end of the Cold War was the beginning of an African renaissance, led by the African Union (AU). Kufuor, the newly appointed chairman of the AU, pledged to continue working with other African nations in their New Economic Partnership for African Development, which he believed would assist the continent in gaining equal footing with other world powers. Kufuor also spoke directly to Africa's youth to persuade them to discontinue what had become a mass emigration and "brain drain" to foreign countries: "The future of this continent is yours; it is your heritage and you must stay and be part of building the well-governed, economically vibrant nations we all aspire to."[49] The next day, Jacob Obetsebi-Lamptey, the minister for tourism and diasporan relations, shared a similar capitalist message regarding Pan-African responsibility at a conference for a mostly U.S.-based contingent of the Universal Negro Improvement Association (UNIA), though his remarks created more breaches and distrust than linkages.

We also have a dream of a free, a liberated, and resurrected African
continent—organized around the United States of Africa, which will include as
the sixth province, the Diaspora.
—Julius Garvey, Universal Negro Improvement Association

The mission of the Ghana@50 UNIA forum was to highlight the initiatives that UNIA and other Pan-African organizations were designing to
strengthen Ghana's economy. During the meeting, speakers expressed
two interrelated outlooks as to why Black Americans should invest in
Ghana: individual capital gain and Pan-African responsibility. The speakers included Keidi Obi Awadu, a Black American radio station host and
owner of Black Star Media, who utilized charts and statistics to recommend
that attendees look to Africa for investment opportunities in underdeveloped areas. Awadu insisted that Ghana should act as the investment portal to other countries in Africa—that economic achievement
would lead to crucial advancements in the livelihood of Africans. The
next speaker, E. Jerome Johnson, a Black American expatriate and author
of *Seven Steps toward Black Re-Emergence*, disagreed somewhat with the
focus of Awadu's presentation. Johnson asserted that a Pan-Africanist
stance is viable only when the people on the ground are involved: "Poor
economic development is a symptom of lack of power. We have too many
people talking about Pan-African business opportunity . . . all of that stuff is
secondary . . . we have to get a mind-set that we are going to regain power
and we are going to confront the people who are taking the power."[50]
Johnson's critique called for an avoidance of a top-down approach—the
political power that he imagined excluded Ghanaian political figures,
who he believed had aligned themselves with the United Nations and
other agencies whose missions were neither progressive nor Black nationalist. He found that most foreign interest in the African continent
was questionable, borderline neocolonial, and therefore antithetical to
Pan-Africanism.

Julius Garvey, Marcus Garvey's son, echoed Johnson's concerns, often
directing his gaze at Obetsebi-Lamptey as a subtle, though unavoid-
able, corrective gesture. Julius Garvey's rhetoric echoed his father's
vision of Pan-Africanism, which was keen on representing the voices
of all African-descended peoples, not simply "the elites at the top who

have co-opted the system and funneled off the resources for their own benefit."[51] Garvey articulated his desire to work with the Ghanaian government in its endeavors, but he warned that the proper infrastructure needed to be in place before he would participate or petition others to do so. His concerns were perhaps reinforced by the fact that the government had close ties to Wolfowitz, who presided over a largely U.S.-controlled financial institution that has been widely criticized for benefiting Western elites at the expense of the world's poor, and had invited him to the Independence Day celebrations. Garvey's caution also may have been a reaction to how the government had been marketing its economic plan to the diaspora through the Joseph Project.

On August 1, 2007, the Ministry for Tourism and Diasporan Relations officially launched the Joseph Project, the purported goal of which was to celebrate African excellence and to welcome diasporans back home—to Ghana. The project's name is an allusion to the biblical Joseph, whose brothers sold him into slavery. Once freed from bondage, Joseph became a member of the noble class and forgave his kin for their disloyalty, a sort of reconciliation that Ghanaian leaders desired to have with the African diaspora. The organizers of the Joseph Project were likely inspired by the nation's 1990s tourism strategy and former President Jerry Rawlings's 1994 declaration of Emancipation Day to atone for Ghana's role in the slave trade as well as to commemorate annually the worldwide liberation of African slaves. The Ghana@50 Emancipation Day theme was "Re-Uniting the African Family," and it was inextricably linked to the nation's ongoing tourism push. In addition to conferences, concerts, healing ceremonies, and PANAFEST, the Joseph Project also sponsored pilgrimages to vestiges of the slave trade that survived throughout the country. According to Obetsebi-Lamptey, the government's desire was to take responsibility for its role in the transatlantic slave trade, to apologize, and to make amends.

Although the now-defunct Joseph Project's website displayed images of and emigrationist quotes by Marcus Garvey and featured a song called "Welcome Home," Obetsebi-Lamptey told the members of the UNIA audience that the Ghanaian government did not intend to initiate a back-to-Africa movement. He insisted:

We're not saying everybody should get up and relocate back in Africa. No, you built the country over there—you built the wealth over there. Why should you give it up? You should use that wealth over there and bring some of it back here to use it to build up here. . . . The Africans have tremendous power in the U.S., power that is not being used for the benefit of Africa and could so easily be used for the benefit of Africa. The Jews do it for Israel. Why don't we do it for Africa? We can and we must.[52]

In addition to the potentially problematic assumption that Black Americans have disposable income that they should spend to support Ghana and Africa (the amount often cited by Ghanaian officials then was $6 billion), the government never explained its plan for how the average Ghanaian was to participate in the reconciliation and Pan-African organizing that the Joseph Project was designed to initiate. Obetsebi-Lamptey mentioned that most Ghanaian citizens had little knowledge about the transatlantic slave trade and that a 2006 national broadcast of Alex Haley's film *Roots* had sparked what he envisioned to be an opportunity to begin educating the nation about the diaspora and Ghana's historical role in the transatlantic slave trade. The Joseph Project's website indicated that the history of slavery would be added to school curricula and that the government would advocate the proliferation of texts about the continent written by Africans to disrupt what had been centuries of relative silence about the institution.[53]

At the Ghana@50 parade, I met Jerome Johnson by happenstance as he braved his way through the restless crowd distributing Pan-Africanist leaflets. I watched as he initiated extemporaneous discussions with various guests until I lost sight of him in the crowd. Johnson's presence was fascinating in that it served as a counternarrative—a moment of rupture in the costly, excessive pomp and circumstance that played out in the background. Despite the uncertainties about the future of Pan-Africanism and his skepticism about the Ghanaian government's intentions, Timothy voiced his agreement with Johnson and other members of the expatriate community that reservations about calls for diasporan financial investments "shouldn't stop Africans from abroad from coming home because this is our home. Africans born in the diaspora have the responsibility to come home even under [European-sanctioned and complicit Ghanaian political figures' embrace of] neocolonialism."

DISARTICULATIONS

Robert E. Lee, one of Ghana's few dentists, was among the first Black Americans to arrive in Ghana in the late 1950s. His intention was to assist his friends and former Lincoln University classmates, Nkrumah and K. A. B. Jones-Quartey, in the building of the fledgling nation. While reflecting on the progress made during his more than fifty years as an expatriate in Ghana, Lee lamented that "'no one seemed to talk about Pan-Africanism anymore.' Instead, people use the term 'diaspora,' which to Lee connoted separateness and individualism rather than solidarity."[54] To be sure, it is not accurate to draw a firm line to suggest that the earliest waves of activist-minded Black American expatriates in Ghana somehow put aside attempts to reckon with their imagined homeland. Angelou's avoidance of the slave castles, even though she desired recognition and the feeling of truly being at home, speaks to how the tropes of longing and dispossession haunt travel toward Africa. With the civil rights movement playing out back in the United States and various anticolonial movements on the African continent to support and learn from, Angelou, Julian Mayfield, Leslie Lacy, and other Black American expatriates and exiles tended to be more concerned with Pan-African inquiries that could perhaps answer the urgency of the struggle back in the United States rather than simply assuaging their individualistic desires.

The question becomes how disappointments lead to the breakdown of Pan-African activity in the post–civil rights moment. The answer, perhaps, lies in the expectations of Africa that go unspoken. Today, several expatriates have difficulties with Pan-Africanism as it is imagined in Ghana because of the perpetual disagreement over what Africa means, the politics and economic reasoning behind who is included, and how membership is conferred. Significant to this homeland exploration have been the moments of breach and misrecognition wherein the Black American traveler—certain of the possibilities and promises associated with his movement—is met with a greeting that designates him as a stranger. Misnaming is a verbal form of cultural distancing, which Black Americans read as a serious affront that runs counter to the traveler's assertion of self. Often, the Black American is rendered an outsider—specifically, a white person culturally—and his intertwined African and Black identities are disrupted and erased. Imagine, then, how this now unsteady footing might translate in various movements that require Pan-African unification (keeping in mind, of course, that the exercise of flight is geared toward suturing this very sort of alienation from the origin). The most devastating of such breaches occurs because of the difficulty of defining a basic grammar to explicate just what is meant when someone asserts Africa. In an interview about her novel *Paradise*, Toni Morrison explained about exclusive, separatist communities that "all paradises, all utopias are designed by who is not there, by the people who are not allowed in."[55] A common occurrence in the various travel narrative manifestations explored herein is this moment of breach, which is aptly alluded to in Morrison's insight. The distinction that the imagination is utilized to construct place by those "who are not allowed in" is quite useful in thinking about the riveting dynamic between diasporan travelers who arrive with romantic notions and peoples in the desired homeland who are facing contemporary realities. Also of import here is the tension inherent when someone who is connected more recently to a place has or asserts the authority to determine who is African and to allow or forbid travelers' attempts to self-actualize by denying or imposing limitations on their belonging.

During the yearlong research stay in Ghana that she chronicles in *Lose Your Mother*, for example, Hartman's already critical eye is sharpened by an uneasy silence aboard the tour bus with her African academic counterparts, who refer to her inconsistently as kin and distant acquaintance: "sister" and "my friend from the diaspora," respectively. Hartman begins to self-isolate as a defense mechanism to combat the constant othering she experiences during the tense disagreements that she has with many of the other seminar members, who have made it clear that Africa did not extend beyond continental borders and certainly did not include her. Hartman's Black American expatriate friends, John and Mary Ellen, had instructed her that "certain things don't catch" in Ghana when it comes to thinking about controversial topics such as Ghanaian complicity in the transatlantic slave trade and domestic slavery, and it appeared that their warning was indeed correct, as Hartman was met with severe pushback when she voiced her perspectives on the very topic of the seminar with her colleagues. The men accused Hartman of being self-centered and unconcerned about how slavery negatively impacted the Ghanaians who remained. Hartman recalls arguing passionately with the African researchers who, in her estimation, had figured African financial losses as more substantial than the generational dispossession experienced by enslaved Africans and their descendants in the Americas.[56] Some of the scholars referred to specific kidnapped relatives and argued that African nations should receive financial reparations, as they were the ultimate losers—given the relative underdevelopment under which most West and Central African nations suffered.[57] The scholars generally agreed that the Africans who had participated in the slave trade were coerced into it, and their refusal to acknowledge the possibility that their ancestors had played a more active role in the trade hardened an already deflated and pessimistic Hartman. She resolved that after six months of being in Ghana as a researcher and diasporan, no one would understand her hurt; in their constant bickering, each side attempted to make the other feel its grief. Hartman's analysis of her travel tragically highlights the inevitable rifts that can occur when linguistically and culturally distinct African-descended peoples attempt to forge political and cultural connections. She later reflects on her initial presumption that the seminar would be a sort of Pan-African think tank, as she and her colleagues had a difficult time developing a "common vocabulary about slavery."[58] Pan-Africanism, she continued, "no longer included the likes of me . . . my self-proclaimed African identity, albeit hyphenated, was fanciful [to them] and my Swahili name an amusement. They could hardly manage to say it without snickering."[59]

What Hartman experiences as a piling on of painful disavowals evidences a breach wherein the indigenous African scholars position themselves as a sort of adjudicating front that claims geographic license to arbitrarily decide who belongs. What is interesting about their ridiculing exchanges with Hartman is that the group itself is a multinational collective; their sense of Africa is imagined, too, and no gauge exists to determine whose version is most authentic unless geography trumps. It is clear, though, that the crux of this series of native/diasporan disagreements is caused by divergent understandings of the temporal stakes. In this case, my thoughts align with Kamari Maxine Clarke's regarding the problematic erasure of contemporary Africa that occurs in some homeward journeys.[60] In general, people more recently from Africa are not as concerned with revisiting the distant past as they are with grappling with their countries' pressing realities. For the descendants of slaves in the

West, the peculiar institution continues to have bearing on the present moment, and they tend to be most concerned with the politics of suturing what occurred in the past through flight and actual engagements with the imagined homeland. This distinction is, in essence, a continuous point of tension between diasporan and Pan-Africanist politics.

Intriguingly, the most recent iteration of Pan-Africanism that seeks to merge the related but competing political outlooks that have been described above is the Diaspora African Forum (DAF), an AU initiative that has an office based in Accra and is headed by a Black American expatriate, Erieka Bennett. The DAF mission statement indicates that its goals are to connect diasporans and continental Africans, and to encourage those "who yearn to be part of their roots and are willing to contribute their time, financial resources, expertise, skills and energies, in the building of a better Africa."[61] John Kufuor, then president of Ghana and chairman of the AU, and H. E. Alpha Omar Konare, chairman of the AU Commission, officially commissioned the DAF in July 2007. Bennett is an elected member of the Economic, Social, and Cultural Council of the Africa Union, has diplomatic status, secured a land grant, and served as an advisor to President Kufuor. She recalls fighting for years to make the diasporan voice heard in Ghana and throughout Africa, though she has not always felt support from fellow members of the expatriate community. Because a number of expatriates have lived in Ghana much longer than Bennett, she notes that there has been some tension in the building the DAF mission with those with different visions, and that she regrets not working more closely with the African American Association of Ghana during the process. Basic philosophical differences regarding how to curry favor with the government has hindered the possibility of full cooperation, as most expatriates were and remain concerned with securing a permanent visa and basic rights as citizens and are perhaps too direct in their opposition to the government's seeming nonchalance, while the DAF mission is concerned more with the AU's and the Ghanaian government's overall economic and redress strategy by way of what many expatriates critique as effectively capitalistic programs such as the Joseph Project. Bennett noted:

Many may not fully recognize that the African diaspora "nation" is within the top ten richest nations in the world. We are coming home with remarkable knowledge, talent, skills. We are absolutely abounding with top scientists, engineers, military advisors, medical doctors, social scientists, teachers, financial executives, and hard workers. We have worked in top institutions, both in the public and private sectors. . . . We now add to that knowledge African holistic connection to the land, the language, the culture, the governing bodies, the civil society, and we will make a powerful partner with our brothers and sisters at home.[62]

Bennett travels throughout Africa often as a strategist and as the appointed voice of the diaspora. When pressed, she concedes that the AU should concern itself with supporting the repatriation of interested diasporans, and she believes that the DAF mission in Accra (and the posts yet to be built throughout the African continent) should couple their focus on economic uplift with plans to assist returnees in their adjustment as permanent migrants. Unprompted, a few expatriates admitted their distrust of the DAF mission's brand of Pan-Africanism, connecting the organization to neocolonialism and blaming its emphasis on diasporan responsibility for their continued displeasure at not being integrated into Ghanaian society as full-fledged citizens with an ancestral right to live there.

The mistrust that arises between these expatriates is caused by an uneven exchange. The Ghanaian government is interested in capitalist ascent through the funneling of diasporic dollars into its economy. Yet the government wishes to accomplish this transaction without bending much to the desires of the very people that they shoulder with the responsibility of funding this redress project. The government articulates its belief that Ghana is Black Americans' home at least symbolically, but temporally and legislatively it has made no major movement toward developing a viable path to citizenship or a diasporan visa option that expatriates have long demanded, as they realize that their engagements with Pan-Africanism require at least some political power. It is as if the diaspora does not exceed the borders of the nation (Ghana), except when it comes to the flow of money. Ghana and, by extension, Africa are presented to tourists as commodities to be consumed during temporary passages. How peculiar it was to witness Obetsebi-Lamptey, then, bluntly advise the UNIA delegation, whose original charter was geared to building the Black Star Line and repatriating diasporans to Africa, that the Ghanaian government did not intend to support permanent migratory efforts, while in the next breath he uttered variations of themes that marked the Ghana@50 and Joseph Project's strategies, which included the reuniting of the African family. Perhaps the Kufuor administration felt that the establishment of a Black American "tribal" voting bloc would pose a risk to the nation. One would not have to look too far in the past to discover historical reasons for this fear: in addition to the brutality of the United States' Federal Bureau of Investigation's Counter Intelligence Program (COINTELPRO), assassinations across Africa, and other Cold War issues, the toppling of Nkrumah's government by a coup assisted by the Central Intelligence Agency was organized in part because of his increasingly isolationist socialist government, in which some of his closest confidantes were Black Americans. Black American émigrés, in general, also have a sort of historical Afro-colonialist rap that precedes them based on the nineteenth-century Liberian settlement, which poised Americo-Liberians in leadership positions as they attempted to Christianize the supposedly heathen Africans and assisted in a peculiar project of modernization—a colonization scheme whose damage reverberates today. Among the current expatriate contingent in Ghana, very few members engage in any sort of radical political activity, even if they initially moved to Ghana with such goals. As I have been suggesting, constant misrecognitions and bipolar naming wherein the expatriate consistently is subjected to the sibling/obroni binary impede Pan-African possibility. It is understandable, then, why the DAF mission is met with suspicion by expatriates, particularly members of the African American Association of Ghana, as Bennett lobbies on behalf of the AU's economic objective to embrace the diaspora as the sixth province of Africa.[63] If unification is the goal, then strategies will have to be enacted on smaller scales as well, especially since breaches and misunderstandings continue to occur in exchanges between Ghanaians outside of the tourism industry and roots tourists.

With her related experiences in Ghana, Hartman finds it doubtful that Ghanaians involved in the tourism industry truly believe the African "mirage" created by their performances for tourists "even when their survival necessitated that they indulge the delusion. . . . What each community made of slavery and how they understood it provided little ground for solidarity. . . . African Americans entertained fantasies of return and Ghanaians of departure . . . we did not see the same past, nor did we share a common vision of the Promised Land. The ghost of slavery [the trace of ancestral Africa] was being conjured to very different ends."[64] Authenticity has no appointed adjudicator, which suggests that sincerity is the appropriate lens through which to think about relationships between subjects.[65] It remains up to individual subjects to gauge the probity of the performance or even to suspend disbelief to feel something for which they had yearned so deeply that they were prompted to travel. Perhaps the tourism industry's strategies to meet roots tourists' psychic needs are devised out of sincere concern, which incidentally results in financial gain. Or maybe it is greed and the employment of trickery and deceit that satiates longing. Whatever the case, it is evident that moments of breach are results of, at least in part, the juncture created by many travelers' expectation that ancestral Ghana has been preserved in the manner in which they have imagined.

Stuart Hall's formulations about the construction of cultural identities are significant here not only regarding diasporans but also concerning what we may think of native and, as such, more "authentic" identities as well:

> The past continues to speak to us. But it no longer addresses us as a simple, factual "past," since our relations to it, like the child's relation to the mother, is always-already "after the break." It is always constructed through memory, fantasy, narrative, and myth. Cultural identities are the points of identification, the unstable points of identification or suture, which are made, within the discourses of history and culture. Not an essence but a positioning. Hence, there is always a politics of identity, a politics of position, which has no absolute guarantee in an unproblematic, transcendental "law of origin."[66]

In essence, the location and repossession of a primeval Africa is always already an impossibility; sincerity becomes the gauge of and speculative activity the test to determine the limits and possibilities of articulation. In Black American speculation, the story consistently has been one of continuous travel toward freedom (figured as Africa), as "curiosity in Africa led one not to any immediate satisfaction but only toward ever-winding avenues of searching."[67]

Refiguring Return and the Hopeful Perpetuity of Afro-Atlantic Redemption Songs

A Journeyman Pictures short documentary titled *Coming Home—Ghana* features Seestah Imahküs, the Pan-Africanist hotel owner who is still fighting to map out avenues for diasporans to return home with full rights as citizens upon landing. The film opens with Seestah Imahküs as she recites to a tour group the horrific history of the Elmina slave castle-dungeon and the legacy that slavery wrought on diasporans. A few men situated behind her, including her husband, Nana, provide a dramatic pulse through drumming and song. The cultural roots tourists listen intently as Imahküs's voice cracks, and she becomes visibly overwhelmed as she catalogs the horrors inflicted on the ancestors and the untold losses that occurred during the transatlantic slave trade. She tells the group of mostly Black American visitors: "You are what we have been waiting for . . . we are no longer coons and niggers. We are proud African people who are here where we are supposed to be. We make no apologies to anyone for what we are doing or how we are doing it. We stand proud as African people."[68] The next scene cuts to reenactments of how slaves were captured: a performance that her company, One Africa Productions, has staged for the tourists. After the presentation, Seestah Imahküs leads the tourists, who are now carrying lighted candles, into the women's slave dungeon as part of her company's "Thru the Door of No Return—The Return" commemorative ceremony. A soprano voice sings the Christian spiritual "Come by Here, My Lord," and someone keens loudly in the background; the cameraperson pans the group to search for the source of the wailing, positioning the camera's gaze on several weeping women. Others utter "hallelujah" and "yes" to affirm the words Seestah Imahküs speaks and perhaps to express relief at being able to travel to bear witness to her description of their ancestors' pain and their own inheritance.

In a later question-and-answer segment about her life in Ghana, Seestah Imahküs expresses her disillusionment with the Ghanaian government's turn to Pan-Africanist rhetoric in the wake of its fiftieth anniversary and the two hundredth anniversary of the abolition of the slave trade: "[They] want us to celebrate the abolition of a slave trade that [they] were responsible for starting or participating in? No, I think that that's hypocritical. And I, personally, would have nothing to do with that." Though Ghana's founding triumphalist narrative continues to inspire the homeland dreams of many diasporans, it is worth noting that after the 1966 coup that deposed Nkrumah, there were indications that the focus of Pan-African thought in Ghana would not be as encouraging of expatriation and exile as Nkrumah had been to the cadre of Black Americans who settled there during his presidency. In fact, most Black Americans were deemed untrustworthy by the military regime that deposed Nkrumah and were forced out of the country. By 1970, Ebenezer Moses Debrah, the Ghanaian ambassador to the United States—who was very popular because of his ventures into poverty-stricken communities and engagement with Black Americans, unlike other African diplomats who refused to involve themselves in U.S. domestic politics—bluntly indicated to *Ebony* magazine that while he desired to serve as a kind of missionary to educate Black Americans about their roots and promote a rise in their self-confidence by sharing Ghana's story of liberation with them, he was not supportive of back-to-Africa migrations. Debrah explained his controversial position in the midst of the rise of Black cultural nationalism in the United States: "There are a lot of skills in Black America that can be utilized in Africa. . . . Blacks and Africans can share profits of these ventures and your profits could be returned to the U.S. to gain additional business capital. . . . American blacks and Africans haven't learned how to take friendship out of the emotion stage and transfer it to the area of substance."[69] In many ways, Debrah's 1970s capitalistic call for Black Americans to lend their skill sets to Ghana presaged the summons made by the architects of the now-defunct Joseph Project and, more compellingly, the AU's focus on recognizing the African diaspora as the sixth region of Africa, on the one hand, and, on the other hand, the AU's bolstering of this seemingly Pan-African inclusion with statistics on how the gesture makes financial sense in reference to the development of Africa.

Though mistrust and misrecognitions continue to hinder the establishment of a true Pan-African column, it remains the case that scholars generally are quite wary of expatriate attitudes like those of Seestah Imahküs and other Black American tourists at sites of slavery, as they find the commentary indicative of Black Americans' attempting to impose their narratives of loss and dispossession on Ghana, thereby privileging Black American ancestral histories over contemporary Ghanaian issues. Salamishah Tillet, for instance, argues that "the myth of the African diaspora, despite protestations otherwise, risks becoming an exclusively and undeniably African American national space."[70] When taken into the context that I have laid out throughout this chapter, Tillet's assertion, which is a quite common critique of these interactions, belies complex and often misleading Ghanaian governmental narratives, informal discussions by tourists and expatriates, and the continuing legal discussions that have been active since at least the 1990s regarding whether Pan-Africanism ought to involve the integration of African-descended expatriates into the Ghanaian nation.

After nearly thirty years of fighting for the diasporan right to return and citizenship status, Seestah Imahküs has not given up on her Pan-Africanist vision, but she has revised it in light of the realities in Ghana, where rifts have hindered the realization of the united Africa that she imagined. Often referred to as "One Africa" by locals in Elmina, this renaming of Seestah Imahküs as her hotel brand indirectly mocks the support that she and her husband (before his untimely death in 2007) provide to local villages, as she receives very little in exchange. Seestah Imahküs explains diasporan claims to Africa and the lack of dual citizenship, for which she and other expatriates had been fighting on governmental record since 1996: "As far as I'm concerned, anywhere in Africa, wherever the spirit leads us to be, we have the right to go there and settle."[71] For Seestah Imahküs, the ancestral imperative exceeds whether or not modern citizenship laws recognize the descendants of slaves. Seestah Imahküs continues to consider herself a gatekeeper at the Door of No Return in Elmina and struggles against government entities and UNESCO, which maintains its policy of preserving the slave castles for tourism by repainting them and by repurposing portions of the structures with tourist lures such as gift shops. Though Seestah Imahküs's resentment about these conservation efforts remains—she even expressed her anger in 2009 about the continued efforts at "whitewashing the Black man's history" by confronting publicly an unsuspecting UNESCO employee during a conference panel regarding contemporary Pan-Africanism in Ghana—she takes comfort in her belief that "the spirit of the ancestors is real and strong, for as much as they paint [the slave castle dungeons], they can't keep the paint on the wall looking white for any length of time. The stone gray cement continues to break through the white wash."[72] The specter of slavery indeed reappears, serving as a subtle reminder of the duplicitousness that can be located in narratives of kinship and progress.

The question that arises is how to reimagine the possibilities for return if literal travels back have proven either impossible or unsustainable due to mutual distrust and misrecognitions, and governmental strategies that are concerned with making economic returns are decidedly and devastatingly aligned with furtive neocolonial projects. Certainly, by titling her travel memoir *Lose Your Mother* in such a riveting manner, Hartman leaves it open to the audience's interpretation as to whether she simply is alluding to a striking phrase from a mistake-ridden letter that is given her by a young Ghanaian man outside a slave castle who intends to acknowledge that Hartman, a potential benefactress, has "lost" ties to her mother[land] because of slavery or whether she is actively imploring the return-minded diasporan reader who has picked up her narrative to disabuse himself of any fantasies that he may have about reclaiming an all-embracing African motherland. Throughout her journeys in Ghana, Hartman expresses an acute longing for recognition, but she is halted at nearly every turn: in the sparsity of the archives, at the lazy forms of memorialization that exist at the slave castle–dungeons, and on the bus with African academics who ridicule her and appear to downplay the interconnections between the diasporan and neocolonial conditions. Hartman indeed issues an undeniable sort of counterrejection of what the silence about slavery's effects and aftereffects have left for descendants of slaves: dispossessed lives that they are charged with making sense of to survive. In the chapter "So Many Dungeons," Hartman briefly catalogs her attempts to attend to this heightened sense of loss by engaging in speculation about slaves who appear in the archives, but whose life stories and fates are deemed insignificant and fall into the gaps, so to speak.

For instance, Hartman notes that accounts of what it was like to experience imprisonment at Cape Coast Castle do not exist in the archives. The closest description was made in a 1787 antislavery tract written by Ottobah Cugoano, a former African manservant who happens to appear as a fixture in an etching with his owners, who describes remembering the groans, cries, and misery of his fellow captives in the bowels of the dungeon. Hartman takes on the task of "[imagining] the boy entering the gates of the fort on the day he lost his name" by speculating about what young Cugoano's life was like before he was strewn into slavery.

"His name was Kwabena," she writes, and she continues by assigning him a home village and a background narrative that leads up to his kidnapping and his internal struggle to make sense of the terror that he experiences.[73] Of course, Hartman cannot save Kwabena from his eventual fate, but the fact that she engages the imagination in such moments of brutality and violent erasure from the historical record is moderately healing for Hartman's psyche, redeeming the sense of hopelessness that threatens to engulf the narrative tone of *Lose Your Mother* in various sections.

Hartman later recalls the 1792 death of an unnamed woman aboard the slave ship *Recovery*. She works to literally rescue the woman's story from oblivion by stating the various recorded accounts given as to why the woman was disrobed, beaten, strung up on a sail, and nonchalantly tossed into the ocean and by speculating on how the woman might have felt at various moments leading up to and during the elaborate process of her murder. In the final, speculative account, Hartman characterizes the woman as a radical who takes back control of her body by refusing to eat and electing not to perform a dance to entertain members of the ship's crew. Instead, the woman chooses death vis-à-vis the path of the Flying Africans that had gone before her: "It worried her that the ancestors might shun her, or the gods might be angry and punish her by bringing her back as a goat or dog, or she would roam the earth directionless and never find her way beyond the sea, but she risked it anyway, it was the only path open. When the two boys plummeted into the sea, they had made leaving look so easy. . . . All they could see was a girl slumped in a dirty puddle and not the one soaring and on her way home."[74] Yet once Hartman descends from her moments of speculative flight, she concludes the chapter thusly: "If the story ended there, I could feel a small measure of comfort. I could hold on to this instant of possibility. I could find a salutary lesson in the girl's suffering and pretend a story was enough to save her from oblivion. I could sigh with relief and say, 'It all happened so long ago.' Then I could wade into the Atlantic and not think of the dead book."[75]

In the age of continued everydayness of the brutality against and the restriction of Black bodies, it is understandable why Hartman feels this way about the seeming interminability of slavery. As stated above, it is unlikely that Hartman is wholly pessimistic about Africa due to her inability to travel through time in the way that she intended to during her journey throughout Ghana. Subjective and mildly egoistic, as one might expect a first-person travel narrative about cultural loss would be, *Lose Your Mother* contains quiet moments of joy enacted as temporary relief, as each speculative episode demonstrates Hartman's burgeoning faith in alternative ways of framing history and the possibilities for return. While Hartman's use of the imagination within the memoir, however brief, does appear to underscore her belief in the futility of attempting to go back to the past to reclaim one's histories and peoples in the traditional sense, it more significantly highlights the promises inherent in seeking out a politics and practice that compel the establishment of speculative, communal fictive and nonfictive spaces of pleasure and possibility in the face of dispossession—perhaps something called neoteric Pan-Africanism, an epistemology by which Africans and all Afro-Atlantic descendants of enslaved persons might begin to navigate the wilderness as they continue to struggle in the "future created by" the era of slavery.[76]

◆　◆　◆

At the end of 2009's Obama Summer, Seestah Imahküs helped welcome to Elmina members of the Association for the Study of Worldwide African Diaspora (ASWAD), which held its biennial academic conference in Accra on dates that overlapped with PANAFEST. In recent years, PANAFEST has lost much of its original luster because of what some of my Ghanaian acquaintances have blamed on the expatriates' usurpation of the programming and crafting of the festival to satiate the longings of diasporans returning home rather than keeping up the Pan-African arts theme that once drew tens of thousands of attendees from across Africa and the diaspora.

During the 2009 festival's opening ceremony at Elmina Castle, an estimated two hundred guests watched a few members of the ASWAD diasporan contingent as they poured themselves emotionally into their offerings of interpretive dance, musical, and poetic performances. Several ASWAD audience members encouraged the performers' expressions of relief at finally being able to return home through impassioned utterances of the Haitian Kreyòl word *ayibobo*, meaning hallelujah and amen. Later in the evening, an all-Ghanaian troupe performed reenactments of slaves being kidnapped from their villages. Actors portraying European men were outfitted in modern outfits (button-down shirts and dress pants), while those acting as captives wore more realistic "traditional" costuming that was crafted from Ghanaian fabrics. As the presentation continued with the portrayal of frightened sons and daughters being stripped away from their villages and bound with iron shackles on their feet and hands, I watched as the mostly Black, American-based tourists seated on the right-hand side of the audience looked on in a dignified manner; they were obviously transfixed and moved by the display. As I turned to observe audience members on my left, my attention was caught by and my gaze fell upon a group of young, unaccompanied Ghanaian children who had perhaps noticed the fanfare of the candlelit processional that opened the ceremony, joined in, and sat along the edges of the expanse of the court-yard to witness Elmina come alive with television news teams, musical acts, bright lights, and speaker systems reverberating against the slave dungeon walls and throughout the town. The children giggled loudly at the performance when the captives screamed in reaction to the strong arm of the slave catcher. I stared at the children. It was as if the more brutal the treatment became, the more raucous the laughter—now not just from the children, but from the adults near them as well. Exasperated, I hoped that those for whom the dungeon remained sacred—those who sat stoically, seemingly unmoved by the frenetic distraction—had truly not heard or perhaps were able to block out the disruption.

It was unclear whether the adults who laughed understood fully what was going on, were reacting to what could have been verbal or body-language cues unknown to me (reminders of something culturally relevant that was out of my scope), or if those who realized Ghana's complicity in the slave trade were struck by shame and attempting to rid themselves of their nervous energy. It is unlikely that they were amused by the fact of the kidnapping, sale, and brutality that ensued during slavery, especially since we were sitting just above the cavities where Africans awaited their cruel fate. Perhaps the positionality of the bemused adults did not require the same suspension of disbelief, and that very freedom had rendered them able to enjoy aspects of the performance that I, the descendant of enslaved Africans and a scholar, was unable or unwilling to enjoy. Certainly, at least I hoped, those who found amusement in the performance had not come to the slave dungeon to observe woeful, romantic Black Americans and other diasporans search for and weep over long-dead forebears who may or may not have originated from Ghana.

To conclude PANAFEST's official opening service, the emcee instructed the attendees to hug those around them, to explain to each other from where they had traveled, and to greet each other verbally with "akwaaba" (welcome). As most of the audience members gleefully stood to participate in this staged, literalized Pan-African embrace, we were then encouraged to join the performance further by singing Bob Marley's "Redemption Song" in unison. Inspired in part by Marcus Garvey's Black nationalist rhetoric, "Redemption Song" was a fitting selection with which to end the opening ceremony, as it contains a speculative insistence on unification and the defining of a political standpoint for African descended people to more assuredly negotiate their lives under neoslavery and global racism:

> Emancipate yourselves from mental slavery;
> None but ourselves can free our minds.
> Have no fear for atomic energy,
> 'Cause none of them can stop the time.
> How long shall they kill our prophets,
> While we stand aside and look? Ooh!
> Some say it's just a part of it;
> We've got to fulfill de book.
> Won't you help to sing
> These songs of freedom?
> 'Cause all I ever have:
> Redemption songs;
> Redemption songs;
> Redemption songs.[77]

At the Cape Coast Intercity STC bus station the next afternoon, as we awaited a bus to take us back to Accra, my friends and I were eating lunch when a Black American woman, whom I had hugged in Elmina Castle at the end of the previous evening's program, walked into the area in which we were sitting. She began waving wildly at us before stating emphatically, "Akwaaba!" The others around me sat silent; it is possible that they did not remember her. I paused at the woman's naiveté and misuse of the term for the current circumstance, but I recognized her face, and I empathized with her longing. É minha cara. Catching myself before the awkwardness of the silence set in, I responded, "Hello, sister. How are you?" We got on the bus.

CHAPTER 3

"We Love to Be Africans"

SAUDADE AND AFFECTIVE
PERFORMANCES IN BAHIA, BRAZIL

Somebody built up a wall in the United States, and
the African Americans are unable to see their history.
Here in Bahia we were able to keep our orixas.
—Marco Reis, a Brazilian tour guide, quoted in
Patrick McDonnell, "Bahia"

The tour bus is often where and how the initial exposure to Bahia, Brazil, takes place—it is the literal vehicle by which guides introduce Black Americans to various aspects of the state and how future expatriates and frequent travelers are created. Tourism professionals have homed in on Black American travelers' curiosity about their Afro-Atlantic counterparts and Black Americans' desire to satiate dispossession by reclaiming a portion of "old world" Africa at sites of imagined authentic vestiges in this northeastern Brazilian state, where 80 percent of the population is widely believed to be of African descent. Inspired by Bahia's cultural retentions and copious narratives of slave revolt, resistance, and triumph, Black Americans travel to Bahia not only to be closer to Africa physically and spiritually but also to become African. Those who lament that a virtual wholesale embrace of the U.S. post–civil rights notion of progress and assimilation find that the spirit that undergirded Afro-Bahians' organic forms of radicalism during slavery thrust them into a fully free, postracial society by the latter part of the nineteenth century. In the minds of many Black American travelers, this imagined efficacious, centuries-long Black social movement positions Bahia as the place to repossess Africa as well as to achieve American dreams. Bahia is situated outside of Africa proper, but as I will demonstrate, it is a fascinating place where longing, invention, and curiosity intertwine on multiple registers.

The legacy of Bahia's Malê rebellion, for example, reveals common desires for Black social life even in the fluidity of radical thought among the peoples of the Afro-Atlantic, momentarily centering our focus back on Ghana. On January 25, 1835, during Ramadan, a group of Muslim slaves in Salvador, Bahia, staged a rebellion that rocked the stability of the Brazilian nation in such a profound manner that the revolutionary moment became central to subsequent Afro-Atlantic attractions to the region. Bahia had been the site of at least twenty major slave revolts from 1807 to 1835, setting the stage for the Malê rebellion, which is thought of widely as the incident that prompted the Brazilian government to reconsider the feasibility of maintaining the institution of slavery.[1] The Malê uprising most certainly equipped the enslaved with a particular type of agency that exceeded the event. The very notion of continuous eruptions of slave violence instilled in each owner's mind that his human property might resist violently at any moment by destroying crops and property, running away, and perhaps even slaughtering the owner and his family.

The Malê slaves split into several small groups, moving quickly throughout Salvador and assaulting soldiers and elite political figures in a dual quest for freedom and retaliation. They were cornered at various sites, where the owners had been warned of the pending uprising by a few loyal, obedient slaves, but the Malê rebels were able to defeat and escape barriers, as sympathizers across the city, most of whom had no foreknowledge of the rebellion but felt duty bound to join the fight for liberty, took up arms and supported their brethren. It is estimated that seventy people died during the one-day conflict, including fifty Africans who were killed in action or drowned during their attempts to escape.[2] The surviving slaves faced sentences that were as severe as the terror that haunted the elite class. The majority of the captured Malê Africans and their enslaved compatriots were sold away to other parts of Brazil, brutally punished by a succession of public floggings, or killed by firing squad. Others were deemed probable architects of future violence who would recruit and train new rebels to participate in unrest and were expelled promptly from Brazil altogether and repatriated to the Gulf of Guinea, where they settled in villages throughout countries now known as Ghana, Nigeria, Togo, and Benin. In 1836, Afro-Brazilian repatriates arrived in Ghana's Ga Mashie kingdom, where they were assimilated readily into the Ga tribe and allotted prime oceanfront property on which to build and settle into their newly established freedom. The repatriated Afro-Brazilians and their descendants are now known as the Tabom community, a name assigned based on the Brazilians' use of the Portuguese phrase *ta bom* (okay; fine) to respond to inquiries about their well-being.

Among the survivals from the Tabom's early community is the primary home, which has been renovated into the Brazil House, a cultural center in the Jamestown community of Accra that strives to preserve connections between Ghana, Brazil, and the transatlantic diaspora. In 2011, the Brazil House featured an exhibit titled *Cartas d'Africa/Letters from Africa*, which was conceptualized as a means of connecting the Brazilian and West African descendants of the roughly 8,000 formerly enslaved people who repatriated to the Gulf of Guinea from the 1830s to the 1900s. The sentiment revealed by the participants in the exhibit's epistolary project was the most striking element not because their writings were profoundly emotional or particularly cathartic but because of the aura of dispossession that haunted each message. Generations after the migrations of their foreparents, each community had mainly held steadfast to oral narratives and fragmentary evidence regarding their ancestral pasts. Handwritten in Yoruba, Arabic, French, Portuguese, and English, the collection of letters expressed the desire of the participants to travel to and connect with their kin in Brazil. Some provided genealogies, detailing when their ancestor left Bahia or arrived in West Africa, while others sent general wishes of good health and success to their relatives abroad. Through photographs and multiple historical installations, the exhibit also highlighted cultural and architectural continuations found throughout Brazil and West Africa. The implied narrative, however, was that each community had experienced significant breaches vis-à-vis transatlantic slavery and the subsequent forced and voluntary migrations. The kernel of that which was lost was not identified explicitly, but the participants' tone indicated a

3.1 The Brazil House in Jamestown, Accra, Ghana. Photo by author.

sense of dispossession nonetheless. The project mediated formal expressions of yearning and proffered hope for possibility of reconnecting long-separated kin.

Since their arrival in Ghana, the Tabom people have largely lost their understanding of the Portuguese language, and most of their oral histories about Brazil have been forgotten, though connections to the ancestral spiritual realm remain. The Tabom cult of Şàngó, a version of the warrior god Xango from the Brazilian Candomblé faith, worships an orisha who is believed to have protected the Tabom and other returnees as they crossed the Atlantic during their "return" passage from Bahia to West Africa. While the majority of today's Tabom community is Christian, some worship Şàngó in highly secretive, ritual ceremonies in which Yoruba dirges are sung to evoke ancestral presences. During these rites, libations are poured to "open the minds of the elders so that they can tell about the past," and worshippers give offerings in exchange for their ability to bring their concerns to Şàngó in hopes of his divine intervention.[3] Mythical engagements with the sole deity from the Yoruba cosmology that is worshipped by the contemporary Tabom people allow evocations of and connections with their Bahian ancestral pasts as well as the old Africa represented by their foreparents. As a traveling exhibit, *Letters* fostered a means by which long-separated peoples were able to acknowledge the

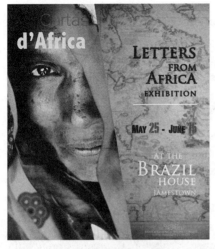

3.2 The *Cartas d'Africa/Letters from Africa* exhibition poster. Photo by author.

3.3 An installation of letters from the *Cartas d'Africa/Letters from Africa* exhibition. Photo by author.

3.4 Detail of a letter from the *Cartas d'Africa/Letters from Africa* exhibition.

IT GIVES ME GREAT PLEASURE TO SEND THIS MESSAGE OF PEACE AND GOODWILL TO MY BROTHERS AND SISTERS IN BRAZIL AND LOOK FOWARD TO THE DAY WHEN I SHALL SEE YOU ALL IN PERSON.
PROF. CYRIL FISCIAN
P. O BOX ACCRA NORTH

existence of and communicate with those who are conceivably kinfolk, though such recognitions do not undo diasporicity or necessarily render longing futile. In fact, the exhibit and other events sponsored by the Brazilian and Ghanaian governments' external relations and tourism boards' economic development strategies in the past thirty years have revealed that while African diasporans generally view the African continent as their ancestral homeland, many members of the Tabom community consider Bahia their joint motherland and long for return, however brief. Described in the *Letters* exhibit as "African in their daily lives, but Brazilian in their memories," the Tabom people's understanding of their ancestral identity as Afro-Bahian and more recently Ga Mashie—in an African nation that, to complicate matters further, may or may not be the original home of each of their ancestors before they were loaded onto slave vessels en route to the New World—is indicative of the complexity of Afro-Atlantic identities.

Portuguese-speaking peoples often utilize the term *saudade* to express this sentiment of nostalgia for some person, thing, or place—a rememory of an essence and a desire for nearness to it again. Afro-Atlantic saudade is an active response to the disconnections that African-descended people feel as a result of slavery and its subsequent diasporas, the sheer lack of historical records and intact cultural memories, and the distance caused by forced migrations. To long for something that exists in the past, then, does not require that an experience necessarily happened to the person who expresses nostalgia, nor does it presuppose that the "yearned for" is fully known, tangible, or recoverable. Whereas Ghana's Tabom people view Brazil as a certain ancestral motherland from which they have been displaced, Bahia's status as an intradiasporic, surrogate Africa is perpetuated by Black American cultural roots seekers; reinforced by a series of performances and circuits of peoples, religions, and traditions in Bahia; and grounded in history and mythmaking.

This chapter is an analysis of the variegated act of Afro-Atlantic saudade that focuses on the circumstances that shape how longing is enacted by Black American tourists and expatriates as well as by Afro-Bahians, who create new and engage with existing speculative fictions that reverberate in Bahia and across the diaspora, positioning us closer to comprehending dispossession in the Afro-Atlantic—where Africa remains a fluid signifier upon which competing desires, particularly yearnings for ancestral cultures and the American Dream's promise of the pursuit of happiness, are ascribed.

Pursuits of Happiness: Historical Black American Engagements with Brazil

"Bahia is the new Ghana," Corrine, a Black American expatriate, proclaimed matter-of-factly as we sat down for an interview and lunch at a creperie in Salvador.[4] Bahia, she continued, has seen increasing numbers of Black American tourists, expatriates, and part-time residents since nearly thirty years ago, when Ghana became less of a destination for Black Americans due to political unrest and the Brazilian currency shift to the *real* made relocation feasible—the exchange rate had fluctuated tremendously until 2002, when one could trade a single U.S. dollar for 3–4 Brazilian reals.[5] In migration literature homeland returns are often figured as "antiprogressive, illogical, and illusory," as it appears nonsensical that a migrant would want to go back to a place from which she fled or was displaced.[6] In the case of expatriation to Bahia, the line of thinking might appear even less logical, as it is a movement from one diasporic locale to another, rather than Africa proper. Stuart Hall suggests that returning to one's origins is "like the imaginary in Lacan—it can neither be fulfilled nor requited, and hence is the beginning of the symbolic, of representation, the infinitely renewable source of desire, memory, myth, search, discovery."[7] Black American expatriation to Bahia illustrates that searches for home are not always centered on geographic Africa—they also include reclamations of Africanist presences throughout the Afro-Atlantic, where one imagines that Blackness is not treated as an impediment or pathology. As another expatriate succinctly explained, Bahia is where there is the "freedom to just be," to attain social life without systemic obstacles.[8]

When he lived in the United States, seventy-year-old Richard explained that he had felt an "internal struggle just to exist." His travels to fourteen African nations in search of another country to call home were rewarding, yet not as fulfilling as he imagined. He has not set foot on the African continent since his first trip to Bahia in 1986, citing the state's African vestiges and his appreciation for the communal lifestyle in Bahia, which reminds him of Black American society before integration in the 1960s "changed things for the worse." Richard reflects: "I love Africa, but I'm so comfortable here. I feel like myself. . . . I've found that 'Africa' is here in a way that I understand it." Another expatriate revealed that his initial visit to Bahia, too, was a cathartic, emotional experience, as he discovered what it meant to finally "live" joyfully and realize his African cultural identity after being displaced in the States:

The first three days [of the initial visit] was a very spiritual experience. I actually cried for three days. It was very emotional . . . the laughs of the kids echoing all around and the kids playing in the streets. They play naturally here like we did when I was growing up. This is it. This is really life—unadulterated happiness. People who don't have much . . . are happy because they haven't been inundated with all of the things we think we need. That just captured my soul. African Americans, come see who you would be if you did not get stripped of your language, culture, or religion. Who would you be? You would be who you see here.[9]

Bahia has indeed garnered and embraced the unofficial nickname Black Rome (Roma Negra) and its capital, Salvador, the moniker the Capital of Happiness. There is a kind of promise for the very cultural and affective satiation that Black Americans desire, then, that encourages the projections that they make onto the state. Aaron's declaration about the inherency of unencumbered access to life and "unadulterated happiness" in Bahia rather than the pursuit of happiness guaranteed by the Declaration of Independence hints at the internal psychological strivings that undergird Black American saudade. Sara Ahmed explains that happiness

is directed towards certain objects, which function as a means to what is not yet present. If objects provide a "means" for making us happy, then in directing ourselves towards this or that object, we are aiming somewhere else: towards a happiness that is presumed to follow. The temporality of this following does matter. Happiness is what would come after. Happiness does not reside in objects; *it is promised through/proximity to certain objects*. So the promise of happiness— if you do this, then happiness is what follows—is what makes things seem "promising," which means that the promise of happiness is not in the thing itself. Consider that a promise comes from Latin promissum "send forth, foretell" from pro- "before" and mittere "to put, send." The promise of happiness is what sends happiness forth; it is what allows happiness to be public in the sense of being out. Objects that embody the feeling are passed around: they are "out and about." Happiness involves the sociality of passing things around.[10]

When slavery ended in Brazil in 1888, the nation maintained a contradictory relationship with the ways in which Africanity permeated society, rendering it imperative to trace the historical moments that impacted Black Americans' protracted association of Brazil with universal access to life, liberty, and happiness. A series of successful and celebrated Brazilian plantation slave rebellions led to escapes to *mocambos* and quilombos—independent communities of runaway slaves who, with the assistance of abolitionists, utilized the underground system to carve out a free life elsewhere. This revolutionary determination to unify despite ethnic differences was read by Brazil's ruling class as defiance and created an anti-Africa backlash well into the twentieth century, resulting in the attempted suppression, but not complete eradication, of publicly expressed cultural activities.[11] In the face of the government's attempts to silence their ancestral histories, for instance, some Afro-Bahians sought out Yoruba-based diviners to engage with the mystical realm with hopes of becoming fully African. Despite evidence that Afro-Bahians began participating in speculative actions early on to undo their dispossession, it is the existence of seemingly authentic African vestiges and spiritual presences in Bahia today that catalyzes Black American travelers' desire to live among people who they feel they could have been.

The myth of Brazil as a racial utopia has drawn the rather sustained interest of Black American travelers since the 1920s, though it should be observed that the country was believed widely in the United States to be postracial even before the institution of slavery ended in Brazil in 1888. Astoundingly, a brief article printed in 1849 in the *North Star*, Frederick Douglass's abolitionist newspaper, commented on the exceptional quality of life for free Black persons in Brazil: "The social state of the population is not marked by the distinction of color . . . but only by that of freedom and servitude. The blacks have access to all, and are in possession of many offices of honor and trust, and engage in every department of business. The white race and the black meet on terms of equal equality in social intercourse, and intermarry without scruple, provided there exists no obstacle in the relative position in life of the respective parties."[12] In 1888,

Black Americans and their variously motivated white allies from the North and South began schematizing a mass emigration of skilled Black American agricultural workers to Central and South America, including Brazil, to forge colonies where they could work and realize social life and true freedom.[13] Adding to the sense of Brazil as a site of possibility was the assignment of Henry Furniss, a Black American, to the diplomatic post of U.S. consul to Bahia from 1898 to 1905.[14] During the early twentieth century, however, the Brazilian government overtly encouraged *embranquecimento*, the virtual whitening of its citizens through racial mixing; the acquisition of wealth; and/or the successful integration into the elite class through education or a significant increase in social status, all of which could render a person white or nonblack, even though he or she would be designated Black phenotypically and regardless of class in the United States. Racial eugenicists championed the whitening of the masses to create a Brazilian race, rendering this complicated process a fundamental component of Brazilian nationalism. The rejection of Blackness, by way of anti-Africa sentiment, led to the government's interest in attracting immigration to Brazil to create a new population of mixed-raced peoples and to assist in the nation's modernization initiative. Interracial minglings certainly occurred outside of governmental imperatives, leading much of the world to continue to believe in Brazil as a protoracial paradise and potential paragon for postslavery nations that were grappling with how to assimilate the formerly enslaved into their societies.

By the 1920s, the Brazilian government elected to advertise determinedly in the United States and Europe to encourage foreign investment and settlement, inadvertently garnering attention from Black American businessmen and nationalists who sought nobler livelihoods abroad. To Black Americans, Brazil's immigration campaign followed, and appeared to confirm, President Theodore Roosevelt's depictions of the society in his travel account based on his explorations in South America seven years earlier. Roosevelt did not detect a color line or substantial racial issues in Brazil. Rather, he startlingly highlighted the successes of Afro-Brazilians, piquing the curiosity of Black Americans who were inhibited and exasperated by racism and the inaccessibility of the American Dream. A 1914 article in the Black newspaper *Philadelphia Tribune* speculated on the possibility of realizing Black nationalist self-sufficiency in Brazil based on Roosevelt's seemingly objective report:

There a man is judged by personal merit. There is no blank wall of prejudice that faces him. All the opportunities of life are open to him. If there is a failure it is by the individual and not from any prejudice on the part of the dominant class to keep him down or to deny to him the rights of a man and a citizen of Brazil. . . . Brazil would be to the educated colored man of today, what the United States was to the European in 1850—a new land and a land of promise. From the point of view of climate and tradition, Brazil is the country peculiarly fitted to receive the colored man of this country, and offer him a vision of freedom and opportunity beyond his wildest dreams.[15]

Black American sentiments about Brazil were and remain bound up with the notion of a particular type of paradisiacal futurity based on the imagined absence of racialized oppressions. In the Black American press during the early twentieth century, Brazil was often touted as a potential haven from racism, where a liberated social existence, the pursuit of capitalistic business opportunities, and personal happiness were possible to achieve. The Brazilian government, however, had no intentions of supporting the migration of Black Americans, particularly because a mass incursion of Black Americans would have encumbered its project to create a whitened Brazilian race. What eventually became clear to Black American travelers is that while segregation was never legally sanctioned anywhere in Brazil as it had been in the United States, de facto racial separation occurred throughout Brazil, tarnishing the myth of the country as a racial paradise.

A visible professional Afro-Brazilian middle class had prompted Black American visitors to believe initially that equality prevailed in Brazil—that there existed no need for protracted civil rights battles to guarantee basic civil liberties. Early Black American travelers to Brazil did not witness or understand fully that class and other complicated divisions made the establishment of a nationwide Afro-Brazilian social movement difficult to nearly impossible during the postabolition period.[16] In newspaper editorials, some Black American writers tentatively applauded Brazil's encouragement of racial mixing and posited that interracial marriage might be the solution to the so-called race problem. In 1920, L. H. Stinson erroneously suggested that the Brazilian government desired "colored North American" migration because it found Black Americans to be "far advanced in civilization and intelligence; hence they [Brazilian officials] believe that his citizenship would be an asset."[17] Three years later, Robert S. Abbott wrote a series of articles for the *Chicago Defender*, encouraging business investment in Brazil and promoting a trade mission for Black American businessmen that was scheduled to sail to Brazil in 1925.[18] Despite the ongoing debate and enthusiasm about the prospect of a better life in Brazil, it was not until after Brazil's First Republic ended in 1930 that Black Americans were allowed to travel there again. As the U.S. government had advised Brazilian immigration officials to reject all visa applications from Black Americans, the First Republic feared Black American emigration schemes such as those led by Abbott and others who would have been eager to bring their tools and experiences from the United States to the Afro-Brazilian fight against racism, and the Brazilian elite was focused on continuous movement toward a more European-complexioned modernity.[19]

A prime example of Black Americans erroneously interpreting Brazilian cultural elements in the early twentieth century occurred in the Black press's 1926 reading of Brazil's *Mãe Preta*. The *Mãe Preta* is a statue of an Afro-Brazilian woman nursing a baby that was erected as a symbol of Brazil's embrace of Africanity and its nostalgia for the past. Micol Seigel cogently identifies numerous narrative threads that resulted in mistranslations by the Black American press about the statue's installation. In addition to nationalist aims, *Mãe Preta* was conceived as a propaganda tool to proliferate the notion of Brazil as a racial democracy to the world. While some Afro-Brazilian citizens viewed the statue as a needed progressive social move by the government, others bristled at the empty, calculated gesture.[20] The crudity of the wet-nurse imagery rests in its recalling of the stereotypical mammy figure, an exaggerated representation of enslaved women who were viewed as docile, nonthreatening, loyal caretakers of white children and their families.[21] Cultural producers, particularly in the postbellum United States, have continued to express a certain perverse nostalgia for the mammy caricature as symbolic of the good old, genteel antebellum days. Coupled with the overarching Brazilian narrative that Black American journalists had disseminated during this period, *Mãe Preta* all but confirmed for many readers that Brazil was indeed a racial utopia. Seigel's analysis leaves open for debate whether the writers at the *Chicago Defender* intentionally mischaracterized and "mistranslated" the condition of Afro-Brazilians to contrast their supposed uplifted status with that of Black Americans, and thereby indicted the U.S. government for failing to make substantial reparations for slavery and subsequent forms of inequality. Seigel maintains that the journalists did not truly believe that Brazil had achieved racial equality and that they actually found *Mãe Preta* problematic, postulating that the journalists championed the narrative of Brazilian progress merely for sociopolitical expediency. Pointing out the firestorm that occurred in the Black American community and press in reaction to a 1923 proposal by the United Daughters of the Confederacy (UDC) to place a similar memorial in Washington, D.C., to honor the mammy figure, Seigel notes the Black American press's contradictory responses and issues a warning against relying on the efficacy of comparative frameworks to address the struggles of Afro-Atlantic populations.

In an effort to further the examination of these Black American travelers and the *Chicago Defender* journalists' seeming complicity in the global transmission of the mythological narrative of Brazilian postracialism, I offer here a more empathetic reading of the Black American actors in this case. It appears to follow that the public spectacle of these distinct, grotesque images would attract a similar response from the Black American press. However, it should be noted that the UDC members celebrate their blood connections to Confederate soldiers, mourn the downfall of the Confederate States of America, and express a desire to possess permanent connections to the pre-emancipation moment. Aware of the sordid histories and the more recent iterations of Black subjugation in the United States, most Black American critics likely interpreted the UDC project as one that was inspired by a covert desire for a return to the Old South, including slavery's social hierarchy, and an indirect approval of contemporary Black social alienation, which was sustained via Jim Crow laws, acute poverty, and domestic terrorism. Brazil's *Mãe Preta*, in contrast, was grounded in political, historical, and social actualities that were quite possibly unrealized and/or misunderstood by many Black Americans, regardless of whether they had been able to travel to Brazil. Rather than rehearse the contradictions in the approach taken by the *Chicago Defender*, I want to concentrate on what is lost often in Afro-Atlantic translations, as this example from the early twentieth century certainly sets the stage for what follows. Brent Hayes Edwards's conceptualization of décalage is useful in making sense of the gaps in time and/or space and the misreadings that occur among African-descended peoples as they attempt to unify based on commonalities and translate materials for consumption in culturally and linguistically distinct societies. Décalage, Edwards posits, is the "kernel of precisely that which cannot be transferred or exchanged, the received biases that refuse to pass over when one crosses the water. It is a changing core of difference; it is the work of 'difference within unity.' "[22] Black Americans had long expressed interest in migration to countries throughout the Americas, as seen in the Black Southern farmers' scheme earlier and other nineteenth-century expatriation schemes promoted by such staunch emigrationists as Martin Delany and Mary Ann Shadd Cary.[23] In the *Mãe Preta* case, décalage might account for the breaches caused by competing agendas and also opens up the possibility that the *Chicago Defender*'s moves were guided by sincere saudade for the freedom that the newspaper associated generally with Afro-Brazilians' seeming possession of what is framed in the United States as the American Dream, and what in later Black American migrations to Bahia, in particular, becomes conflated with the related desire for Africa. Pronounced feelings of nostalgia often compel contemporary Black American travelers to believe what they think they see, and they firmly begin to project their desires onto Bahia and other surrogate homelands.

Between the 1940s and 1960s, Black American optimism regarding Brazil as a racial utopia began to subside. The gradual erosion of their belief in Brazil as a site of possibility during this period can be attributed to the growth of a progressively more militant Black political consciousness in the United States in opposition to the continuing racist laws and practices throughout the country, Afro-Brazilian involvement in the establishment of Black studies, the UNESCO antiracism studies of the 1950s, and the ability of a more diverse cross section of Black Americans to travel within the United States and other nations such as France and Ghana in search of a truer sense of freedom.[24] When reports surfaced that the Brazilian government categorically opposed Black American immigration, critics began to scrutinize more closely the racial dynamics in the country.[25] During his visit to Brazil in 1940, the journalist Ollie Stewart was disturbed to find that "the government does not encourage visitors to touch Bahia when they go into the interior. You have to have a pretty good reason before you will be issued a permit. Perhaps they don't want the natives to get ambitious."[26] Stewart does not qualify his usage of the term *ambitious*, but his tone indicates that the Getúlio Vargas dictatorship, which had indeed shuttered Afro-Brazilian political organizations such as the Frente Negra Brasilera a few years earlier, suspected that Black Americans might bring their history of struggle to Brazil, exacerbate the already rebellious Afro-Brazilian spirit, disrupt the status quo, and ultimately inspire a social uprising of some kind.[27] The Brazilian government's mistrust of outside agitators certainly echoes the U.S. government's concerns about worldwide Black unification and Pan-Africanism during this period, as several sub-Saharan nations were fighting for or had achieved independence from colonial powers, inspiring Black diasporans who were suffering under repressive regimes transnationally. Other writers, such as James W. Ivy, disputed that a color line existed in Brazil, especially not to the degree experienced in the United States. Ivy maintained that while prejudice exists in Brazil, "Brazil has freely accepted educated, cultured colored persons as members of Brazilian society, as human beings, as equals."[28] George S. Schuyler, however, detected a distinct color line, beginning with a Brazilian hotel's refusal to recognize the reservation of a prominent scholar once the hotel discovered that she was Black. Schuyler continues by pointing out aptly the effects of racism in various facets of everyday Brazilian life such as housing and education, noting that because so many differently complexioned people intermingle, it would require a more sustained—what we might refer to today as intersectional—analysis before one could determine the country's suitability for expatriation.[29] As the U.S. Black social movement transitioned from the contradictory successes of the civil rights era to the Black Power movement and eventually cultural nationalism, emigration-minded Black Americans began to dismiss Brazil as a site of possibility because they determined erroneously that Afro-Brazilians were ashamed of their Blackness and that Brazil lacked visible radical organizations that touted racial pride.[30] Instead, some of these Black Americans refocused their attention on postcolonial African nations that seemed to more fervently embrace uplift ideologies grounded in socialist thought and Pan-Africanism, while others gave up hope of realizing the American Dream in Brazil.

In *Orpheus and Power*, Michael Hanchard provides a historicization of Brazil's Black social movement that counters these Black American misreadings by clarifying that the Afro-Brazilian *movimento* consisted of diverse factions and organizations across the political spectrum, including some that were Afrocentric and inspired by anticolonial groups on the African continent proper and throughout the diaspora and others that were more aligned with integrationist ideals and U.S. notions of progress that embraced capitalism and individualism.[31] A significant cultural development of contemporary Brazil's movimento is often referred to as the 1970s renaissance, a period that many scholars refer to as the re-Africanization of the country. However, what some outsiders, particularly Black Americans, understood to be indicative of a wholesale Afro-Brazilian embrace of African cultural projects and the existence of a race-based politics, including the inauguration of the radical organization O Movimento Negro Unificado in São Paulo, which created the National Day of Black Consciousness in 1978; the rise in all-Black Carnival associations; and what Black Americans understood to be a general Brazilian concern for the welfare of the Portuguese-speaking peoples in African countries, were actually pieces of a far more complicated set of revolutionary political strategies to realize true democracy.[32]

The significance of large-scale cultural performances and narratives about African retentions in Bahia, to be sure, are not solely the figments of Black American imagination. Carefully crafted accounts of postraciality and equality tend to dominate discussions about the nation for tourism purposes especially, assigning a mystical quality that has revived Black American aspirations mainly in the northeast region of the country, where happiness and, in some cases, the realization of a particular kind of Afro-Atlantic cosmopolitanism is thought possible. While the personal reclamations of Africa in these outward behaviors might indeed be crucial to the concretizing of certain Afro-Bahians' local, national, and diasporic identities, my analysis here is not centered on that particular debate, but on the external ends of these cultural performative acts.

During a visit to a beach in Rio de Janeiro in the 1980s, the journalist Eugene Robinson was struck by Brazil's seeming racial utopia, as its shades of brown and Black reminded him of those of the Black American community. In his travel narrative, *Coal to Cream*, Robinson speculates about the prospect of forging connections with Afro-Brazilians based on this presumed sameness: "There would be thousands of people, almost certainly many thousands, whose ethnicity was made from precisely the same recipe as mine, with the same ingredients in just the same proportions. We're so far removed physically and psychologically from Africa that the continent itself is more a pleasant daydream than anything else, a source of a possible identity that we can no longer confirm. . . . After only five minutes in Brazil, I knew instinctively that belonging was not only possible, but somehow already half-accomplished. I felt oddly at home."[33] Brazil's seeming Blackness had figured it as a surrogate homeland for Robinson.[34] The belief in the possibility of reclaiming Africa and its associated cultures, according to Robinson's reflections on his initial response, was grounded in fantasy. When warned by a colleague that the construction of race in Brazil was more complicated than it appeared, Robinson dismissed him outright: "I thought, frankly, that as a white American, despite all his experience and all his facility with the language, he just couldn't see the situation as clearly as a black American. He was analyzing the country intellectually, while I was *feeling* its presence" (emphasis added).[35]

Robinson's narrative weaves present and past events together, as he grapples with how racial oppression had affected him in the United States, specifically since he spent his childhood in segregated Orangeburg, South Carolina, where the unforgiving one-drop rule had relegated race to a biological condition. In Brazil, he felt a sense of "freedom" and "weightlessness" from the United States that compelled him to ruminate about the futurity of Brazil.[36] Robinson's imaginings about the possibilities, it turns out, were short-lived, and his beach epiphany was ruined by an experience at the Carnival festivities in Rio, where the spectacle of a group of middle-age and elderly Afro-Bahianas dancing a quickly paced samba laboriously along the scorching parade route infuriated him. Distracted by the Afro-Bahianas' pained expressions and lack of opportunities to rest, Robinson opined aloud to no one in particular that the women needed to be assisted before they became ill. A white American couple seated next to him commented that the women were "tough" and were used to working hard. The spectacle of the elder women's performance despite the obvious agonizing pain they endured for the pleasure of strangers, coupled with Robinson's earlier experiences in Brasilia with acute segregation and discrimination, caused him to reach a sobering conclusion about his imagined utopic "future that never came": "structuring a society so that black people didn't 'have to be black' didn't seem to do much good for the black people at all. . . . [I]n fact, it seemed to do them harm, to hold them down—worse, to deny them the language to talk about it and the anger to do something about it. Amid all the beauty and excitement and joy of that evening, I saw something that was backward and ugly and wrong."[37] It took a trip to Bahia for Robinson to come to terms with the letdown. While in Bahia, he journeyed through historic Salvador and Cachoeira, absorbing lessons about the history of slavery, music, and religious practices, some of which he had learned on his first trip to Bahia with his family—but the details somehow spoke to him more profoundly on this second trip. Strikingly, Robinson compares his emotions in the Pelourinho district of Salvador to his previous visits to a preserved auction block in Charleston, South Carolina. Both places brought about a sense of shame about slavery that overwhelmed him, though he could not articulate exactly what prompted this emotion. In the countryside of Cachoeira, Robinson's agnosticism about African gods dissipated once he received a reading at a Candomblé house of worship and observed how the religious experiences in these spaces offered the opportunity for one to realize the sense of freedom and weightlessness that he had felt in Rio earlier: Afro-Atlantic flight—physical, spiritual, and temporal ascension over worldly circumstances—to its members. He explains about this epiphany: "Sometimes you had to escape from [societal injustice], through transcendental ceremonies in the *terreiro* that featured hypnotic music and rhythmic chanting and that drew worshipers out of their earthly bodies, into a better place. . . . I had reached across the many miles, across the yawning centuries, and touched ritual and belief that went all the way back to the West African village, the place from which my ancestors had been untimely ripped."[38] Robinson's visit to Bahia did not induce him to support Brazil's racial ideologies wholly, but he did find "a measure of racial identity that embraced *me*, that reflected my history, that gave me instruction on how to live my own life."[39] The tourism juggernaut in Bahia caters to a perceived African diasporan need for racial recognition, as Bahia, like Ghana, offers catharsis through engagements with traces of slavery. Through their fantastic performances of Africanity, Bahians mediate Black Americans' imagined recuperation of an African identity, while at the same time, the very presence of Black Americans journeying in northeast Brazil legitimizes and reinforces the

African identity that many Afro-Bahians assert and perform through their kinesthetic imaginations.

Cultural Roots Tourism in Bahia

In December 2002, the U.S. Congressional Black Caucus Foundation (CBCF) set its sights on Brazil by signing a landmark "Memorandum of Understanding" to unite Black-owned U.S. businesses with those run by Afro-Brazilians. In a press release, the CBCF's president, Weldon J. Rougeau, expressed the foundation's sense of diasporic responsibility to the African- descended in the Southern Hemisphere: "Afro-Brazilians . . . are striving to learn positive growth strategies from African American business leaders. They face many of the same roadblocks and economic issues that we faced in the 1960s—lack of business opportunities and the tools to organize into a cohesive unit."[40] Encouraged by this diasporic union, César Nascimento, the founder of an organization called Integrare, devised plans to establish a combined airline and travel service, to be called Avocet, with the Black American businessmen Ira Moseley and Clarence Smith. The proposed airline was conceived to establish regular, direct flights from major U.S. cities to Bahia. Moseley rationalized the business plan this way: "Brazil has much to offer. Much more than any place on the continent of Africa. The environment here is stable; there is no civil war here. There are no famines on the scale of what a visitor would encounter in Africa."[41] Nascimento added: "Our expectation is that when [the Black American tourist] comes here, it won't be just for one time. We're not targeting the person that will want to come here just for the sun and the beach."[42] Avocet's flights, to be sure, were imagined to be those that would launch roots tourists into primeval Africa as preserved in Bahia.

Though the Avocet business plan failed due to an admitted inability to transcend personal differences regarding business strategy, Nascimento continues to act as an informal consultant to Bahia's state government as it strategizes roots tourism schemes driven by thoughts similar to Moseley's comments about Bahia's serving as an Africa by proxy. Nascimento remains active with Integrare, too, by inviting Black American trade missions to Brazil's financial center, São Paulo, and recommending strategically that these potential investors visit Bahia for the cultural experience.

Inherent in this northward nudge to Bahia is the hope that a connection, spiritual or otherwise, will increase the likelihood of further business relations and the transition of Brazil from its status as an emerging market to an international economic power. In 2007, the state of Bahia and city of Salvador began taking considerable steps to expand the cultural roots tourism industry.[43] African descendants and their imagined lost cultures, once thought antithetical to Brazil's modernizing effort, have become crucial to current pecuniary aspirations at the local and state levels. Of course, the Bahian government and local businesses are not the only entities that benefit from tourism schemes that at once embrace and disavow Africa.

Like the now-defunct Avocet venture, several travel agencies have fashioned their business plans around the desire of Black Americans to discover Africa in Brazil's northeastern region. Brazilian and U.S.-based websites promoting Bahia boast about the state's rich African cultures and underscore its historical richness through visual indicators of the authentic such as images of darker-complexioned Bahians celebrating Carnival or enjoying the beach and women outfitted in head wraps, face paint, beads, and other seemingly traditional African garb participating in a ritual or dance. There is an attraction to Bahia that goes beyond the aesthetic— Black American tourists are drawn to its people's seeming ability to maintain that which is thought to have been lost through their assimilation into the social fabric of the United States. Black American curiosity about Bahia is related to Africa, but, more specifically, it is a confrontation with how things might have been for them, if only. To some tourists, contemporary Africa is not the answer; their longing is for authenticity and what they imagine is endemic to the source. African-descended peoples' ability to maintain their ancestral religions and cultures despite slavery and discrimination renders this bastion of old Africa—where the ancestors are thought to dwell—attractive, and there is an acute desire for nearness to it.

In 1985, UNESCO named the Pelourinho district in Salvador, Bahia, a World Heritage Site, which inadvertently helped jump-start governmental efforts to rid the area of its poverty-stricken citizens as well as drug infestation, violence, and prostitution, all of which officials deemed detrimental to the preservation and marketing of its historical attractions from the sixteenth through the twentieth centuries. For years, the Bahian government had articulated plans to gentrify the area, but it was

3.5 Bahian drummers perform in Pelourinho. © Corbis Images.

not until 1991 that the first phase of revitalization commenced to preserve and commercialize the former pillory, a slavery-era public whipping post. Prompting the mass state takeover was the international success of the musical group Olodum. Founded in 1979, Olodum arranged regular Tuesday night rehearsals in Pelourinho that "reinvented the old custom of the benediction, a six o'clock evening mass at the Church of the Rosario in Pelourinho," gradually attracting hundreds of local youths and international tourists to these weekly musical sets and, by extension, visitors to the whole Pelourinho.[44] As one of many activist *blocos afro* in Bahia, Olodum incorporates an awareness of history and social issues and disseminates its radical ideologies through its music. In the 1990s, the state-funded Institute of Artistic and Cultural Heritage sought to reinvent the area by relocating the poor constituents for whom Olodum advocates. These revitalization measures displaced longtime residents who were paid meager sums to vacate their homes, while gun-wielding state police officers intimidated those who protested against forced removals.[45] Despite the dispersal of this largely Afro-Bahian underclass, the African-descended population and Olodum were and remain crucial to the marketing of Pelourinho, which is now a gentrified district of cobblestoned streets, countless pastel-colored souvenir shops, baroque and

3.6 A Bahiana in Pelourinho awaits passersby. © iStock by Getty Images.

neoclassical buildings, restaurants, museums, and centuries-old cathedrals. Past meets present in this historical center, as attractive Bahianas outfitted in colonial-style hoop dresses of white Brazilian lace, clinking earrings and bracelets, bold red and pink headscarves, and generously applied make-up, sell souvenirs and charge onlookers to take photographs with and of them. In the midst of this parade of smiling beauties are several establishments that utilize *Africa* or *diaspora* in their names to denote their social or political awareness; many of these businesses offer Afro-Brazilian dance, drumming, and other for-purchase cultural instruction to tourists. Local capoeira groups and drum corps create energetic, impromptu spectacles for tips; while hawkers descend upon tourists, offering them mass-produced "authentic" Brazilian jewelry and other kitschy items.

When one takes the Elevador Lacerda down from the upper city of Pelourinho to the lower city, one is confronted with a full-fledged market, the Mercado Modelo. A large, canary yellow structure, this is an indoor marketplace composed of narrow pathways between tables and make-shift storefronts overflowing with local crafts and souvenirs. Outside of the building stand additional kiosks at which a hodgepodge of fren-zied exchanges between insistent sellers and curious tourists haggling toward a fair sale takes place. By most accounts, the Mercado Modelo was established in 1912 and filled with vendors that sold fresh foods and general household products. In response to several devastating fires over the years, the building was relocated to the former Customs House in 1971. Today's structure is the result of a 1984 renovation after yet another inferno ravaged the building—after which the city of Salvador acted de-finitively by shifting the merchandising focus from foodstuffs to crafts.[46] Of great interest to cultural roots tourists, in addition to the prospect of purchasing a variety of souvenirs, is what lies below the bustling bazaar on its lowest level.

There is no signage to indicate the location of the entry to the base-ment of the market. One must already have knowledge of the significance of the place. Situated in a corner between two merchants is a doorway to a narrow staircase, which leads to an eerie and damp brick-walled room with several archways, light fixtures, and strategically placed concrete platform risers to allow safe movement across the room, which is located below sea level and often floods. Local lore maintains that the cavern-ous basement is a former slave holding cell, which (minus the lights and concrete slabs) bears a striking resemblance to what remains of the slave castle-dungeons in Ghana. Similar to witness's accounts from Elmina and Cape Coast, some of the Mercado Modelo's security officers have reported hearing the ghostly clinking of chains at night.[47] This fabled remnant of the slave trade and the African performances and purportedly authentic

3.7 A view of the Port of Salvador in All Saints Bay, Bahia, Brazil. © Corbis Images.

goods sold in Pelourinho and throughout Bahia have continued to serve as a marketplace much like the vestiges in Ghana; Charleston, South Carolina; and other places in the U.S. South where slave holding stations or slave markets have been repackaged as a sort of old world for cultural roots tourists' consumption.[48] In her discussion of New Orleans's cultural tourism industry, Lynnell Thomas offers a reading of how Blackness and Africa are at once embraced and disavowed in former sites of slavery that reverberates across the Afro-Atlantic, though her temporal bracketing and the ends of such bipolar relations with African-descended populations and "African" cultural elements no doubt differ from one tourism site to another:

> In the post–civil rights era, tourism promoters recognized black tourists as both a new niche market and a potential threat to the city's racially exclusive tourist image that views the old South with a sense of loss and nostalgia. . . . [T]ourists were directed to adopt the white supremacist memory of slavery and black culture. . . . In effect, the city's promotion of black cultural consumption produced a desire for blackness at the same time that this blackness was used to signify the disaster of black emancipation and desegregation and the perceived social ills of poverty, crime, immorality, educational inadequacy, and politi-

cal corruption of the postbellum and post–civil rights eras. . . . In the end, these competing impulses of desire and disaster facilitated the symbolic continuance of slavery as the appropriation of black labor and denial of black history and agency even as they highlighted the city's black cultural contributions and appealed to black residents and visitors.[49]

The underbelly of the Mercado Modelo is not commonly included on cultural roots tour itineraries, it should be noted, as the atrocities of slavery—detailed accounts of public lashings in Pelourinho, rape, the separation of families, and so on—are not belabored in a way to evoke inconsolable grief. There is something oddly disturbing about how strategic silence (about Brazil's slavery past and the continued struggles of many Afro-Brazilians in the aftermath of the institution) is utilized in Pelourinho tourism in service of promoting the district and, by extension, Bahia as jubilant and paradisiacal. In *Revolt of the Saints*, John Collins argues:

> The Pelourinho project is instead an approach to development and capital accumulation that rests on a UNESCO-supported canonization of selected residents of the neighborhood as producers of practices that function as both commodities and a civilizing, supposedly shared milieu called "culture." The resulting attempts to purify the Pelourinho and its populace, a project officials often referred to until quite recently as a "moralization of the soil," gave rise to the expulsion of nearly all residents in the period between 1992–2006. Only people with close relationships to politicians, able to "shake down" IPAC [Institute of Artistic and Cultural Patrimony] bureaucrats, or who produce especially valuable expressive culture and whom IPAC thus deems ready to represent Afro-Brazilian culture to the world, have managed to remain.[50]

Pelourinho's overarching master narrative as a historical center, paradoxically, is that of elation that Afro-Bahians were able to establish a free social existence steeped culturally in Africanity despite the strongholds positioned to defeat them. As will be shown in the following chronicles of a Black American tour group's travels around Bahia, after their initial exposure to sites of Bahia's triumphalist mythologies and myriad performances of Africa, numerous Black American visitors

3.8 A cobblestoned street in Pelourinho. © iStock by Getty Images.

describe a yearning for Bahia's affective feeling that inspires them to return permanently.

A SALVADOR CITY TOUR

As I walked into the Vila Galé hotel lobby to meet the Sankofa tour group, I immediately encountered a series of small pockets of Black American tourists speaking quietly to one another as they awaited their tour guide's arrival. Among those with typical traveler's gear—consisting of lightweight fabrics, sensible shoes, and fanny packs—were others wearing dashikis, dresses, and headgear designed from ornate African-styled fabrics. In a sudden disruption of the relatively quiet space, their tour guide, Joel Gondim, enthusiastically rushed through the entrance wearing a bold T-shirt emblazoned with the slogan "we love to be Africans." Joel's presence transformed the lobby's atmosphere into one of palpable anticipation and excitement, though what stood out most to me was that his T-shirt design demonstrated just how mistranslations often reveal intent. The shirt, whose back featured the landmasses of Brazil (Bahia was highlighted) and Africa, was designed as a souvenir for sale to members of his tour groups. The utilization of the infinitive "to be" in the shirt's declaration reveals unstableness and potentiality. The phrasing asserts that performative acts and improvisation are required for one to appear African. Conversely, the usage of the participle in "we love being African" would have been a more precise phrase, as this revised proclamation reads as if the state of the wearer's Africanness is definite. Joseph Roach aptly contends about cultural memory and performance:

> Memories torture themselves into forgetting by disguising their collaborative interdependence across imaginary borders of race, nation, and origin. The social processes of memory and forgetting, familiarly known as culture, may be carried out by a variety of performance events, from stage plays to sacred rites, from carnivals to the invisible rituals of everyday life. To perform in this sense means to bring forth, to make manifest, and to transmit. To perform [is] also, though often more secretly, to reinvent. This claim is especially relevant to the performances that flourish within the geohistorical matrix of the circum-Atlantic world. Bounded by Europe, Africa, and the Americas, North and South, this economic and cultural system entailed vast movements of people and commodities to experimental destinations, the consequences of which continue to visit themselves upon the material and human fabric of the cities inhabited by their successors. As the most visible evidence of an oceanic interculture only now beginning to be reclaimed on its own terms, performances reveal what it means to live through memory in cities of the dead.[51]

Joel's T-shirt foreshadowed the cultural performances to come and elucidated a significant fact: the production of Africa and return in Bahia sets up a moment of contact between distinct diasporic groups that are both imagining and attempting to locate an elusive Africa through their speculative actions. Their incidental collaborations, then, result in the validation of Africa in Bahia.

Joel's tour script did not offer a surface history lesson about Bahia; instead, he highlighted the traces of Africa that remained in Bahia and accounted for the state's rich cultural heritage. Joel's company, Sankofa Tours, provides consultations and tours almost exclusively for African diasporic agencies because he finds it a burden to censor his script for travelers who do not possess a personal stake in the uplift of African-descended peoples. Throughout his excursions with diasporan tourists, Joel's mission is to discuss politics and inequalities in Brazil with visitors whom he determines are able to relate to the Afro-Brazilian plight. In his estimation, the struggles and successes of other diasporan Africans are so similar to those of Afro-Brazilians that such discussions might result in a sort of unification that would potentially broaden the mind-sets of everyday Afro-Atlantic persons. Joel rationalizes that

> If we don't have someone to [whom to] compare [ourselves], we won't go anywhere. But if more African Americans come, things would start changing a lot because we're learning with you guys and you're learning with us. We are learning to use our strength to be more rebellious against the system—to demand rights. Thirty years ago, you wouldn't have seen a bunch of African-Bahian guys in front of the police [station] demanding for less crime in the communities . . . stopping traffic [with their protest]. What they do is an influence of the civil rights— the human rights movement 40–50 years ago in America. There is a deeper reason for African Americans to come to Bahia.[52]

The "deeper reason" that Joel taps into is expressed astutely by his decision to refer to the Ghanaian precept of sankofa in his company name. Joel presents Bahia's history by interspersing introductions to how Africa has survived in Bahia with moments of Afro-Atlantic similarity (even its negative aspects) to articulate a connection between Afro-Bahians and those based in other nations that purportedly have not maintained deeply rooted cultural elements—he suggests that Bahia's history is indeed part of the diasporan travelers' as well.

The Sankofa city tour's first stop was at a nearby favela. The impoverishment of much of Salvador's *negro/preto* community became evident as the bus climbed the hill and parked on a street alongside a sea of stacked, multicolored shanty houses. Despite a sudden rainstorm, we got off the bus, and Joel's assistant, who recorded the tour and later created DVDs to sell to the tourists, kept his video camera rolling. Children of all ages and their families, who knew Joel well because he often takes groups to the community, poured out of their homes to collect the school supplies and other gifts that the tourists had brought for them. Some of the children screamed gleefully as they accepted the items and hugged or high-fived the tourists. Their loved ones smiled approvingly and posed for pictures without hesitation. Many of the tourists said that they had never seen children so excited to receive gifts as seemingly insignificant and relatively easy to come by as writing materials. During an extended period of silence aboard the bus just after the brief favela stop, a female voice rose to break the stillness, commenting that most children in the United States would never have been that appreciative of the items that they had donated. A few others mumbled sentiments in agreement. The majority of the tourists, however, remained quiet, processing the emotional jolt that they had just experienced.

Cultural roots tourism is a spiritual quest that is gauged by the traveler's cathartic reaction to what are presumed to be authentic experiences. The Sankofa tourists sought to bear witness to the evidence of the Africa that once was and the reality of that evidence in the present moment. When a Black American traveler meets non-U.S. descendants of slaves during roots tourism, it is as if there is an expectation for her not to forget. She is endowed with the responsibility of maintaining somehow that initial connection. The physical existence of souvenirs, photographs, and/or videographic reminders of various stops along the journey is important. However, it is the impact on the tourist's psychic memory that becomes crucial in the preservation of these newly forged kinships. Thomas, a seventy-something art gallery owner from Baltimore, for example, became overwhelmed emotionally during a tour of the Afro-Brazilian Museum in Pelourinho.[53] As the group paused to admire intricate wood carvings of the Candomblé orixas, a nervous Thomas asked for everyone's attention as he tearfully shared his wish that wayward Black American youth from his Baltimore community could see what we were witnessing. His voice cracked as he expressed his belief that if the younger generation were endowed with knowledge about the history of slavery and its impact on the descendants of slavery in a setting like Bahia, then they might be inspired to commit themselves to bringing about positive changes in their lives. Members of the tour group applauded his speech and patted Thomas on the back when he finished speaking. Thomas's revelation and the previous silence that had swept over the heretofore gregarious Sankofa tour group aboard the bus in the favela are significant in the positioning of their seeming shame and disappointment regarding younger Black Americans' disconnect from their cultural histories in the post–civil rights era over what might have otherwise been critiqued as travels that attend solely to individual dispossession.

As we carefully negotiated the uneven cobblestoned hills of the district after lunch, Thomas excitedly informed me that he would love to retire in Bahia and that he planned to discuss the idea with his wife. Was it possible that he missed Bahia already? Joel explained to me that of the members of his past tour groups, "many come more than twice to Bahia. They miss it. That's the mission—that's the fruit of the mission. To make them feel that they miss this place—they miss the food; they miss the people; they miss the atmosphere; they miss the spirituality here." Joel facilitates saudade, nostalgia for Bahia, by striking a balance between how he presents the familiar and the exceptional. Certainly, such connections do not always happen because of a larger tourism entrepreneur's script. They can and do occur when tourists, for instance, backpack across the country alone or visit Bahia during a business trip. Once the Salvador city and Bahia state governments began to embrace African heritage tourism's economic power, it became commonplace for the average Brazilian to recite portions of the historical importance of Bahia and recommend that Black tourists visiting other parts of the country travel to the Northeast. Similar to the "Akwaaba! Welcome home!" that diasporans encounter when they travel to Ghana, Bahia's greeting comes across as a "welcome to the closest thing to Africa outside of the continent proper." To follow the metaphor, it is a reunion with a brother or sister who remained physically and culturally closer to the mother. Haunting this discussion is a sense of urgency that is not only about alleviating saudade but also about attending to an imagined deficit, a grappling with why and how Afro-

Bahians have been able to retain so much of an Africanist presence and U.S.-based diasporans have retained seemingly so little.

TOURING AFRICA IN BAHIA THROUGH
RELIGION AND RITUAL

We African Americans talk about our connection to Africa, but we don't have that much evidence for our connection. But we go to Brazil and Cachoeira, and it's all so evident and meaningful.
—Wande Knox Goncalves, a Black American tourist in Cachoeira, quoted in Patrick McDonnell, "Bahia"

These women kept their tradition, their clothing, their language, the religious practices. You come here and you can see what slavery was like.
—Renee Padmore-Baccus, a Black American tourist in Cachoeira, quoted in Patrick McDonnell, "Bahia"

Two hours northwest of Salvador in the interior of Bahia sits the tiny colonial town of Cachoeira, which is surrounded by former sugar plantations and located on the Paraguaçu River. Cachoeira is the site of an annual commemoration of Nossa Senhora da Boa Morte (Our Lady of the Good Death) during a popular three-day celebration in mid-August that attracts thousands of tourists, including a substantial contingent of Black Americans, each year. The sisterhood, Irmandade da Boa Morte, was founded in 1821 by manumitted slaves, and their community is regarded widely as a site of resistance because of its status as a Candomblé religious stronghold during and since slavery as well as for its continued commitment to freedom, women's rights, and social justice.[54] On August 15, the Catholic Church commemorates the Assumption of the Virgin, which is an integral element of the sisterhood's syncretic faith as it celebrates Mary's death and perfect passage to her heavenly home, a Christianity-based account of ascension that, fascinatingly, has inspired these African descendants' belief in the promises of flight. Our Lady's divine death—coupled with elements from traditional African beliefs—has given slave-descended Candomblé worshippers and cultural roots tourists faith that regardless of the social alienation that they might experience, their physical deaths, like Mary's, will be good, as they will finally be at home and free.

According to a 2007 *Los Angeles Times* article, some tourists at the Boa Morte festival opined that there is a disconnect between Black

Americans and the African homeland because there are no significant remnants of Africa in the United States.[55] The publication's selected interviewees lamented a lack of African traditions in the United States, which a Bahia-based tour guide, Marco Reis, echoed and explained as evidence that a wall was built to prevent Black Americans from seeing "their history." The underlying thread here is a mutual misrecognition that posits that Black Americans' traditional African core was defeated by slavery, while that of Afro-Bahians prevailed somehow. The performance of Africa in the Boa Morte rituals and processionals, African-derived cuisine, and musical elements had indicated to these visitors that their own connections to the ancestors were insignificant or nonexistent. Prior to the commencement of the second day of the celebration, members of the Sankofa tour group rushed to take pictures with the Boa Morte sisters and expressed pride in their revolutionary legacy. The tourists were enthralled by the Boa Morte story, which is very much akin to other narratives of triumph such as those portrayed in trickster tales that highlight the ingenuity of enslaved persons who somehow trump the power of the master's whip. These real and imagined rebellious accounts lend a sense of pride that refigures how Black Americans process their dispossession.[56] The group's witnessing of a once-enslaved community maintaining a portion of its Africanity despite slavery and the postemancipation prohibition of Candomblé until the 1970s was at once intriguing and sobering for them.

The Sankofa tourists attended a funeral rite at which the sisters of Boa Morte sat together at the front of their small cathedral adjacent to a statue of Our Lady that was positioned in a coffin. A priest led a mass to venerate Our Lady, the *iyas* (female ancestors) celebrated in Candomblé, and deceased former members of the sisterhood. Afterward, the sisters rose and led a solemn, candle-lit march as they carried "the statue through the streets in a funeral procession accompanied by mournful music from one of the town's two bands. The statue [was] then placed in the museum of religious articles contiguous to the church, where it [remains] during the year, and a standing statue of Our Lady of Glory is [later] taken from the museum into the church. Sisters and people who have attended the mass touch the statue to request the saint's blessings, and the congregation eventually disperses."[57]

When the crowd of attendees and multiple media crews gathered to join the sisters in this closing act of the evening ceremony, the processional

3.9 Members of the Irmandade da Boa Morte/Sisterhood of the Good Death gather around a statue of the Virgin Mary. Photo by Mario Tama, © Getty Images.

around Cachoeira, numerous Black American tourists, including the Sankofa group, became part of the spectacle as well as the history and culture for which many of them longed and, thus, contentedly endured the accompanying rainstorm.

To an even greater degree, the tourists' reckoning with loss was evident when they visited a *terreiro* (house of Candomblé) for a ceremony. Candomblé and a sense of Afro-Bahian spirituality as seen at terreiros and in celebrations like Yemanja Day are significant lures that entice the growing expatriate collective. Outfitted completely in white, a color deemed inoffensive to the deities, the group members traveled over an hour by bus to observe an evening Candomblé ritual, which lasted well into the next morning. The ceremony commenced with animal sacrifices, and afterward the estimated three hundred attendees were invited to lay offerings on a shrine. For several minutes, the Sankofa group members stood motionless, with the exception of Joel and the group's American-based leader, Pat. The tourists were unsure of and possibly intimidated by the spectacle. As other attendees eagerly participated and demonstrated how to posture before the deities, several Sankofa tourists reticently approached the altar. Some later confessed that their

3.10 Devotees celebrate Yemanja Day in Salvador da Bahia, Brazil. © Corbis Images.

own understandings of religious expression conflicted with the elaborate, costumed celebration of deities through dance, drumming, trance, and other esoteric activities enacted to connect to the orixas. At various points throughout the evening, Pat, who incidentally had been installed as a nonresident chief of a village in Ghana some years earlier and wore traditional garb befitting her status, stood behind the Sankofa group to narrate the activities. She whispered variations of "That is African. You would not see any of this in America," which legitimized and reinforced the exotic spectacle as one that indeed was from the source. Pat was determined to ensure that the evening's ceremony produced Africa for her clients.

Patricia de Santana Pinho examines the politics underlying how blackness is constructed in Brazil, making a convincing argument about how myths of a maternal Africa, such as that which is validated by Pat, have been utilized to establish authentic markers as to who and what counts as Black and African in Bahia. Though her analysis centers on Afro-Brazilians as the actors in various performances of Africa, Santana Pinho directs some attention to Black American traversals of Bahia, notably thinking through how circuits of roots tourists have rendered some "[Afro-Bahian] expressions . . . more ethnic than ever because of the seal of approval provided" by Black Americans and their continued interest in Bahia.[58] Santana Pinho makes a salient point regarding the ways in which these Afro-Atlantic groups' engagements with the African imaginary solidify mythmaking. The persistent refiguring of Africa in Bahia suggests that literal migrations from the United States to Bahia, as well as the flights of the imagination that guide cultural productions in Bahia, are indicative of Afro-Atlantic peoples' concurrent traversals of a spectrum of fantasy. Relatedly, African religiosity has remained a hotly contested issue in Brazil, as the Yoruba/Nagô Candomblé worshipped in Bahia is viewed widely by many as traditional and closest to the source, while other iterations from the religious universe—the Umbanda, Bantu, and Macumba worshipped mainly in other parts of Brazil—are discounted mainly because of their level of syncretization.[59] What Black American roots tourists witness as authentic African vestiges in public, tourist-friendly Candomblé ceremonies and festivities such as Boa Morte have actually been marked by a "continual search for information about African religions, and the resumption of journeys to Africa . . . [that] are expressions of this quest for African purity."[60] Afro-Bahian interpretations and performances of Africa, then, are the result of the tourists' imaginations, cultural essences, and perpetual searches for authenticity through book knowledge and practitioner trips to Africa proper.

The tourism professional's task, then, is complicated. One can anticipate how the staging of interactions between diasporans with sacred spaces and cultural elements might unintentionally lead to falsification, which is not to suggest that cultural roots tour operators are exploitative but to propose the reading of these interactions through the lens of sincerity. John Jackson explains: "Authenticity presupposes a relation between subjects (who authenticate) and objects (dumb, mute, and inorganic) that are interpreted and analyzed from the outside, because they cannot simply speak for themselves. Sincerity, however, sets up a different relationship entirely. A mere object could never be sincere, even if it is authentic. Sincerity is a trait of the object's maker. . . . [S]incerity presumes a liaison between subjects—not some external adjudicator and a lifeless scroll."[61] When Pat identified the "authentic" elements in the Candomblé ceremony, the Sankofa tourists nodded affirmatively as she spoke the words "that is African," but it remains unclear whether they were using the physical movement to confirm that they were listening to and processing her explanations, were already aware or had gathered that the performance was African, or simply agreed with Pat to be part of something they felt (but did not know) was authentic. Roots tourists who depart this symbolic Africa with the vexing belief that the entirety of their lives has been spent operating at a cultural deficit often describe a sense of disquietude as they witness their diasporic counterparts in Bahia living a life they might have had. In turn, many of them expatriate to Bahia to discover who they might have been.[62]

"Africa Is Alive and Well and Living" in Bahia: Come Be Who You Would Have Been

In his 1975 essay "Africa Is Alive and Well and Living in the Diaspora," Stuart Hall examines the necessities, complexities, and contradictions that mark return among Afro-Atlantic peoples by exploring the case of how ethnically diverse Jamaican slaves utilized cultural elements to establish a political column. Unconcerned with notions of preserving authenticity, these slaves cobbled together an amalgamated, symbolic Africa, asserting a mode of resistance against the colonizer's primary goal of robbing them of their ancestral cultures and, by extension, denying them access to a means by which to coordinate and fight for political power. Imaginings of Africa throughout the Afro-Atlantic, it follows, "preserve, borrow, alter, and transpose elements in order that the historically developing and emergent trajectory of the masses and classes in struggle can find articulation."[63] As shown in the aforementioned tourists' sentiments and the expatriate stories that follow, the perceived Blackness in Bahia, bolstered by the persistence of its evocations of Africa, facilitates the refiguring of their identities, lending credence to Hall's finding that even outside of literal travels throughout the Afro-Atlantic, "cultural identities undergo constant transformation . . . .[and] are the names we give to the different ways we are positioned by, and position ourselves within, the narratives of the past."[64]

Thirty-eight-year-old Tamara noted that as she prepared to flee the United States for Bahia in the early 1990s, her family expressed concerns as to why she would leave without a guaranteed job or adequate financial preparation. Tamara explained her quest to self-actualize: "What I find happens when you move to another country—if you allow it—is you can really lose your identity, which helps you find your identity. . . . There are some things that you do because you've been taught to do them, and that's not necessarily who you are. You don't figure that out until you leave. . . . You have to go to Bahia being really open to it transforming you because it has that power. It is a very powerful place."[65] Tamara moved to Salvador permanently in 1994, despite knowing that she would lead a more difficult lifestyle than she had in the United States. Shortly after her arrival, she found a roommate with whom to share a modest apartment outfitted with the absolute basics: a table with two chairs and two mattresses. To pay her portion of the rent, Tamara taught English to Bahian high school students. With a combined one hundred dollars left each month to pay for food and other expenses, Tamara and her roommate learned to barter for groceries at the end of each day when food that was near its expiration date and dented canned goods were sold at reduced rates. After a year-long exile in Bahia, she returned home to San Francisco, California, where she spent much of her time longing for Bahia, as it had left an "indelible mark. . . . I have never felt that kind of attachment on a soul level." She began taking an Afro-Brazilian dance class and seeking out new friends who were from Latin America or who had lived abroad. Tamara explained: "I am a hybrid and a modern nomad. I feel like I belong to a wandering tribe. Bahia is the home of my spirit—of my heart. I needed to wake up in Bahia, and I would be happy. Even when I was really sad, my spirit and my heart felt supported in some way [in Bahia]."

In 1995, Tamara returned to Bahia and went "through this phase where I tried to detach from American identity. . . . If I saw an American coming, I would walk the other way. I wouldn't speak English. . . . I really made a point to integrate myself into Bahian culture." Now a flight attendant for a major international airline, Tamara splits her life between New York City and Brazil. Her realization of an actively crafted Afro-Atlantic identity, despite her financial struggles in the very place that had and continues to affect her so profoundly on the "soul level," is striking in its romantic quality, particularly because not all expatriates have experienced such spiritual growth and happiness in the face of Brazilian social realities.

Above I have shown that Black American travelers move toward sites of imagined racial progress in the post–civil rights moment by reclaiming Africa in Bahia, which has situated them squarely in the midst of distinct Brazilian entities that utilize and conjure Africa to various ends:

Afro-Brazilians who wish to maintain their ancestral identities and embrace cultural productions as a means of protest; and local, state, and national governments that usurp the Afro-Brazilian culture as a means by which to realize their economic and first-world aspirations. While the continued presence of Black Americans in Bahia assists in the legitimization of these African imaginaries, breaches occur when expatriates who have bought into the myth of equality ultimately are confronted and impacted by racial realities in Bahia. Disenchanted and chagrined that the history of radical Black social movements throughout Brazil has not resulted in the utopic levels of social progress that they had envisaged, some Black Americans problematically not only assume critical positions that frame the case of Black American progress as the paragon of Afro-Atlantic radicalism, but they also couple their critiques with the outright rejection of contemporary Africa.

Isaac, a retired international developer and manager of a prestigious fashion house, settled in Salvador in 1999. As he trekked around Bahia during his visits as a tourist, Isaac found the state to be an "amalgamation of several places" to which he had traveled in the past as a sort of sophisticated, cosmopolitan figure, only the phenotypic Blackness and African cultural richness in Bahia offered him a unique sense of identity that European destinations had not.[66] Isaac believed absolutely in Brazil as a racial paradise and moved to Salvador, where he invested $1 million to renovate a long-deserted, dilapidated building into a boutique hotel. Soon after the construction began, he made the untoward discovery that he had not escaped racism in his flight to Bahia. Convinced that his investment in Salvador's economy should automatically afford him, at the very least, a modicum of political power, Isaac took his concerns to local politicians to no avail. Instead, he began working on the micro level to address issues by hiring darker-skinned Afro-Bahians for positions at the reception desk and committing himself to improving their professionalization rather than relegating them to more menial positions as was common in Salvador. He explained that he wanted to offer opportunities for workers who would have a difficult, if not impossible, time acquiring such employment given the societal preference for *good appearance*, a form of discrimination that increased the likelihood of generational poverty among the African-descended population. Isaac lamented: "The thing that made Salvador attractive [originally] was that it was a predominantly Black community. And that was the lure. Everybody seemed happy, and it seemed like an ideal place to want to be . . . to live. And it is an ideal place to want to be—on vacation." Interesting here is his notation that roots tourism in Bahia thrives off façades powerful enough for him to sell most of his possessions, leave family behind in the United States, and devote a lifetime's worth of savings to be near the sensation that emanates from the place. Perhaps the joy that Isaac and other expatriates saw in the faces that could have been theirs during their initial visits was a kind of outward, radical expression of Afro-Bahians' determination to survive despite their political marginalization.

Outside of the stressors that came along with the hotel's construction, Isaac encountered firsthand how racial issues arise in everyday ways when he witnessed the treatment of Afro-Bahian workers who were forced to utilize separate restroom facilities from their "white" coworkers at the behest of their boss. Isaac bristled at what he surmised to be either the Afro-Bahian construction workers' complacency about or obliviousness to how their skin color was used as a rationale for discrimination. By the time of our first meeting, his decade-long immersion into Brazilian society had transformed a once naive Isaac into an individual who was hyperaware of his surroundings. Bahia had failed his imagination, and he was disappointed in himself for believing what he thought he saw as a tourist. Just before our first meeting, Isaac made the decision to sell his hotel, though he fretted openly that his staff might not adjust well to the new European ownership. As we spoke, Isaac was visibly distracted and discomfited by the sight of the white owners poring over business records at the reception desk and pacing about the expanse of the ground floor of the hotel with authority. He explained that while he had lost a significant amount of money—more than half of his original business investment because of missteps in decision making and falling victim to fraud—it was the reality of what he viewed as the unchecked racial oppression in Bahia that remained the greatest disappointment: "Now that I understand how society is structured here, I get mad with the Black people; I'm furious because I see that they are too passive. The mentality of slavery still exists here and it stresses me; it frustrates me. And you have to live here to experience that."

Isaac's arrival was predicated on a wish to live in a postracial Black utopia, and this unmet expectation was central to his decision to depart.

Paradises and "utopias always have entailed disappointments and failures. They cast a harsh light on the limits of our imagination, underscore our shortsightedness, and replicate the disasters of the world we seek to escape. Utopia never turns out to be the perfect society."[67] Isaac reflected on his initial understanding of Bahia's societal structure: "There is, initially, an illusion that the Blackness here gives one an anchor—gives one an identity . . . but then you come and you don't look African and the people don't recognize you as being African or Black. And maybe you have a few ducats in your pocket, so that eliminates you from their definition of Black because their definition is: poor and uneducated." What Isaac found to be overwhelming evidence that Brazil "is racially sick" Denise Ferreira da Silva simply explains through the phrase, "Brazil Is Not (Quite) the United States."[68] At a follow-up dinner meeting with Isaac, he divulged somberly that Bahia "was not what I'd hoped it would be. I came under false pretenses . . . it was 100 percent my fault. It was by far—I can say this now with conviction: coming to Salvador was the biggest mistake I've made in my life. But my life isn't over, so I can correct it by leaving."[69]

In an e-mail to me in late 2007, Isaac concluded: "It's definitely time for me to leave this place. And despite the picture of gloom and doom that has been painted for me by friends in the States now, I'd rather take my chances there as a Black person than to remain here as a nonentity. With [Barack] Obama's candidacy [for president], I see a glimmer of hope—something that has always and continues to elude life in Bahia for descendants of Africa!"[70] The Black American relationship with the nation is always already fraught due to the community's status as an outsider within, but mobility reveals a paradox: some expatriates who flee the United States because of its racialized oppression and sluggish advancement toward progress return to or long for the known in America, when they recognize the plight of African descendants abroad. In Isaac's case, Obama's soaring rhetoric of hope and popularity among members of all political parties and across racial lines offered a "glimmer" of a chance that Isaac's postracial longings might be realized. As Houston Baker once noted and Isaac found, "No matter where you travel, you still be black."[71] No matter how far he travels, he is still an American.

The imagined African "bloodline of the Brazilian people" brought expatriates Charles, Kevin, Donald, and Allen to Bahia.[72] As the following exchanges reveal, when their returns to Bahia prove that who they would have been is not fully liberated—that is, when they find that the vast majority of Brazil's African-descended population is fighting struggles similar to theirs in the United States, the men express a bevy of contradictions regarding whether and how to embrace their American and African linkages. Born in the U.S. South and active in organizations such as Students for a Democratic Society (SDS), the Student Nonviolent Coordinating Committee (SNCC), the National Association for the Advancement of Colored People (NAACP), and/or other civil rights organizations, each of these expatriates expresses disappointment in the failures of the United States in the post–civil rights period, which is marked by the continued unattainability of social life for all citizens. In the decades since the passage of the 1960s civil rights acts, activism to ensure that those laws were enforced and to strategize for the actuation of additional social transformations has decreased exponentially as the Black American community of the pre-1965 era has been swept into a period of neoliberal individuation. A combination of the persistent renovations of the slavery-era geography of containment, the inaccessibility of true mobility in the United States, and yearnings for a cultural compass compelled these expatriates to set their sights on Bahia with hopes of realizing the social evolution for which they had fought during the freedom movement in the 1960s.

The dialogue that follows is a compilation of portions of my interviews with retirees Charles and Kevin, who had been highly educated in the United States and had successful careers, despite the turbulent historical period in which they were (partially) raised in North Carolina and Florida, respectively. Charles was raised in New Jersey but spent a great deal of our conversation reflecting on the portions of his childhood spent in segregated North Carolina with his extended family. Active in civil rights organizations—including SNCC and SDS—as a teenager and college student, Charles also served in the military, though he was able to avoid deployment to the Vietnam conflict. Charles retired from working in the fashion industry and relocated to Bahia in 2003 because of the high quality of life he is able to have there (he owns a condominium in the city and a country home) and because the Afro-diversity of Bahia reminds him of his adulthood home, New York City. Kevin, the former director of a university-based general equivalency diploma outreach program, also chose Bahia because of its seeming embrace of Blackness and relaxed way of life, which differed significantly from the culture of fear that he believes has enveloped the United States since 9/11. Before retiring in Bahia in 2004, Kevin traveled to India for a month to decompress at a spa retreat and to wash his connections to America away symbolically. Moving to Bahia, he explained, was his escape from racism, injustice, and the ever-present threat of brutality.

MC: How do you define freedom?
CHARLES: Ooooh freedom, baby![73]

Charles's sociable disposition became solemn suddenly. He closed his eyes and began to clap slowly, rocking back and forth in his leather armchair, as if he had been transported elsewhere. I watched and listened intently as Charles sang a mournful, improvised spiritual. His tenor voice thundered against the walls and up to the far reaches of the ceiling of his expansive living room. Charles's utterance of each syllable was deliberate, resonating as a profession of a pained history.

CHARLES: (Singing) Freedom, freedom, freedom, freedom, freedom, freedom! (Now speaking) My parents and their ancestors and how they held that vision [of freedom] in spite of the chains—both physical chains and mental chains . . . blockages in every way. And how the holding of that vision enabled my generation to go to the universities of our choices. Freedom, on a personal level, has a relationship to prosperity. The freedom of movement. It's very difficult to have monies . . . access to capital . . . The freedom to self-express.
MC: In what ways has being an American in Bahia been an asset? A liability?

Kevin answered that being an American is an asset because one is granted preferential treatment as an American (regardless of race) who is assumed to be rich. He answered the "liability" portion of the question by stating that it is difficult to develop trustworthy relationships because there is a history of Black Americans being exploited financially. Kevin became much more animated and loquacious when he began describing his disgruntlement with often being challenged by Brazilians to account for the pervasive atrocities committed by and through the administration of President George W. Bush, the Iraq war, and America's historical role in the demise of other nations.

KEVIN: I've decided I am not going to listen to any anti-American propaganda or anti-American remarks from people. I'm not going to apologize for being an American, and after seeing the situation of Black people here, in Togo, Mexico, Puerto Rico, and Cuba, I'm glad my [foreparents] stayed on the [ship] until they said, "The last stop: the United States." I'm glad I wasn't born in Brazil as a Black person because I think people here have almost no rights, no respect, and no opportunity. And so I'm not going to apologize for that anymore, and when people say stuff, I'm going to be right down their throats. . . . As a Black person, I'm not in love with the United States. I was so angry about the racism that I experienced on the job. I was very bitter and wanted to get away. [The United States] is just one of the best places that I could have been born because I've seen the plight of Black people in other countries, and they don't have opportunity. At least in the United States you have an opportunity. In that sense, I'm glad I was born there.[74]

MC: What are your opinions about race in Bahia?

CHARLES: Bahia is still stuck in the mind-set of the [postslavery] Reconstruction period in the States. I see things happening here that I would never see in the States. [Afro-Bahians] make the best out of their particular lot. They are joyous. I don't think that they have the desire to make a demand on the powers that be for change.

MC: Based on your experiences here, what advice would you offer to a Black American who wishes to settle in Bahia?

CHARLES: I think that one of the problems of African Americans when they come to Bahia [is that] they get so caught up with the exterior that they let go of a lot of the warning signs they would use back in the States to direct and to guide them in their business decisions and social decisions. They drop them here. [In the future, Black American migrants should] come with an open heart and a shrewd mind. . . . I think it is a great place for us as a people to make a great contribution and to be rewarded socially and financially. I think it's wide open for Black Americans. Wide open. They need our intellectual, historical, and financial resources—they are desperate for them. And we have them. As bad as the States has been, quote end quote, it has been great for many Black Americans, and when you travel outside of the States, you have the chance to really compare our lives to the lot of Blacks around the world, and I think we come out on top. . . . They don't have the tradition of the social institutions that we have. The long tradition of lawyers, doctors, schoolteachers, ministers, business people—we carved that out in the wilderness. We carved it out; I don't know how, but we did! We're some of the most dynamic people on the face of this earth—Black Americans.

Throughout the dialogue, the expatriates discuss some of their experiences using defensive, disparaging language, yet the question becomes how to frame these moments of décalage. Certainly, some of the sentiments are indicative of the arrogance inherent in exceptionalist American postures. Though the majority of the retirement-age expatriates arrived in Bahia with a tremendous amount of financial resources and a few have achieved what elsewhere might be described as cosmopolitan lifestyles, it is not exclusively due to a herculean ability to carve success "out of the wilderness," but to various forms of U.S. imperialism that created and relegated so-called second- and third-world nations to their particular places. These privileged Black American expatriates, especially those who have reached what they refer to as the twilight of their lives, are exasperated by the reality that full equality probably will not be realized in their lifetimes. Kevin's declaration of pleasure that slave ships displaced his ancestors on American shores rather than in what he deems as less-desirable nations reads as an endorsement of the United States, but as he continues, it is clear that he was affected profoundly by segregation and other discriminatory policies that impede Black Americans' chances at the American Dream. A measure of fault lies, certainly, with the manner in which these travelers ascended into flight. Each attempted to self-actualize by eschewing psychic returns to Africa and instead literalized their flights through physical movements toward an Africa that no longer exists. Over the years, many Black American travelers with earnest projects to "uplift" Bahia's African-descended population, as Charles champions, have come and gone. Those who remain dismiss these former volunteers as idealistic activists who failed to educate themselves about Bahian society.[75] Isaac argued that "the social problems here are so tremendous. Any of these 'goody two shoes' projects, to be effective, [is] going to need the government's financial and moral support. I can't tell you how many people that

I know that have been to Salvador working on children's projects.... These projects are momentary distractions."[76] Despite this widespread sentiment, empathy catalyzed Isaac and the majority of the expatriates to become active in Bahian social programs, some of which have resulted in long-term commitments.

Witnessing the subtle and blatant forms of racialized oppression play out in what had appeared to them initially as an Africanized paradise affirmed for Allen and Donald, academics who have been traveling to Bahia for nearly forty years, the import of the U.S. Black freedom movement and the establishment of a political column to address contemporary forms of oppression. Both travelers have held fellowships and teaching appointments at universities in Bahia, possess scholarly interests in Bahian cultural practices, and are active followers of Candomblé. Yet when asked to muse about Africa generally, Allen and Donald offered startling perspectives:

ALLEN: The corruption, the wars, hunger, disease, and AIDS. No potential. I see Africa as lost. I [appreciate] what folks like Bill Gates are trying to do [to] educate folks, but educate for what? Educate how? If you're an African in Africa, what are you going to want to be? You want to be an American? You get a free computer ... what is that going to give you access to? I don't think I'm a pessimist. I'm a realist.[77]

DONALD: It became very clear to me early on that I was African—that I was the *other*. Once one discovers that one is, in America, an African, you have to say what are you going to do about that. Are you going to forget it or try to forget it? You're not going to be an African in terms of Africa because you've lost certain fundamental contact points and lines of heritage and inheritance ... being an African American is a challenging intellectual feat. Once I became conscious, once I woke up—fortunately, I did not wake up angry. I channeled my energy into art from the very beginning. Africa, Africa—everything. Everything that makes me happy [and] makes me sad—that lives in my imagination and stimulates my work ... that causes me stress and disappointment—that energizes, frustrates. Everything. Where I'm from; where I'm not from. Africa: Where it all began; where it all ends. Where everybody rushes to; where everybody rushes from. Where everybody invests; where everybody steals.[78]

Disappointed in the fallacies expressed in Brazil's (and America's) national myth of supposed postracial progress, these travelers employed invectives to rail against Brazil and, in Allen's case, to dismiss contemporary Africa as a site of Black possibility even for the people who still live on the continent. In the midst of this cacophony of contradictions echoes Charles's impassioned song of "freedom," an unexpected, powerful moment that encapsulates the impetus behind my call for more measured examinations of décalage in circuits of return. Given the expansiveness of structures of domination, one's relative wealth or nation cannot undo the fact of one's being Black and all that that entails under structural racism. Yet it would be remiss to downplay the fact that it is the dual Black American quest for both the American Dream and repossession of Africa in Bahia that stalls the prospect for sustainable returns. This is not to say that life, liberty, and the pursuit of happiness are insignificant goals, of course, but that the inward focus—the individualism that marks American exceptionalism—conflicts directly with these travelers' reclamation of cultural identity, rendering it more possible to travel (across the world, up social and financial ladders, and so on) as well as overlook and generally disconnect themselves from the very people whose appearances legitimized Bahia as an Africa by proxy. Richard Iton comments on the power of these despotic systems, underscoring why they must be rejected: "The forces that both make and disrupt the virtual Africa, and encourage blacks elsewhere to internalize stigmatized notions of the 'African,' are the same pressures that make settlement unavailable elsewhere and diasporize all within and without the continent. It is in this modern matrix of strange spaces—outside the state but within empire—that naturalization and citizenship are substantively unavailable, regardless of geographical position."[79]

The varying relationships that the Black American expatriates discussed here have had with Bahia are indicative of individual intradiasporic quests for contentment on emotional, economic, and societal levels. The journey is consistently capricious. Blackness is the imagined connector, but disparate historical relationships to their respective nations often lead to misrecognitions and breaches between Black American travelers and Afro-Bahians. Consequently, literalized Black American flights throughout the Afro-Atlantic hinge on the question "where to now?"— that is, their speculative imaginations are ever-employable. Corrine, for instance, considers Bahia her permanent home, but relayed her desire to travel to the "Door of No Return" in Senegal: "As a diasporan, you need to know other languages. What's the *source* looking like? Not this romanticized source that we have in the diaspora when we're Africanist. I need to live that experience." For now, however, Bahia serves the overwhelming majority of this collective as an imperfect paradise. Time will tell if Bahia remains sufficient for them. The fact of Afro-Atlantic dispossession and the attendant histories of domestic and international Black American radical flights since the Middle Passage to address social alienation suggests that it will not be, without the intentional, self-reflexive modification of their exceptionalist views on the function of return.

Coda: Collective Returns

In the book-length poem *Song for Anninho*, the Black American author Gayl Jones performs the speculative act of what Toni Morrison refers to as a "literary archaeology," the painstaking task of developing a narrative from the historical record, fragmentary evidence, and the author's imagination.[80] Jones utilizes speculation to explore Afro-Atlantic identity via a loving relationship between Anninho and Almeyda, two fictional members of Palmares, a quilombo community in Alagoas, Brazil, where escaped slaves defended their fugitivity and created new radical generations for the better part of the seventeenth century. Jones's version of this highly regarded and oft-mythologized narrative of Black resistance begins just after the final, devastating assault on Palmares. During the fictionalized battle, Portuguese soldiers brutally sever the breasts of the protagonist, Almeyda. A conjure woman, Zibatra, assists Almeyda's physical recovery and also facilitates her reclamation of memory about her ancestral past, the history and future of Palmares, and Almeyda's relationship with her husband, Anninho, who is missing when she regains consciousness. The poem is a lyrical expression of Almeyda's yearning to be reunited with Anninho in the midst of her considerable physical and emotional pain as well as an articulation of her desire to retain connections with the local and distant pasts through rememory and the spiritual realm. Through Zibatra's mystical mediation, Almeyda is able to communicate with the deceased Anninho, offering wisdom from her grandmother that is instructive about the Afro-Atlantic expressions of saudade that I have analyzed throughout this chapter:

She said, You are the granddaughter
of an African, and you have
inherited a way of being,
And her eyes stayed on mine, Anninho,
until all her words and memory
and fears and the tenderness
ran through me like blood. . . .
That was the moment when I became
my grandmother and she became me.
Do you know what I mean?
Yes.
Our spirits were one.
Yes.
But it was more than that.
Yes. We are never alone.
We keep everything.
Yes.[81]

In reciting her grandmother's words, Almeyda reinforces the idea that while the foremothers may no longer exist in the flesh, there is an African interiority that remains in all dispossessed descendants of slaves. Many stories are unknown, lost to time. Afro-Atlantic speculative acts to reclaim Africa in Bahia and in places throughout the African diaspora are deemed by Black American travelers and Afro-Bahian cultural producers as necessary for tapping into that which they feel is inherent yet deeply obfuscated. If African-descended peoples are always already connected to their ancestors and have retained everything in cyclical fashion, as diasporan lore maintains, then it follows that dispossessed individuals will continue to utilize literal and figurative flights to return.

By broadening typical explorations of Black American exceptionalism, which tend to be wholly dismissive and suspicious of Black American flights, I have argued that saudade functions as a manner by which many African-descended peoples mourn and recover as well as re-create and radicalize how they understand Africa. As shown above, returns that inspire Afro-Bahian cultural production and Black American expatriation are not always connected to legible, regenerative political projects, but at the core they are revolutionary in their resolve to embrace and remember the African ancestral past and in their rejection of transnational postemancipation narratives of progress and postracialism. Almeyda and Anninho recall about the fantastic flights that signaled the conclusion of the war at Palmares:

> And didn't the war end like that?
> Only cliffs to be jumped from, or surrender?
> ... And our brave Palmaristas,
> jumping from cliffs rather than surrender.
> Oh, if they could have become birds then!
> Even now, I watch for birds,
> hoping it's some Palmarista!
> We are blessed because we did not just survive
> that, but we survived it loving.
> We never stopped loving each other.[82]

The history of postwar mythmaking about Palmares in cultural production exalts the courageousness exhibited by the Palmaristas and propagates a triumphalist narrative about the radical potentiality in collective flights, love, and unification even after liberation and across difference. The question becomes: how might a unified psychic return to Africa be actualized into a more direct, unified politics of nonsurrender?

CHAPTER 4

Crafting Symbolic Africas in a Geography of Silence

RETURN TRAVELS TO AND THE RENARRATIVIZATION OF THE U.S. SOUTH

they ask me to remember
but they want me to remember
their memories
and i keep on remembering
mine.
—Lucille Clifton, "why some people be mad at me sometimes"

In the late 1990s, I took an evening walking tour called "The Ghosts of Charleston," a guided encounter with the supernatural in Charleston, South Carolina. As we strolled around the city's downtown area and through winding cobblestoned streets, admiring the horse-drawn carriages and rainbow-colored buildings, we paused often at cemeteries, centuries-old homes, hotels, a former jail, and markets to witness the locations of the occult. Our guide opined that a range of elements whereby widespread death occurred—hurricanes, floods, fires, and the Civil War—had rendered the city ripe for paranormal activity. The dead, he intimated, have unfinished business. What struck me about the tour and the numerous visits that I had made to plantations throughout the Lowcountry throughout my childhood in South Carolina during school field trips and family excursions, as well as a researcher in more recent years, is that other than in passing references, Charleston's history as a major slave port is glossed over in the larger tourism industry to promote representations of the imagined antebellum South of the Lost Cause. In downtown Charleston, a former slave market sits quietly near a more recently constructed block called the Market, which is surrounded by expensive hotels, eateries, and boutiques that serve as background for a sort of souvenir bazaar at which Gullah women and their children weave and sell seagrass baskets crafted using what are believed to be West African techniques passed down from their ancestors.[1] The silence about slavery betrays the trauma, dispossession, and death suffered to build and sustain the wealth that, if one looks at and listens critically (even to the silence), hovers over the area, mocking the evidence of the great injury that was the transatlantic slave trade.

"The Ghosts of Charleston" tour guide's lone story that described the spirit of a slave was about a boy named George, a decidedly gentle spirit who is said to pester guests impishly at the 1837 Bed and Breakfast. George drowned in 1843 after he jumped into the harbor in pursuit of a ship that was transporting his parents to a Virginia plantation. Today, George taunts hotel patrons by shaking the bed in one room and by turning the lights on and off repeatedly in another. He is sometimes seen playing in the building or swaying in a rocking chair. George's nuisance, the story goes, is remedied easily when one cracks a whip to frighten him. To relegate Charleston's cruel history of slavery to the margins of the historical master narrative by repeating stories about slaves that make light of the institution while reinforcing its horrors—ships utilized to separate parent from child, the horrific struggle that ensued as the child fought drowning, and the whip's lash—rewounds. Most disquieting is that 1837's guests are encouraged to participate in the past, wherein it becomes a diversion to threaten the spirit of a slave with force, reenacting the role of the master. The lore identifies a playful ghost rather than a sad spirit who is frightened, crying, screaming, gurgling as he writhed in the ocean, or gasping for air. Why is it that the unsilenced ghostly specters of slaves in these Lowcountry master narratives are not enraged and vengeful?

In the post–civil rights moment, Black Americans are not only returning to the South to live permanently in a reverse migration that has befuddled onlookers, but Black American cultural producers are also working against the region's geography of silence to illustrate how the ideologies that undergirded past social configurations in the South redound in the present, moving toward a broad Black fantastic frame. Through analyses of these points of return and revision, this chapter contends that Black Americans embrace speculative thought to recast cultural production about the South; challenge what is commemorated as significant in historical preservation; and create alternative "African" worlds in the purview of the racism and the often spurious narratives of progress that reign in the South, particularly at sites of slavery. Such fantastic reimaginings contest and thereby perform a democratization of contemporary master narratives and, for some, attend to the desires of those who are determined to realize Black social life in the American South despite its sordid histories.

Troubling the Silence in Southern Master Narratives

"Growing up in Midway with the coloreds, I spent the night at Molly Montague's house in the bed with five niggers—spent the night with them. In the same bed, eat from the same table, drink from the same thing, play with them every day. I mean, they were family. I mean, as far as I was concerned. They loved you."[2] Winston Silver's curious memory of a colorblind childhood in North Carolina in the pre–civil rights era reflects a disturbing disconnect that his cousin, the film critic and novice documentarian Godfrey Cheshire, explores in the film *Moving Midway*. The film was conceived initially to chronicle the relocation of the home at Midway Plantation to a quieter tract of land away from the urban sprawl in Raleigh, North Carolina. Yet as Cheshire scoured historical records and interviewed members of his mother's family, he found that most narratives about slavery at Midway went unspoken, though it once was a thriving tobacco plantation. During his search, Cheshire discovered that there existed a branch of Black people on his family tree who might be able to assist him in developing a more complete narrative about his familial history. The film, then, traces two interrelated stories. The first is a catalog of a white Southern family's desire to preserve its plantation home, the "grand old lady" and "sacred center of the family" that sat on property that was settled by their ancestors in 1739. The second story is that of Cheshire's chance encounter with Robert Hinton, a Black American history professor whose grandfather was owned by Cheshire's great-great-grandfather. Hinton's inclusion in the film acts to challenge the myths of purity that the majority of Cheshire's maternal family members had embraced about their ancestral past.

Perhaps the most compelling thread examined centers on Cheshire's family's holding steadfastly to memories that were imparted to them by their ancestor Mary Hilliard Hinton (Aunt Mimi), who was fascinated with the idea of pastoral pasts and constructing genealogical maps that connected the Hinton family to the British aristocracy, despite her certain knowledge that various indiscretions by the Hinton slaveholders had resulted in mixed-race Black American kin. What Cheshire reluctantly finds and attempts to rectify is how he is implicated in what he sets out to explore—the lengths to which crafters of genteel, idealistic Southern myths often go to extricate slavery, violence, and racism from how the past is articulated. While the slave plantation serves as a place for wistful Americans to recall the zenith of white superiority, these vestiges of slavery also haunt the region and negate narratives of progress. Black Americans have begun visiting plantation sites and often become vocal about how the lives of their ancestors are erased from the tourism scripts. The moments of rupture in *Moving Midway* are indicative of what happens when the Black and white branches of a Southern family attempt to come to terms with their ties to blue-blooded ancestors, whose wealth was accumulated through their continued participation in the violence and inhumanity that marked slavery.

Robert Hinton appears throughout the film as a historical expert and also as someone who Cheshire initially and naively believes holds an emotional stake in ensuring that the land upon which Midway sits and the home itself are preserved positively in the collective memory. Hinton tours the plantation site in search of evidence of slavery and his long-dead ancestors, seeking out slave quarters and grave sites and showing very little interest in Cheshire's family's romantic stories about Southern gentility. Early in the film, Hinton is asked to attend a Civil War reenactment with Cheshire and Cheshire's mother, Elizabeth. This moment highlights the rifts that would arise later between Hinton and Cheshire, who had become friendly during the making of the film. At the reenactment, Elizabeth attempts to convince Hinton that the Civil War was about states' rights unlike what the (liberal) media and historians suggest about slavery's significance to the conflict. When Cheshire questions

Hinton about his response to the reenactment, a tense moment occurs between him and Cheshire, whose film narration theretofore had been somewhat progressive in its historical analyses of race and slavery in the South:

HINTON: It looked like it was fun for the people involved, but it—it represents to me a misremembering of the war of Southern history and why all this stuff happened. I think the absence of Black people at a thing like this encourages people to think that the Civil War was not about slavery.

CHESHIRE: Right. But also, there was the argument that was of states' rights. That that was—wasn't that the argument? But I mean, don't look at me like that. That was the argument that was put forward, right?

HINTON: I just think the whole argument about states' rights is an avoidance, and if slavery had not been an issue, the issue of states' rights would have never come up. My attitude about this is that I'm perfectly happy to have [the Civil War reenactors] keep fighting the war as long as they keep losing it.

[Both men laugh.]

Cheshire's momentarily aggressive insistence that Hinton not cast his gaze upon him in a dismissive fashion indicates Cheshire's sudden understanding that Hinton had little investment in the parts of Southern mythology to which Cheshire subscribes. Hinton's presence throughout the Midway relocation process forces Cheshire and his family to grapple with unspeakable issues that they had long avoided. When some family members are pressed in Cheshire's interviews with them about the family's role in slavery, they counter that the Hinton slaves were treated benevolently and were not violently terrorized as enslaved persons were on other plantations. Cheshire's situation of the filmic narrative forces these comments and Winston's contradictory love for his "nigger" childhood friends to stand on their own, as he makes no attempt to correct or validate their racial tone deafness. Hinton's role, then, becomes that of a foil for the backward thinking that is expressed, but he also suppresses any postracial, quixotic homecoming that Cheshire may have desired to construct surrounding Hinton's quasi-return to the plantation. "When I think about Midway," Hinton matter-of-factly reveals to Cheshire, "the house is the last thing I think about 'cause I think about the folks working in the fields, growing cotton and tobacco." Cheshire's inquiry about Hinton's emotions as he witnesses the house lifted onto the truck's risers in preparation for its move to a more rural location is met with aloofness as well. Hinton responds that it is important that the home remains in Cheshire's family as they find it to be a constituent element to the framing of their white, Southern cultural identities. However, Hinton elatedly remarks that he has "the pleasure of knowing that what used to be Midway Plantation will soon be covered with concrete and asphalt" and turned into a shopping center. Furthermore, Hinton appears pleased that the slave burial ground, though overgrown with brush, would remain untouched, as it is legally recognized as a cemetery. Hinton's indifference about the fate of the home rattles Cheshire, and the men have another testy exchange:

> CHESHIRE: Oh certainly, surely, you can't like that [the land will be rendered untillable].
> HINTON: Yes, because nothing significant will ever grow there again.
> CHESHIRE: Well, why is that good?
> HINTON: That's good 'cause my folks did the growing.
> CHESHIRE: Well, don't you want to see . . . to see their, you know, legacy continue on growing?
> HINTON: This is all of their legacy I need right here.
> CHESHIRE: That's all you need, huh?
> HINTON: That's right.
> CHESHIRE: But didn't the land mean something to you?
> HINTON: Well, only if [the slaves] ended up owning it.

Peculiarly, Cheshire assumed that the Black descendants of the Hinton slaves would feel the same sense of pride that he and his family did upon beholding the grand home and the still-fertile land upon which it stands. Robert Hinton maintains that the land would have meant something more to him only if any of the Black people who worked tirelessly on it somehow had been able to take ownership of it and renarrativize the space. The selling of the land to corporate interests is ironic, given that the transaction falls in line with the capitalistic impulse that propelled plantation slavery. The real estate deal would render Midway invisible in Hinton's estimation, though it is evident that he is keenly aware that an erasure of the original plantation site would not negate history or the remnants of slavery that continue to affect its descendants. In fact, since the last white male Hinton passed away at the turn of the twentieth century, it is solely the slave descendant who carries the surname of the original Midway Plantation owners.

Toward the conclusion of the film, Abraham Lincoln Hinton—the nonagenarian great-grandson of Ruffin Hinton, who was the child of Charles Lewis Hinton and his slave cook, Selanie Toby—arrives at the new Midway location to participate in a celebration of the extensively renovated and relocated home. As the elderly man is assisted out of his vehicle, the awkwardness and profundity of the moment is palpable. Standing before the white Hinton descendants was a confirmed Black blood relative who had spent his childhood walking past Midway Plantation with the knowledge that his family had ties to the place. When Charlie Silver, Midway's current owner and Cheshire's cousin, invites Abraham into Midway, Abraham is taken aback, as his years of socialized deference to white Southerners and his and his family's general exclusion from the home as guests caused him to pause and question diffidently the casual access being granted into the former plantation home and white social space: "Come in? Oh, I can go in? Huh, can I come in?" As the men pass through the entrance of the home, Silver mentions that Midway has been standing since 1848, the year of Ruffin Hinton's birth. Abraham expresses surprise at the age and condition of the home, to which Silver replies, "That's because your family built it. Ain't that right?" Abraham laughs, but seemingly is discomfited as he replies, "Yeah, yeah, that's right. Yeah." The men's laughter breaks the tenseness of the moment—the shame and sadness—that no doubt overcame them, though at closer inspection, Silver's utterance of "your family" versus "our family" elides the postracial narrative of progress that the white Hinton descendants had attempted to embrace throughout the film. Silver's recognition of the slaves' highly skilled, unpaid labor did not somehow make the home, which is passed down to the eldest male heir, accessible to or a birthright of every descendant, as race trumps bloodline and Abraham Hinton, decades older than Charlie Silver, is not Midway's owner.

Cheshire once referred to *Moving Midway* as a "personal excavation" that allowed him to better comprehend the past and initiate the process of uniting his white and Black family members so that they might confront a long-repressed history.[3] While relations across the Hinton family color line have not been transformed in any dramatic fashion, Cheshire expresses faith in the possibility for reconciliation, focusing on the purported love that once existed between the races on the plantation: "That whole little thing that [Winston] says [about sharing a bed with Black people] just in a few words conjures up the paradox of race in the South, especially from people with a plantation background where you could have been so close to these people that, you know, there was love there and there was affection and yet you're still seeing them as this different class of people."[4] Cheshire's utilization of "still" indicates a racialized, temporal disjuncture that remains unspeakable and seemingly irreparable in the U.S. South in general and is not aptly dealt with throughout the film in particular, though it would have been an obvious thread for Cheshire to examine given that the Black Hintons failed to benefit from their supposed loving connections to Midway and largely led difficult lives after emancipation. Winston Silver's declaration that "they loved you" rather than "we loved each other" or "I loved them" indicates that the interracial relationships that he celebrated were not about mutual affection and respect. Rather, they demonstrate his ignorance of the racial power dynamic that existed on the plantation site even after slavery and among children. Silver implies that Black Americans were joyful and forgiving despite their lot in life, an observation that functions as a way for him and some of the other white Hinton family members to absolve themselves of any lingering feelings of shame and guilt. To counter such misreadings. Black American cultural producers have taken to public spaces and sites of slavery, as they have understood since the end of the Civil War, the sense of liberation that comes with reclaiming historical narratives and unraveling obdurate Southern mythologies such as those echoed in the Hinton family story, which is bound in perpetuity to supremacist foundations and rearticulated in service of upholding the region's old order.

Confronting Symbolic Annihilation at Southern Sites of Slavery

On a scorching summer afternoon a few years after my "Ghosts of Charleston" tour, I traveled to Boone Hall Plantation in Mount Pleasant, South Carolina, in search of Gullah craftspeople. When I attended the Gullah Festival that May, I was told that the Gullah women not only set up shop along Highway 17, a popular coastal passageway that extends from Florida to Virginia, but they also work at local plantations in the region to sell their crafts. Their handiwork allowed the estate owners to claim that Black Americans were represented by the slave descendants' presence during the tours, though the atrocities of slavery and the role of the peculiar institution in the continued wealth of "one of America's oldest working, living plantations" went untold.[5] At the Boone Hall ticket office, I was informed matter-of-factly that the Gullah basket weavers were stationed in the slave quarters. Stunned, I walked down a dirt road to a set of neatly tucked away, small brick buildings, where I found a woman in her sixties and her young granddaughter working steadily on new baskets as they perspired profusely in the stifling, unforgiving Lowcountry heat. It was unclear whether they had been assigned space in the slave quarters or if they had chosen to work there to force tourists who were interested in their craft to engage, if only briefly, with the forsaken evidence of former slave life on the grounds. The subject of plantation slavery and the inheritance of social alienation remain ghostly matters whose "absence [from the script] captures perfectly the paradox of tracking through time and across all those forces that which makes its mark by being there and not there at the same time."[6] The Lowcountry's ghosts are part of a carefully constructed master account that suspends the Old South in time for a particular sort of roots tourist who desires a triumphalist narrative that reestablishes the Confederate States of America and relies on the silence about and the existence of the dishonored, alienated other. The heritage tourism industry in South Carolina's Lowcountry is substantial, in part because its plantation home tours promote a genteel Southern ideal that markets the region to white tourists and indirectly revels in its slave culture, though tourism scripts hardly make mention of such atrocities. The presence of slave quarters often goes underacknowledged, and the descendants of the original owners, who sometimes live in and maintain the homes, offer few or no explanations.

The center of slave communal life on plantations has remained a contested space, as local activists, anthropologists, and other scholars have highlighted the continued erasure of slave histories from contemporary mythmaking about the Old South.[7] Jennifer Eichstedt and Stephen Small refer to the expunction of Black life from the construction of Southern histories as a "symbolic annihilation," where "slavery and the enslaved are either completely absent or where mention of them is negligible, formalistic, fleeting or perfunctory."[8] To symbolically annihilate Black life from the narrative requires willing, active forgetting. Slave quarters have been

4.1 Boone Hall Plantation. © iStock by Getty Images.

4.2 Slave cabins at Boone Hall Plantation. © iStock by Getty Images.

torn down or left to deteriorate; in the most egregious cases, they have been transformed into restaurants, restrooms, and "charming" bed and breakfast cottages by proprietors who maintain that they are not responsible for history and refuse to engage critically with the spaces that they inhabit. Sanco Pansy's Cottage at Prospect Hill Plantation Inn in Charlottesville, Virginia, for instance, is constructed as a bungalow dedicated to a faithful enslaved charge and advertised as "[the original] sleeping quarters of a loyal slave who would spend four years fighting alongside his master in the War Between the States. Now our most-secluded luxury cottage, it epitomizes Southern plantation living . . . elegance without being pretentious."[9] Like the crafters of grand American mythologies regarding liberty, recent raconteurs of Southern lore about racial progress often cleave to stories that are immersed in apocryphal claims of paternalistic, requited affection and respect between the races, while disavowing the former plantation owners' connections to the fear, brutality, and geographies of containment that buttressed the era of slavery. To be sure, the virtual silencing of the plantation South's entanglements with the peculiar institution commenced long before slave cabins began to rot and the outward celebration of racialized hierarchies fell out of fashion among the privileged class.

After the Civil War, for instance, Black Americans began commemorating the sacrifices that Union soldiers had made to defeat the Confederacy by decorating their graves with flowers. The practice, which began in May 1865, led to the establishment of Decoration Day, which later became known nationally as Memorial Day to honor fallen soldiers. Black Americans also began to renarrativize Charleston, which describes itself as America's "most historic city," by publicly staging events to celebrate their freedom and flaunt their mobility. As Blain Roberts and Ethan Kytle note about this moment:

> In early 1865 the grounds [at the Citadel Green] where white cadets, charged with protecting the city against slave insurrection, had regularly conducted public exercises became the gathering point for a parade of black Union soldiers and countless local African Americans. On March 21 this large procession set out through the city streets. Publicly ridiculing the system under which they had suffered for so

long, some of the demonstrators conducted a mock slave auction while others displayed a hearse that proclaimed, "Slavery Is Dead."[10]

For a decade, those newly freed Black Charlestonians continued to march at various public sites on Emancipation Day and Independence Day and openly "mocked, critiqued, and vandalized these memorials to [John C. Calhoun], South Carolina's leading antebellum politician, thereby rejecting the claim that he—and all he stood for—deserved to be recognized in the city's public space and public memory."[11] Their attempts to build monuments in commemoration of those who challenged the Southern cause failed, however, as they struggled with white local and state officials over the inclusion of white Union and abolitionist allies in Southern memorialization. The Black Americans' assumption of a radical, defiant posture in a moment of defeat and indignity for the South grew out of their unified resistance on the plantation. White Charlestonians actively reimagined history to determine who was significant to the cultural memory, excluding figures who were instrumental to the emancipation cause by driving them out of what eventually became the heritage tourism corridor proper and into the fringes of local memorialization. Thus, while slavery was indeed "dead" in the sense that the institution proper had been defeated legally, new forms of containment and disfranchisement were enacted—from the Reconstruction Era's Black Codes and the twentieth century's Jim Crow laws to more recent iterations of police surveillance and stop-and-frisk policies, all of which obstruct the mobility of Black Americans, relegating them to the periphery of society yet rendering them hypervisible.

In the post–civil rights moment, very little has changed regarding who is allowed to craft or perhaps even revise historical narratives throughout the plantation South, particularly when it involves the history of slavery in the region. Decades of public outcries regarding the symbolic annihilation of Black histories in the Lowcountry of South Carolina have not gone completely unheard; there have been some victories in formal and informal historic preservation projects such as Charleston's Old Slave Mart Museum. In addition, a growing number of plantation sites throughout the South, generally tourist attractions with high visibility, have begun to renovate their slave cabins and include more direct narration about slavery in their tourist scripts to address the complaints leveled by Black American tourists about the historical erasure of Black lives from the South's tourism narratives.[12] Yet these revised narratives typically are admissions of what is generally known—that, yes, slaves labored here. Memories of slave humanity, their names, how they were treated, and the violence that contained them do not pass most tour guides' lips. In reaction, Black Americans concerned with public memorialization have developed creative ways to address the silence.

Joseph McGill, a historical preservationist and Civil War reenactor, initiated the Slave Dwelling Project in 2010 to underscore the necessity of preserving the long-forgotten remnants of slave life on plantations throughout the former slaveholding region.[13] When he learned about Charleston's Magnolia Plantation's plan to renovate its long-neglected slave cabins, McGill asked for and was granted permission to sleep in one of the dilapidated structures, which was overgrown with plants and inhabited by wildlife. McGill outfitted himself in shackles overnight to produce what he imagined to be a more authentic experience and later stated that he was frightened by noises in the decaying cabin, but found this temporary discomfort necessary to educate the public and increase the possibility for raising money for preservation efforts. He has since traveled to scores of plantation sites, sometimes with interested Black American tourists, to reengage in the act of resting where former slaves once lived because it makes "the history come alive."[14] McGill's intention is to visit every former slaveholding plantation that still stands to draw attention to the lack of preservation funds directed to memorializing the slaves whose unpaid labor supported the big house and its inhabitants. Though McGill maintains that his project centers on attracting financial support to fund the restoration of sites of slave life and not about reparations, he admits that shame compels some of the owners to allow him access to their homes: "Sometimes I sense guilt is part of what's driving people, but whatever it is, having me visit and acknowledge their preservation of these places makes them feel they're doing the right thing. . . . It's not a cure-all for what happened in the past, but it's a start."[15] McGill's desire for connections with the ancestors, like his participation in reenactments of the Civil War, is personal, yet there is fantastic potential in forcing the reconstitution of historical narratives vis-à-vis the staking out of a Black presence at sites from which Black Americans, regardless of their bloodlines, have been disinherited.

Asked in a 1989 interview to reflect on what had compelled her to write her Pulitzer Prize–winning novel, *Beloved*, Toni Morrison responded that the story had developed out of her concern about the very apathetic silence that McGill's project seeks to disrupt:

> There is no place you or I can go, to think about or not think about, to summon the presences of, or recollect the absences of slaves; nothing that reminds us of the ones who made the journey and of those who did not make it. There is no suitable memorial or plaque or wreath or wall or park or skyscraper lobby. There's no 300-foot tower. There's no small bench by the road. There is not even a tree scored, an initial that I can visit or you can visit in Charleston or Savannah or New York or Providence, or better still, on the banks of the Mississippi. And because such a place doesn't exist (that I know of), the book had to.[16]

Inspired by Morrison's words, the Toni Morrison Society founded the Bench by the Road initiative to create "outdoor museums" throughout the Afro-Atlantic that are integral to African diasporic memory.[17] In 2008, the society placed the first bench in Sullivan's Island, South Carolina, to memorialize the 40 percent of Africans who were brought to the United States through this port into South Carolina or further dislocated throughout the country, while another bench was placed to mark the former site of the Port Royal Experiment in Mitchelville, South Carolina, a town established in 1862—after General William Tecumseh Sherman's march through the region during the Civil War—on the Drayton Plantation on Hilton Head Island to redistribute land to runaway slaves, refugees, and others in the area who became free after the Emancipation Proclamation. These newly freed slaves had no place to turn, as their former owners left them behind when the war escalated. Allotted plots of land on which to farm and donated materials to build homes, these Black Americans proved their ability to be productive citizens.[18]

While McGill's and the Toni Morrison Society's attempts to repossess and revise narratives have been fairly successful due in part to the shame of the white descendants of slave owners, most projects aimed at preserving historical moments central to the lives of Black Americans are subject to severe opposition by white citizens as well as by local and state governments. Plans to establish a monument dedicated to preserving the memory of Denmark Vesey's heroic quest for freedom in 1822, for instance, were met with resistance in the late 1990s, and the situation was not resolved for more than a decade, as Vesey was a radical former slave who, along with his co-conspirators, strategized but failed to execute an insurrection in Charleston that likely would have resulted in the widespread death of white people. Vesey sought a liberated existence and the ability to lead a mass migration of Black Americans to Haiti. Though an enslaved informant foiled the rebellion, Vesey inspired a legacy of coordinated Black resistance and political thought throughout the New World that continues to be antithetical to Southern master narratives and the related national mythmaking about postracialism. During his trial, Vesey allegedly became defiant and proclaimed to the courts that the "work of insurrection would go on" whether he was executed or released.[19] Vesey's strategy of violent resistance likely spurred the consciousness of radical Black freedmen and slaves such as Nat Turner, whose storied rebellion in Southampton County, Virginia, in 1831 struck fear into the hearts of the Southern planter class, as it led to the deaths of sixty white people. Reactions from laypersons, political figures, and academics in the Lowcountry regarding whether to recognize Vesey in the public memory, then, were steeped in uneasiness, and many labeled him a murderer and "terrorist" who should have utilized the proper channels to achieve freedom.[20] A 2014 letter to the editor complained about an article published in Charleston's *Post and Courier* that purportedly lacked objectivity and seemingly supported Vesey's ideologies: "Contrary to this slanted story, Vesey was no heroic figure battling for education and freedom, but was well-known in the community as a brutal and violent man obsessed with vengeance. In real life he got the monument he deserved—the hangman's scaffold."[21] The letter writer's presentist outlook disregards the lack of civil liberties and the ruthless violence that sustained the era of slavery and promoted Black social death, rejoicing in the fact that justice had been served when Vesey was executed. Despite other disturbing protestations from other citizens and after nearly twenty years of negotiations, the Vesey monument was ultimately unveiled in Hampton Park in February 2014.[22]

Similarly, in Savannah, Georgia, Abigail Jordan donated most of her life savings to support the dedication of a bronze statue of a contemporary Black American family breaking the chains of slavery, which lay broken at their feet. The Savannah City council and several white residents bristled at the quote from Maya Angelou that accompanied the statue, insisting that Angelou's words were distasteful in their resurrection of horrific memories: "We were stolen, sold and bought together from the African continent. We got on the slave ships together. We lay back to belly in the holds of the slave ships in each others' excrement and urine together, sometimes died together, and our lifeless bodies thrown overboard together."[23] Feigning concern for the River Street heritage tourists, those who objected to the quote reacted as if the words, which recalled the horrors of the Middle Passage, somehow inflicted a wound on them rather than simply challenged the carefully constructed master narrative that is rehearsed in Savannah. After a decade, the objectors were successful in forcing the African American Monument Association's hands, and the organization contacted Angelou, who until then had had no involvement with the monument, to request that she amend the quote to render it more palatable to those who might take offense. Angelou obliged by adding a vague additional line: "Today, we are standing up together, with faith and even some joy."[24] The struggle against the original quote, of course, was more about ensuring that the words aligned with narratives of democratic racial progress than preventing tourists from being disgusted as they read about the conditions suffered by Africans on slave ships and the unremitting significance of slavery to contemporary American life.

Each of these historical preservation and memorialization examples illustrates how Black Americans have actively inserted themselves into master narratives since emancipation to fight against the erasure of Black life and sociality. One hundred and fifty years after Black Charlestonians established Decoration Day, the Gullah people in Beaufort County and other Black Americans continue to solemnize the final weekend of May, opting to venerate their ancestors alongside—and in some cases instead of participating in—the local, patriotic Memorial Day activities. The annual Gullah Festival, which celebrates the culture of the Black sea island people during a full weekend of events, including performances by griots, musicians, actors, and artists, culminates with an official rededication of the commemorative marker ceremony held in Port Royal, South Carolina, to honor the African ancestors at the foot of 11th Street, where some slaves are thought to have been brought into the area during the slave trade. During the service, a libation is poured to honor the ancestors, hymns are sung, and guests are asked to form a circle to read a litany to their African ancestors, which includes the following passage:

CALL: O ancient African souls hear our voices—it is because of you that we are—and as long as the sun rises in the East we will forever remember the days when you, our women, men and children were chained, whipped, raped, lynched, tarred and feathered, stripped of our African God, languages, names, and families then sold on the auction block to the highest bidder.

RESPONSE: We are your African children born in America and we honor you, we remember you, we claim you right now.

CALL: Oh sacred ancestors, your blood that was spilled all over this land, your sweat and toil in the heat of the day for more than 300 years built this land, your technology built this land, your African genius built America and you were never paid reparations for the work you gave.

RESPONSE: We are your African children born in America and we honor you, we remember you, we claim you right now.

CALL: May your supreme struggles, sacrifices, the battles you have fought for us, and the victories you have won be our guide and protector in all that we do every day.

RESPONSE: We are your African children born in America and we honor you, we remember you, we claim you right now.[25]

The recalling of African ancestors and the pledging of a commitment to Black life worldwide signifies the Gullah people's insistence on maintaining connections to an African sensibility while also demanding recognition and equality as American citizens. Specters of Africa continue to reemerge as points of connection for Black Americans returning to the U.S. South and in cultural production about the region, as Black Americans attempt to reclaim Southern spaces through the cultural and religious nationalism that began in earnest in the late 1960s and continues through the intransience of the Oyotunji African Village.

Literal and Figurative Returns to Africa in the U.S. South

During the Great Migration, approximately six million Black Americans relocated from the South, a pattern that began during the postbellum Reconstruction era. Though there was a net emigration of Black Americans from the South from 1880 to 1970, movements to the U.S. North, Midwest, and West decreased exponentially in the late 1960s due to deindustrialization and globalization, crime and poverty in urban areas, and the passage of the civil rights acts, which made life in the South more attractive.[26] Though it might have appeared nonsensical to casual observers that Black Americans would want to return or migrate to a region that historically had been the site of economic hardship and violent racial oppression, the five-year period between 1975 and 1980 alone saw a net migration of 108,000 Black Americans to the South, and the numbers have risen significantly since then.[27] In her ethnography *Call to Home*, Carol Stack found that the return migrations of Black Americans to the South from the 1970s to 1990s consisted of "[those who are] leaving cities where the economy has stagnated and returning to places where the economy has all but disintegrated."[28] Informed by decades of interviews and observations, Stack found that returnees actively were disregarding "the postmodern world" in their reclaiming of life in the rural South.[29] Black American quests for home, family, and reattachments to ancestral places and cultures were imagined to be far more crucial to these travelers than individual upward mobility and financial ascent.[30] About the cultural pulls that propelled her and other Black Americans' return passages to the South, Angelou confirmed Stack's findings, asserting that "the American South sings a siren song to all Black Americans. The melody may be ignored, despised, or ridiculed but we all hear it. . . . After generations of separation and decades of forgetfulness, the very name brings back to our memories ancient years of pain and pleasure."[31] Also important to the foundation of this 1970s focus on the South was the resurgence of cultural nationalist movements and the rise in cultural production about the region, including the publication and subsequent network television production of Alex Haley's *Roots: Saga of an American Family* which compelled Black Americans to trace their heritages and reunite during annual family reunions, create genealogical maps, and take pilgrimages to the U.S. South and imagined African ancestral sites around the world. For many Black Americans, voyages back to the South are returns to "the earth and to roots, to a 'homeland' and to a past. These roots are merged in various pasts which connect individuals to Africa; the South is the home of the ancestors, immediate (parents and grandparents) and remote (African slaves); here the soil is said to be 'baptized with the blood of the ancestors'; and it is here where African gods were first brought to America and where they are, it is felt, most accessible."[32]

Lamenting the lack of cultural ties to a "geographical center somewhere"[33] in the United States where there is a history for slave descendants who, due to migration, have lost their connections with the ancestral South, the author and cultural nationalist Gloria Naylor reflects on the Southern landscape and its influence on her crafting of the setting of her novel *Mama Day* in Willow Springs, a fictional separatist island that is both inside and outside of the South as it is connected by a bridge at the point at which South Carolina and Georgia converge but is not beholden to either state or the United States by order of its most recent charter, which has been in the possession of the Black protagonists' family since 1823.[34] Naylor maintains that "[Willow Springs] offers redemption through holding out the basic tenets that have kept the Black community strong, which is a sense of history. . . . [I]t offers redemption if a person is willing to grasp on to what is there in Willow Springs. For me Willow Springs was to be the ideal black community. And that's why it is separated from the mainland. But there is a bridge where people can go back and forth. You know. No one's a prisoner there."[35] Willow Springs' founding myth is grounded in a somewhat opaque memory that is passed down orally and retold in myriad ways about an enslaved African woman named Sapphira Wade, who used her mystical powers to dupe Bascombe Wade—a Norwegian-born slave owner and father of one or more of her children—into deeding the land to her sons, which ultimately allows the island's residents to maintain their separation and autonomy from the United States. Though Sapphira Wade lost her life to afford the African-descended islanders freedom, the narrative voice of the island informs the reader that "she got away from him and headed over here toward the east bluff on her way back to Africa. And she made that trip—some say in body, others in mind."[36] Naylor notes that in this narrative of return, "Sapphira Wade had no boundaries on herself. She [killed Bascombe Wade and] elected in her own mind to be free. And once you decide that you're going to be free, then people cannot imprison you."[37] To the people of Willow Springs, who were called "un-American" in their rejection of land claims by officials of South Carolina and Georgia, it was not a source of shame to be descendants of slaves, as they possessed the redemptive narrative and were not forced to endure new forms of enslavement and restriction that had been reinforced on the mainland after the Civil War (5).

Mama Day is a multilayered narrative—it is a posthumous conversation between lovers and a speculative narrative about the importance of being rooted in traditional ways through travels to this symbolic site, which was built by African-descended people who resisted assimilation into American society for well over a century. For the purposes of this examination, I turn to an analysis of *Mama Day*'s significance as a literary political project and an intervention regarding return to the U.S. South and the necessity of Black American reunification through the simultaneous travels of Ophelia "Cocoa" Day, a returnee who is thought by her great-aunt, Mama Day, to be too removed physically and mentally from Willow Springs; and George Andrews, Cocoa's husband, who grew up in a New York City orphanage, where—lacking thorough knowledge of his familial history—he was taught by the white directors to reject dwelling on the past because in their estimation "only the present has potential" (126). As the couple prepares for their initial trip together to Willow Springs, George consults maps and atlases to determine exactly where he is going, though Cocoa has informed him that the mystical island was not recognized or recorded. Incidentally, Naylor includes a family tree, a map of Willow Springs, and a bill of sale for Sapphira Wade in the novel's frontmatter that legitimizes the woman, myth, and geographic space for the reader. In a recollection of his first journey to Willow Springs, George tells Cocoa:

> You had not prepared me for paradise. And to be fair, I realized that there was nothing you could have said that would have made any sense to me. I had to be there and see—no, feel—that I was entering another world. . . . How do I describe air that thickens so that it seems as solid as the water, causing colors and sounds and textures to actually float in it? . . . And if someone had asked me about the fragrance from the whisperings of the palmettos, or the distant rush of the surf, I would have said that it smelled like forever. . . . The closeness of all this awed me—people who could be this self-contained. Who had redefined time. No, totally disregarded it. . . . I thought it was unique that you had a heritage intact and solid enough to be able to walk over the

same ground that your grandfather did, to be leading me toward the very house where your great-grandfather was born. Even your shame was a privilege few of us had. We could only look at our skin tones and guess. At least you knew. (175–219)

Representative of the dispossessed roots traveler, George expresses admiration of the Day family's ability to remain cohesive and rooted in their history and traditional core through various cultural expressions. As much as he desires to experience Willow Springs organically, and though he makes the romantic observation that the island "called up old, old memories" of unknown ancestors, George relapses often into his pragmatic, detached manner, attempting to apply scientific and logical analyses whereas Willow Springs residents rely on folklore and traditional ways to complete everyday tasks and understand the world, even hoping for the opportunity to check Willow Springs' founding myth with archival materials (184). Although Cocoa embraces American ways in her life in New York City, she maintains an affinity for and permanent connection to her homeland by taking annual excursions home. The omniscient narrator ruminates on the recentering that occurs during Cocoa's returns: "Home. Folks call it different things, think of it in different ways. For Cocoa it's being around living mirrors with the power to show a woman that she's still carrying scarred knees, a runny nose, and socks that get walked down into the heels of her shoes. . . . Home. It's being new and old all rolled into one. Measuring your new against old friends, old ways, old places. Knowing that as long as the old survives, you can keep changing as much as you want without the nightmare of waking up to a total stranger" (48–49). When George meets Mama Day and Cocoa's grandmother, Abigail, for the first time, he is struck by the familial language with which the elder women greet him: "Up until that moment, no woman had ever called me her child. Did they see it in my eyes? The intense envy for all that you had and the gratitude for their being willing to let me belong?" (176). In this moment of embrace, the South as enacted by Willow Springs serves as a symbolic homeland that is open to return by Black Americans despite their lack of known ties to the region. A literal orphan, George represents dispossessed Black Americans and is welcomed into an existence with the power to liberate him from the burden of loss and social alienation; it is a "landscape [that demonstrates] a state of mind, if you will, or a metaphysical situation."[38] Such points of connection compel George to express a desire to spend forever in Willow Springs, but the precariousness of his acceptance of Willow Springs as a place and ideology become apparent when he finds himself involved in a convoluted series of supernatural occurrences.

Mama Day is a fictitious account of a symbolic Africa that exists in the geographic U.S. South and offers George Black social life if he embraces return as a politics and point of connection with his ancestral cultures. As a novelist, Naylor's employment of the fantastic is unrestricted—the slave descendants in Willow Springs have the freedom to elect whether and how they travel to the United States or engage with American people and U.S. narratives of progress, which tend to erase the histories of African peoples. Naylor reimagines what Black history and culture could be, speculating on what it might look like if America were decentered in the formulations of Black cultural identities of Willow Springs, thereby constructing an imperfect yet paradisiacal social structure that very clearly draws inspiration from the relative seclusion of the Black sea island peoples (Gullah or Geechee), particularly their ability to sustain an African cultural sensibility. Her imaginings of Willow Springs as a Black fantastic place also appears to be modeled on the Port Royal Experiment mentioned above, and the continued existence of these communities simultaneously hearkens back to early all-Black towns such as Africa Town, Alabama, and Promiseland, South Carolina—and, most especially, the 1960s Black radical interest in settling new nations in the region, such as the establishment in Sheldon, South Carolina, of Oyotunji Village, a Yoruba revivalist community and the self-proclaimed first authentic African village in the United States.[39]

Naylor's musings about what draws her and other Black Americans to the South is instructive for locating why Black writers, laypersons, and tourists continue to engage with and center the South as the site for realizing an ideal Black American social existence: "There is something very seductive, though, about our roots in the South. That South is the closest we'll ever come to Africa. . . . for some writers the South might be the closest thing we have to our connection to the Motherland."[40] Naylor comments on the 1960s moment and political and cultural disconnections among Black Americans in the post–civil rights era, issuing a directive that heralds the promise of separatist ideologies:

Black activists were always split between self-determination or assimilation. . . . What we have found out since the Civil Rights Movement is that integration does not work. . . . What we need to do is some backtracking and begin from the cradle to build self-esteem in our young. We should go grassroots in the community and build up our own organizations. So I believe assimilation can be extremely dangerous. It does not exist in fact in America and to buy into it is to hinder your own psychological health. African Americans exist in two worlds. You never have full acceptance when you are on your own soil.[41]

Despite her beliefs in separatism, Naylor resists crafting Willow Springs as utopic. A critical moment occurs at the end of *Mama Day*, for example, when Cocoa is relegated to her bed as she struggles physically and mentally from a curse placed upon her by a jealous hoodoo roots worker; in a sudden, underexplained twist in the narrative, George is charged with saving Cocoa's life. During a brief moment at the Other Place, the transcendent site of her family home and cemetery, a year before George's visit, Mama Day had warned Cocoa that "people see what they want to see. . . . And for them to see what's really happening here, they gotta be ready to believe" (97). Unable to suspend his disbelief, George's ultimate act of relying on his logic—rather than following the instructions that Mama Day, a longtime, proven medicine woman and healer, had given him to do his part in an esoteric ritual to save Cocoa—is a rejection of the African cultural core that undergirds Willow Springs. George's fate is sealed, and he perishes in the flesh in a sacrifice that ultimately allows Cocoa to survive. Because Naylor crafts such rounded characters in this novel and George comes across as affable, if hyperanalytical, readers often question the necessity of his death. Given Naylor's nationalist leanings, George is martyred to show that social alienation will continue if Black Americans buy into narratives of progress and individuation and fail to return wholeheartedly to psychic, political, and cultural African centers. Naylor and other post–civil rights Black American cultural producers' fascination with the South as a symbolic African space and site of the ancestors suggests that the incessant nature of flight in search of spiritual restoration and social life will continue. They create and re-create spaces that feel free with hopes that one day they will be correct. Disillusionment catapults the dispossessed toward imagined

Africas as they hold onto faith that home is or can be forged out there, somewhere.

THE CONSTRUCTION OF BLACK SEPARATIST LANDSCAPES AND REPARATIONS DISCOURSE

Will any of us leave our homes and go to Africa? I hope not. . . . Let no man of us budge one step, and let slave-holders come to beat us from our country. America is more our country, than it is the whites—we have enriched it with our *blood and tears.* The greatest riches in all America have arisen from our blood and tears—and will they drive us from our property and homes, which we have earned with our *blood?* They must look sharp or this very thing will bring swift destruction upon them. The Americans have got so fat on our blood and groans, that they have almost forgotten the God of armies. But let them go on.

—David Walker, *Walker's Appeal*

In the late 1960s, Black radicalism grew in reaction to what some Black Americans saw as the United States' dawdling advance toward equality. Black members of multiracial civil rights organizations such as the Student Nonviolent Coordinating Committee (SNCC), the Congress for Racial Equality (CORE), and the Mississippi Democratic Freedom Party began to embrace the more revolutionary ideologies of Black Power and the teachings of leaders such as Malcolm X, and the organizations eventually transformed themselves into the Black Panthers for Self-Defense and other radical groups. The widespread idea that true equality had taken root as a result of the passage of the civil rights acts of the late 1960s illustrated to Black nationalists that their focus on Black self-determination was as crucial as ever.[42] With the de jure defeat of segregation came the growing disinterest of white allies in the civil rights fight to address inequalities such as joblessness and poverty, which continue to plague the Black community in the post–civil rights moment. As detailed in previous chapters, Malcolm X presciently observed in his autobiography that Black Americans would need to return to the Africa of their imaginations to organize properly and to develop transnational strategies to ensure the realization of a more authentic sense of freedom for Black Americans in the United States and for diasporans and continental Africans abroad. With this charge to radicalize the Global South in mind, Black nationalist offshoots from the U.S. Black social movement of the mid-twentieth century demanded financial and land reparations for slavery to establish, particularly in the southern United States, organizations steeped in Black autonomy and cultural nationalism. Appeals in the post–civil rights era for the redistribution of land in the South recall the Port Royal Experiment in which General Sherman allotted Black sea islanders (contrabands of war) forty acres of land. His orders declared: "No white person whatever, unless military officers and soldiers detailed for duty, will be permitted to reside [there]; and the sole and exclusive management of affairs will be left to the freed people themselves, subject only to the United States military authority and the acts of Congress. By the laws of war, and orders of the President of the United States, the negro is free and must be dealt with as such."[43] The "forty acres and a mule" standard, whereby each former slave would be allotted these items to begin a new life as a free person, lasted for roughly as long as it took for white Southern plantation owners to return to the region and petition President Andrew Johnson to terminate the land redistribution project and transfer their abandoned properties back to them. Disgruntled by the failures of the civil rights acts to improve Black lives, various radical organizations began discussing the possibility of crafting separatist communities, while other activists demanded that the U.S. government apologize for and acknowledge the nation's complicity in the peculiar institution and subsequent forms of oppression; take sincere strides to account for and eradicate the systemic disparities that disfranchise Black Americans; and revise historical records and master accounts that had diminished or erased Black American experiences, all of which were requirements that were guided by what Salamishah Tillet describes as "a deep, ethical commitment to creating an alternative racial framework for the future."[44]

In 1968, Gaidi Obadele and Imari Abubakari Obadele convened a conference of five hundred militant Black nationalists in Detroit, Michigan, to formalize their intentions to establish a Black nation in the U.S. South, which they saw as "the promised land" to which Black Americans, particularly the poor, could journey and "leave the struggle of the ghetto and make a better life."[45] One hundred attendees signed the Declaration of Independence for the new nation, the Republic of New Africa (RNA), which considered itself the provisional government of Black Americans and was grounded in self-sufficiency and a cooperative economic structure modeled on the Tanzanian concept of *ujaama*. To finance its separatist nation, the RNA expected personal donations from members and demanded millions of dollars in reparations from the U.S. government as well as an allotment of land in what they determined to be the five "subjugated states" of Louisiana, Mississippi, Alabama, Georgia, and South Carolina to recompense the descendants of slaves. The RNA proclaimed: "We claim no rights from the United States of America other than those rights belonging to human beings anywhere in the world, and these include the right to damages, reparations due Us for the grievous injuries sustained by Our ancestors and Ourselves by reason of United States lawlessness."[46] If state and national governments had failed previously to acknowledge slavery in the form of legislation to better the lives of Black Americans, apologize for the institution and subsequent social tools used to relegate Black Americans to the borders, and commemorate Black life in cultural memory through historic preservation initiatives, then it is not surprising that the RNA's strategy to achieve Black separation on the one hand and political power on the other hand was met with the government's calculated silence as well.

Undaunted, the RNA forwarded a written request to President Richard Nixon, demanding $400 billion in compensatory damages on behalf of all Black Americans, but Nixon did not dignify the petition with a response. Instead, the president ensured the effective dismantling of the RNA by stunting its efforts using the counterintelligence program of the Federal Bureau of Investigation (FBI)—in concert with local law enforcement support in Mississippi—which began an intimidation campaign against the RNA to evoke fear and prevent members and potential allies from moving forward. The RNA had intended to inspire a fantastic, mass Black American exodus to the South to "become a majority voting bloc in order to control the five states, county by county," which elided the goals of most Black organizations at the time that did not view reparations or schematized migration to the South as feasible.[47] Though they intended to negotiate peacefully with the U.S. government, leaders of the RNA learned hard lessons from the FBI's invasions of their offices and the widespread unregulated utilization of violence against Black bodies during the civil rights movement. With the formation of its Black Legion military arm, the RNA fortified itself in preparation for potential future conflict, recognizing that "right now the trouble is that our land is not free; we are not in charge of it. White people are in charge of our land, and they act as *if* they are in charge of *us*. Our land and our nation are, therefore, *captive*. And our government is a government-in-captivity."[48] As was the case with its response to most radical movements against the geography of containment that has sought to surveil and hamper Black mobility from slavery to the present moment, the government was quite fearful of what its officials viewed as treasonous behavior and implemented tactics to defeat the development of a revolutionary Black political column. The final encounter with government-sponsored resistance took place in August 1971, a critical moment at which the RNA had splintered into two factions due to ideological differences.[49] The FBI and the Jackson, Mississippi, Police Department descended without warning upon the RNA headquarters with weapons, an armored vehicle, and tear gas to serve warrants for the arrest of several RNA members. When no one answered the initial calls, the police fired a shot into the building. Fully armed, the RNA defended themselves in a shoot-out with law enforcement officials, resulting in the death of one police officer, the arrest of eleven RNA members, and the eventual conviction of eight RNA members to life in prison for treason and murder, among other charges. While the government's aggression subdued the RNA briefly, the organization maintains a membership in the thousands and holds onto the speculative hope of one day repossessing the Deep South.[50]

In 1969, after the failure of the RNA to resettle land throughout the Deep South and realize Black economic and political power in the decade after the civil rights movement, Floyd McKissick, the former national director of CORE, busied himself with "an imaginative concept" to found a utopic community, Soul City, in Warren County, North Carolina.[51] This was a significant moment that saw a narrative shift in which government officials throughout the U.S. South were attempting to rid themselves of the stigma of racism and promote a progressive narrative via symbolic propaganda. They failed, however, to ratify broad legislation that would reinforce and render sincere their verbal posturing about American values and the nation's status as a hallmark of equality. McKissick imagined that Soul City could serve as a sort of fantastic litmus test—a multiracial model after which other cities in the United States in general and the South in particular could fashion themselves in the era of desegregation. Soul City was also conceptualized as a rural alternative to the out-migration of Southern Black citizens to urban centers where Black life was largely reduced to impoverished conditions. McKissick argued that Soul City would attend to the acute poverty and joblessness that plagued the community by attracting major manufacturers and other private industry. To be sure, though Soul City was grounded in Black nationalist ideals such as self-determination and economic uplift, McKissick's plan was not concerned with radically separating Black Americans from the larger nation, unlike the socialist RNA. In fact, McKissick succeeded in marketing his scheme to officials and other benefactors by stressing that while Soul City would largely be administrated by Black Americans, it would operate under a capitalistic framework and be available as a multicultural residence to all Americans, regardless of background.

A mere few years after the passage of the civil rights acts, postracialism was celebrated at Soul City's groundbreaking ceremony. This was a certain indicator that the federal interest in the community's successful establishment was guided by a desire to actualize America's founding myth and begin repairing the Southern reputation. While McKissick attempted to realize self-determination and a fruitful Black future through a neo-accommodationist stance, the U.S. government postured similarly to maintain control of and remain privy to the goings-on in the potential postracial community. At the Soul City groundbreaking on November 9, 1973, North Carolina Governor James Holshouser remarked,

> This land we stand on today was once the site of a plantation that depended on the labor of slaves. It is significant of how far we have come that Soul City is being built here as a "freestanding" community with its own industrial base to be developed [by] black-controlled corporations, but to be open to people of all races. Perhaps some of the men and women who will make their homes, who will build their lives in Soul City will be descendant[s] of some of the very men and women who toiled on the old Satterwhite Plantation. Many of Soul City's citizens are certain to feel a spiritual kinship with those slaves.[52]

Guided by the possibility that slave descendants might begin supporting this Black capitalist endeavor, Holshouser's comments preemptively emphasized Southern progress and the possibilities for Black return to redeem the plantation, and by extension, the region from its reprehensible history.

After convincing Nixon and other—mainly Republican—leaders that there would be significant short- and long-term strides in terms of job growth that would attract increasing numbers of Americans back to the rural South, McKissick secured $14 million in bonds from the Model Cities Program of the Department of Housing and Urban Development, headed by George Romney. A number of Black Americans and journalists criticized McKissick for playing respectability politics, befriending Nixon, and outwardly acting as a surrogate for the Republican cause during election season. McKissick defended his curious tactics: "If Blacks are ever to be liberated, they must adopt a philosophy of sophistication, competence, and strategy."[53] The period between 1964 and 1980, to be sure, marked a curious, bipolar Republican courtship and rejection of Black Americans, whom Republicans briefly viewed as a potential, untapped voting bloc but whom they later demonized as pathological—finding that approach to yield more political capital. McKissick's success, then, was due in large part to a Republican desire to illustrate the party's commitment to bettering Black American lives as well as to attracting white Republicans who appreciated a more moderate brand of conservatism: "As a civil rights veteran backing Nixon, McKissick tempered the anti-Black tone both for disillusioned Democrats and for moderate Republicans who found the GOP's southern strategy unsettling. Above all, McKissick furthered an image of a Republican Party that, publicly at least, presented itself as neither openly hostile to the principle of civil rights nor willing 'to be held hostage' by the current group of civil rights leaders."[54] In 1973, McKissick and his family relocated from New York to North Carolina to transform the former antebellum plantation site into an imagined Black utopia in the "new" South.

It should come as no surprise that the Soul City enterprise, under the auspices of an American political system that had demonstrated marginal concern for Black Americans before and after the passage of the civil rights acts, failed to thrive. On election night 1972, McKissick sent a telegram to Jesse Helms, who had been elected senator for North Carolina, to congratulate him and to extend an olive branch to propose that though they had staunchly divergent political beliefs, McKissick believed that there existed numerous bipartisan issues on which they could work together. Helms responded frostily with a promise that he would soon launch an investigation into Soul City's finances and management, which he indeed conducted during the second half of his first term. In an ostensibly concerted effort, newspapers across the nation took notice and also began to criticize Soul City for offenses such as nepotism and financial negligence, as well as likening the conferring of grants on such a project to the distribution of welfare. The vast majority of these claims were later deemed unfounded or exaggerated, but the damage to Soul City's reputation among potential investors and political allies was irreparable. Though he named Soul City's streets after Black freedom fighters such as the enslaved insurrectionist Nat Turner and the Haitian freedom fighter Touissant L'Ouverture, who challenged international white supremacy and whose actions still spark controversy among those who would rather forget America's past improprieties, McKissick had conceived of the fledgling city as "an attempt to move into the future, a future where black people welcome white people as equals."[55]

McKissick's romantic focus on postracialism, futurity, and soul—the last of which was a vestige of the 1960s moment's focus on Black life and empowerment—was rejected not only by Helms but also by politicians across party affiliations and fatigued white North Carolinians, who were not prepared to take or approve of governmental strides toward a more real sense of racial progress. To be sure, despite McKissick's fantastic, egalitarian stance, an influential faction of white Americans remained unwilling to accept Black people as equals. Soul City was defunded gradually by 1980, and while the city still exists, very few residents remain. In fact, in the contemporary moment, Soul City is home to a member of one of America's most booming economic sectors—the prison-industrial complex. Warren Correctional Institute purchased Soul City's sole industrial site in the late 1990s, an ironic purchase given the city's original charter, which was based primarily on assisting Black Americans in achieving the American Dream. As Devin Fergus laments, "the same able-bodied young African American men whom McKissick had optimistically envisioned returning south to be gainfully employed in Soul City did return, but they did so, in the words of the state prisons director, as 'out-of-state inmates back home, back home so they can be with families, back home where our employees can work with them in our facilities.'"[56]

After its demise, Soul City was referred to in the national media as "little more than a fantastic dream."[57] This outright dismissal of McKissick's limited speculative vision was a foreboding sign about the possibilities for Black life in the South as well as the prevarications about the state of racial progress throughout the nation. Even the hopeful moments during the institution of the Soul City project, which piqued the imaginations of Black Americans and saw local, state, and national organizations eagerly strategizing together to build a city from the ground up, quickly dissipated as political interests undermined the passage of legislation and the budgeting of financial support to usher Black citizens more democratically into the American social fabric. Soul City's current status as a prison site confirms that there is more political and financial potential in the continued restriction of Black bodies than there is in the promotion of a truly liberated Black American future. The Soul City and RNA cases illustrate the lengths to which federal and state government officials went and could proceed subsequently to temper Black speculative elements that effectively contest and dismantle exaggerated narratives regarding American democracy. Furthermore, they confirm that the establishment of a Black nation in the South or anywhere else within the United States will be impossible to achieve, if revolution is and remains bound up with petitions to the federal government for financial backing or compensatory measures to account for the damage perpetuated by America's original sin.

"YOU ARE NOW LEAVING THE UNITED STATES OF AMERICA": SPECULATION AND REDEMPTION AT OYOTUNJI AFRICAN VILLAGE

[Oyotunji's] primary purpose is as a monument to our ancestors. . . . How could this many people be on this side of the water and not have a monument to the past?
—Adenibi S. Ajamu, quoted in Laura Marble, "Villagers Maintain Traditions"

On November 9, 1971, an editorial was published in the Charleston *News and Courier* that excoriated the Black nationalist settlers at Oyotunji African Village, a community situated nearly sixty-five miles away in Sheldon, South Carolina. Critiquing the Oyotunji people's ideology and mocking their attempts to get even with "the man" by rejecting America in favor of life in a conceptual African homeland, the editor castigated the members' use of welfare monies to fund their lives in a separatist nation.[58] Oyotunji's Oba (King) Oseijeman Adefunmi I responded brusquely to the sarcastic editorial lashing, employing the language of debt to illustrate the moral and legal right that slave descendants have to speculate in the South and to secure financial support from the U.S. government to compensate them for the hundreds of years of free labor provided by their ancestors. Oba Adefunmi I confronted Hunter's contemptuous editorial in a response titled "Pay for Slavery," which read in part:

> Your editorial quip 'Without the Man,' regarding the use of U.S. Government food stamps at Yoruba Village, represents one of those shortsighted but influential remarks responsible for so much mischief in common race relations, and much vicious legislation on professional levels. For our temporary dependence on the U.S. Department of Agriculture represents a miserable and grudging return for the 250 years of free labor and ideas which Yorubas supplied to that department during its infancy and ignorance. . . . You could have reminded all Americans that having gotten something for nothing, it's time to pay back; also, that an honorable people, rather than hide behind guilty welfare programs, would be paying the blacks unconditional reparations in cash, land, technology and material. . . . If the American power structure is not ready to comply with such measures to liquidate its debt to us, then spare us your proud prejudices, and let us hear no more suggestions that the Yorubas are getting something for nothing.[59]

Not too long after their settlement in Sheldon, the Oyotunji residents faced pushback from local residents not only regarding their seeming laziness and supposed abuse of food stamps, but also for their esoteric cultural elements and the feared radical nature of the community. Over the next decades, the community was subjected to ongoing scrutiny and surveillance. In 1981, the FBI alleged that Oyotunji Village was harboring a former member of the Black Liberation Army who was suspected of conspiring to ship guns from South Carolina to New York, as well as people evading tax bills. Beaufort County residents and curious tourists alike referred to the village as an eyesore, bristled that polygamy was practiced there, and objected to Oyotunji's tribal scarification of children.[60] Reduced in reports in more recent years as fake, weird, tacky, oddball, and alien, Oyotunji Village has withstood the criticism. Despite attempts to utilize local laws to surveil and intimidate, Oyotunji Village has suc-

4.3 Sign just off Highway 17 at the entrance of Oyotunji Village in Sheldon, South Carolina. Photo by author.

ceeded as a separatist community in South Carolina since its founding in 1970 by maintaining what its residents deem to be an Africanist sense of culture and values without an overreliance on reparations demands or support from governmental sources.[61] With its symbolic return to Africa through the construction of a homeland and the assertion of a religious nationalism that elides Western dogma, the Oyotunji ideology works to suture not only the dispossession of its members but also that of African-descended tourists, as it centers return to Africa as most constitutive to the construction of their identities as they repossess the South.

Steeped in religious and cultural nationalism, Oyotunji (which means "Oyo rises again" in Yoruba) prominently asserts its status as an authentic African village in the United States. The village's bold roadway signage contains the quirky subtitle "as seen on TV," which serves to legitimize Oyotunji Village's potential to tourists who might feel tentative about stepping onto the grounds and subtly announces that while the production of a modest African livelihood is the Oyotunji residents' objective, they must engage in Western capitalism through the tourism industry to support the village. The approach into the ten-acre Oyotunji Village down Bryant Lane is a descent into the Lowcountry bush. One must tentatively maneuver along the winding, narrow dirt road, as potholes make for a bumpy ride, and the forest on either side seemingly drops off to unknown depths. Upon entering the Oyotunji property, one notices the castle-like edifice with pointed battlements at the entrance and an assortment of fading wooden signs, a small marketplace, guesthouse, and tiny huts whose agedness lends a sense of authenticity to the place. Vibrantly colored and decorated orisha temples adorn the major thoroughfare, which has residents' living quarters at each end. On a typical day, several traditionally dressed residents mill about the village carrying on daily tasks and manning various posts, while children chase each other around playfully, peppering their English-language conversations with Yoruba expressions. Oyotunji's continued existence in the American South serves as a perpetual reminder of the African presences in the region and the continued audacity of Black Americans in openly forging communities that create and embrace African retentions in the Lowcountry, despite national and local exhortations that American progress necessitates cultural assimilation. Commenting about Oyotunji's political stance in the post–civil rights era, Oba Adefunmi I asserted: "To integrate was a kind of cultural suicide. It's unnatural for blacks to try and graft a European history and culture onto themselves. . . . In the '60s people were searching. Today, the black movement is stagnant. The leaders have no knowledge of Africa."[62] With Black cultural loss in mind, Adefunmi and his followers declared spiritual warfare on what they viewed as the moral, political, and social hold that the United States has on persons of African descent.

Adefunmi had founded the Yoruba Temple in Harlem on 116th Street in the mid-1960s, but he later realized that the syncretization of traditional African religiosity with Western faiths did not mesh with his evolving radicalism. During his initiation into the priesthood years before, a Cuban soothsayer had informed Adefunmi that he was a king sent to destroy a king, whom a more politically radicalized Adefunmi determined years later to be Jesus Christ. With the charge in mind to defeat the West's cultural and political influence on Black Americans and to reestablish linkages between Black Americans and their ancestors, Adefunmi established Oyotunji African Village as a Yoruba-based revivalist community that has

4.4 Thatched-roof homes at Oyotunji Village. Photo by author.

fashioned much of its societal structure after village traditions that its
founders researched and witnessed during pilgrimages to Nigeria. Unlike other manifestations of Yoruba religions in the diaspora, such as the
Cuban Santería that Adefunmi outright rejected and the related Brazilian
Candomblé, the Orisha-Vodu practiced at Oyotunji—though informed
by several Africanist cultural elements—is strictly Black nationalist and
rejects syncretism with Western faiths. Oyotunji's creation of a religious cultural nationalism revises and "(re)constructs the symbolic imagery of Yoruba people from the past, prior to the colonial conquest of
the Oyo Empire and the formation of nation-states. Practitioners have
created a deterritorialized kingdom situated on the outer perimeter of
Beaufort. . . . Using concepts of nationalism and invocations of transnational racial alliance, members of the Oyotunji leadership have decentered the significance of territory to imagine an 'African' political
community in the United States."[63] In fact, outsiders are alerted by a sign
at Oyotunji's entrance that a shift will occur as they cross the invisible
border into the village: "You are leaving the US. You are entering the Yoruba Kingdom. In the name of His Highness Efuntola, peace. Welcome to
the sacred Yoruba Village of Oyotunji. The only village in North America

4.5 A shrine to the orisha Osun at Oyotunji Village. Photo by author.

built by the priests of the Vodun cults as a tribute to our ancestors. These priests preserve the customs, laws and religion of the African race[.] Welcome to our land!"

In its print and online advertisements, Oyotunji frames itself as a place of restoration for African-descended people who are curious about their ancestral culture and desire to return to their heritage.[64] As the founder of this symbolic Africa, Adefumni stressed the necessity of Oyotunji's presence in a 1980s pamphlet that railed against Black American cultural amnesia about Africa and condemned Black Americans for "begging and whining for deliverance and resurrection from an alien god."[65] He celebrated the Yoruba at Oyotunji for having, in his estimation, "succeeded in fashioning in their tiny community a place in point and time where each night they lie down in a world governed by African rules and awake each morning to a world governed by African forms, [illustrating] the evolution of true Afro-American freedom."[66] On the fortieth anniversary of the village's founding, Iya Oba Adaramola recalled the difficult early years of transitioning the grassy landscape into a lively, functional African village: "In 1970, we came in the middle of the night. The road was not as wide as it is now, and the trees hung over the road and met in the middle. I thought to myself, 'I'll be leaving in the morning.' When I woke up the next morning, it was so beautiful and peaceful. I didn't leave."[67] Bolstered by the Black social movement's shift to nationalism, coverage in major Black publications such as *Jet* and *Ebony*, performances in the *Roots* miniseries, and a general print and television media obsession with new forms of radicalism, Oyotunji Village was legitimized as a conceptual, even primeval, Africa for a wider audience, drawing thousands of curious African-descended tourists, initiates, and migrants from around the world.[68]

By the late 1970s, the village was its most active and vibrant, as it was home to an estimated two hundred people and had a steady flow of visitors, who arrived to take tours, obtain spiritual readings, and undergo initiations into the priesthood. By the late 1980s, the village's governing body, the Ogboni council, forbade the utilization of U.S. governmental assistance by Oyotunji residents and ceased using legitimating rhetoric concerning reparations, effectively ending any dependence on outside entities for sustenance. This modification of Oyotunji law has had an unfortunate impact on the full-time resident population, which has dwindled to thirty or fewer persons largely due to economic hardship. Former residents have been forced to search for jobs in other cities, where they have instituted satellite communities to remain connected to their Oyotunji roots.[69] In response to judgmental lines of questioning that insinuated that the village's decreased population somehow indicates that new generations of Black Americans reject linkages to Africa and that Oyotunji's Black separatist politics are becoming irrelevant, Adefunmi retorted: "Why don't you ask how many this community has influenced? That's more important."[70]

During a visit in the spring of 2013, I arrived at Oyotunji Village at a busy time for the Black American heritage tourism season in Beaufort County. Thirty minutes away in the city of Beaufort, the annual Gullah Festival was in full swing. Select Oyotunji residents were included in the opening ceremonies as traditional African dancers and drummers, but the festival itself was a celebration of the history and cultures of the Gullah community—that is, a commemoration of the lives that enslaved Africans and their descendants made on the Sea Islands.[71] As I prepared to go through the gate at Oyotunji, a tour bus pulled up nearby, and twelve of the estimated thirty tourists from New York and New Jersey— mostly middle-aged Black Americans—filed out. The driver warned them emphatically that they had twenty minutes to take a tour before they needed to reboard and head back to Beaufort for the festival. Those interested in Oyotunji as a critical place to engage with the ancestors expressed their displeasure with how rushed they felt and their disbelief that their counterparts who remained on the bus outright dismissed the significance of Oyotunji. The divisions among the group intrigued me, and I hastened to join their tour to get a better sense of their expectations.

The guide, aware of the time constraints, offered short explanations at each of the village's eight orisha temples and explained the history of the community, interspersing his personal journey into the script. At one point, a seemingly staged spectacle occurred as a young Oyotunji member shouted greetings to the guide in Yoruba, to which the guide responded; they continued to exchange pleasantries as we watched and listened to the authenticating performance. The guide referred to the land around the Lowcountry as "old country" marked by violence and slave resistance. He took great pride in recounting the story of the Stono Rebellion, a 1793 uprising led by Congo slaves who raided a store, stealing weapons and killing several whites on their march toward freedom along the King's Highway, which is now called Highway 17 and situated just outside of the village. The rebel slaves overtly marched toward freedom, waving flags, beating on drums, and yelling "liberty" as they fought off the opposition. Though the slaves did not make it to the freedom they were promised in Spanish Florida and were either killed or sold in retaliation, the guide's retelling of this narrative of ultimate defiance historicized the region as a site of Black radicalism, political activity, and triumph that lent a sense of empowerment to the enslaved and their descendants. Some of the tour group nodded knowingly as he recounted the story, while others expressed surprise at the audacity of the slaves in carrying out such a feat.

Triumphalist narratives play a central role in the ways in which the Oyotunji people have imagined themselves, a sense of redemption that is transferred indirectly to Black American tourists so that even if they do not become practitioners, the refashioned history in the symbolic African nation offers a place to return physically and spiritually to experience liberation from dispossession. Kamari Maxine Clarke explains:

4.6 A tour group listens intently to the tour guide at Oyotunji Village. Photo by author.

As the object of practitioner pride in African heritage, ritual in Oyotunji Village is the means through which the Yoruba nobility is held in tension with the dueling remnants of slavery. Ritual combines the realities of historically inscribed hegemonies in the realm of nobility and the grandeur of precolonial governance. It is through these dueling forces that a cartography of moral redemption is articulated, and the imagination becomes a conduit through which to articulate the past. Given that the politics of racialization have dominated black Atlantic zones of exchange, people in contemporary movements also reproduce typologies of racial continuities to debunk the cultural logics of white racial superiority.[72]

The influence of such redemptive narratives on tourists was evident as we paused at the temple to the goddess Yemoja, the mother of all bodies of water. An elderly tourist rushed to pose for a picture with a statue of the orisha. Once her photograph had been taken, she commented to her friend: "You know, I'm happy now. At least I'm [going to] have *something*." She then turned to face the group and stated emphatically: "Stuff like this is real. You'll never forget it. You can say, 'I've been there. I've seen it.'" Seconds later, the bus driver blew the horn insistently to indicate to the tourists that their time at Oyotunji was over. A handful of the

4.7 A shrine to the orisha Yemoja at Oyotunji Village. Photo by author.

tourists were amused by the driver's impatience and moved toward the exit, but the elderly woman stood still and complained in the direction of the sound, though she was standing far beyond the driver's earshot: "We didn't come all this way to see nothing. I want to know."[73] The woman desired to bear witness to Africa and to possess evidence of having gone back, even briefly. This fleeting moment of contact attended to her shame of not knowing, of being disentangled from her roots. There was a sense that she and the others who had gotten off the bus wanted to feel a part of something distinctly African and from the source. The fashioning of Africa at Oyotunji Village and the continued presence and commemoration of the ancestors in the Gullah community in the midst of Southern master narratives provide symbolic spaces for Black Americans, particularly those who live outside the South and made pilgrimages to the land of their enslaved forbears, to reckon with their dispossession.

While it is the case that Oyotunji's Black cultural nationalism, with its radical reframing of territory, maintains transnational ties to Yoruba communities and has devoted nearly fifty years to renarrativizing the South Carolina Lowcountry, the village residents' politics are not without fault. At issue here are the temporal fissures that accompany global alliances and how people connect to and imagine Africa. Oyotunji Village's narrow focus on precolonial Africa presents a significant caution concerning the sustainability of speculation as a means through which to move toward the Black fantastic. As we walked between orisha-dedicated temples during another tour, for instance, an Oyotunji priest and tour guide inquired about my research, confiding that he wished to travel to Brazil, a place he considered more accessible, authentically African, and relevant than present-day Africa itself. This was perhaps the most provocative and confounding moment that I experienced at Oyotunji. It echoed a sentiment that Black American expatriates of various political and religious leanings had imparted to me in Ghana and Brazil about their failed quests to repossess the Africa of their imaginations. Yet the tour guide's declaration that ancestral Africa was only accessible outside of the continent itself seemed to undermine Oyotunji's self-proclaimed legitimacy and contradict its political ideology, which advocates Pan-Africanism—an outlook as much concerned with the past and future of the African-descended as it is with the present. In fact, Oyotunji Village is the site of the annual Pan-African Grassroots Assembly conference, at which discussants converse about how to apply ancient Yoruba ways to their contemporary lives and how to become more self-sufficient. The question becomes, what is at stake when one embraces and recreates imagined pristine African homelands and cultures while simultaneously rejecting contemporary Africa, which in many ways is still reeling from colonization, the transatlantic slave trade, and the continued plunder of its land? Though this book heralds the promises of Afro-Atlantic speculative thought—of using Africa as a vessel for dreaming about other possibilities for life and as a radical manner by which to subvert U.S. national mythologies regarding liberty, equality, and the realities of the continued subjugation of much of its citizenry—the Oyotunji case demonstrates that the unchecked use of speculation has the potential to impede the very transnational revolutionary work that U.S.-based Black separatist communities intend to achieve.

Coda: Ascensions into Thin Air

In June 2015, Brittany "Bree" Newsome, a North Carolina–based activist, filmmaker, and producer of speculative fiction, traveled to Columbia, South Carolina, with the intention of removing the Confederate flag from the State House grounds after a white supremacist, Dylann Roof, murdered nine members of the Mother Emanuel African Methodist Episcopal Church and several Black churches were set ablaze across the South in the aftermath. Newsome yelled out during her courageous feat of scaling the flagpole: "In the name of Jesus, this flag has to come down. You come against me with hatred and oppression and violence. I come against you in the name of God. This flag comes down today."[74] Shown across social media platforms and praised or rebuked in the news media, Newsome was widely deemed a heroine of the progressive cause, and her likeness was even turned into a futuristic, speculative comic figure that was reposted tens of thousands of times on social media platforms. Newsome joined a cohort of brave Black South Carolinians and their allies who had been fighting in myriad ways for decades against the placement of the Confederate flag on the State House dome in 1961 to honor the centennial of the Civil War and the flag's removal in 2000 to a memorial on the grounds as part of a compromise. And while Newsome was rightly lauded for removing the rebel flag during a contentious, fascinating moment in South Carolinian and American history in which Black people were being killed during heavy-handed encounters with brutish police officers and politicians from both sides of the aisle were seemingly becoming more vocal about the necessity of removing the Confederate flag from public memorialization in various states after the Charleston tragedy, a decidedly more dramatic spectacle took place in 2002.

That April, a Black American man who went by the name of Reverend E.X. Slave (né Emmett Rufus Eddy) clad himself in a black Santa suit despite the unforgiving South Carolina heat, used a ladder on which he had written the names of various Black radicals and organizations to scale a fence, and shackled himself to the flagpole before cutting down the Confederate flag and setting it on fire.[75] Eddy was seen often at the State House staging a one-man protest outfitted in chains and torn overalls and armed with signs—including one that read "Nothing without a Demand," a reference to Frederick Douglass's 1857 statement about the significance of protest and rebellion to the Black American fight for freedom and equality, "power concedes nothing without a demand," and others that read "I Too Sing America" and "I Too Am America," which are lines from Langston Hughes's poignant poem, "I Too." Eddy had been arrested several times prior to this incident for his demonstrations against

4.8 Brittany "Bree" Newsome removes the Confederate flag from a pole at the South Carolina State House, in Columbia. © Corbis Images.

what he read as systemic and perpetual American racism and Black oppression in the afterlife of plantation slavery. The reference to himself as an "ex" or former slave is an indication of a shift in his mind-set and a radical desire for flight over his circumstances. Certainly, life in a state that was filled with streets, buildings, monuments, counties, and schools named after Confederate heroes and whose legislative policies continued to fail Black Americans offered constant reminders that South Carolina possessed a staunchly romantic view of the antebellum period, particularly its ignoble proclivity for restricting the movement of Black people. In a near-slapstick moment befitting the intriguing scene, police officers attempted to use pepper spray to force Eddy from the flagpole, but the mist from the spray fell into the officers' eyes instead. A crowd of curious passersby gathered to observe the commotion as the officers struggled to coax Eddy down, and while some of those onlookers cheered Eddy on, a disgruntled man driving past reinforced the solemnity of Eddy's protest when he shouted to the officers, "String him up right there"—a sordid demand that evoked the region's history of terrorizing and lynching Black bodies. Eddy was later arrested, fined, and banned from the State House grounds for defacing a public monument, but his insistence on challenging notions of American progress via his protests at a certain site of hypocrisy in the seat of the former Confederacy remains a radical speculative act of renarrativization that ought to be recollected alongside Newsome's renowned chronicle. In a statement for the Blue Nation Review website in the aftermath of her civil disobedience, Newsome shows reverence for those who had performed various forms of resistance in protest of the Confederate flag prior to her act, demonstrating her steadfast understanding that this radical, long lineage underscores the importance of reimagining nation in the U.S. South via its premier modern symbol, the flag. Newsome reflects on her family's Southern history, effectively forcing the democratization of obstinate Southern master narratives:

> Even if there were borders to my empathy, those borders would most certainly extend into South Carolina. Several of my African ancestors entered this continent through the slave market in Charleston. Their unpaid toil brought wealth to America via Carolina plantations. I am descended from those who survived racial oppression as they built this nation: My 4th great grandfather, who stood on an auction block in South Carolina refusing to be sold without his wife and newborn baby; that newborn baby, my 3rd great grandmother, enslaved for 27 years on a plantation in Rembert, SC where she prayed daily for her children to see freedom; her husband, my 3rd great grandfather, an enslaved plowboy on the same plantation who founded a church on the eve of the Civil War that stands to this day; their son, my great-great grandfather, the one they called "Free Baby" because he was their first child born free, all in South Carolina.
>
> You see, I know my history and my heritage. The Confederacy is neither the only legacy of the south nor an admirable one. The southern heritage I embrace is the legacy of a people unbowed by racial oppression. It includes towering figures of the Civil Rights Movement like Ida B. Wells, Martin Luther King, Jr., Fannie Lou Hamer, Rosa Parks, Medgar Evers and Ella Baker. It includes the many people who rarely make the history books but without whom there is no movement. It includes pillars of the community like Rev. Clementa Pinckney and Emanuel AME Church.

The history of the South is also in many ways complex and full of inconvenient truths. But in order to move into the future we must reckon with the past.[76]

What we learn from Newsome, Eddy, the Oyotunji villagers and tourists, and the quotidian activists who dream of escapes from U.S. racism whether they move into the air or back to the land is that Black American cultural producers in the post-1965 era, regardless of their success in disrupting narratives permanently, actively democratize master narratives by centering on the significance of Black social life. Through cultural materials centered in alternative homelands, historical preservation efforts that remember those who have been erased from the histories of otherwise renowned plantation homes and other sites of slavery, and the staking out of nations in the region's geography of silence, these producers determinedly resist Southern mythologies of progress. In his musings about the possibilities for achieving the black fantastic through politically conscious cultural production, Richard Iton posits:

> To the extent that simple recognition is an important political goal for political actors, the different media of popular culture provide a means by which this need can be satisfied. While simply *being seen*, in and of itself, is rarely translated into an acknowledgment of the legitimacy of one's interests or action on behalf of those concerns, pop culture's ability to render the invisible visible (in an Ellisonian sense perhaps) or the unheard audible—and possibly, to borrow from Ellison and Fred Moten, the invisible audible and the unheard visible— gives it a certain political legitimacy. . . . It could be argued that the development of broader solidaristic sensibilities, which are crucial to sustaining a progressive politics in an era of neoliberal individuation, is *best* accomplished by means of the actions of creative artists.[77]

Given the diversity of the Black renarrativization projects that are active in the U.S. South, these cultural efforts, though not exclusively pop culture per se, render Black lives visible and audible and certainly fall under the scope of Iton's imagining of Black fantastic politics as that which unsettles nation-states that marginalize African-descended peoples. Indeed, the active narrative contestations that I have examined in the

United States are as imbued with possibility as the travels that I explored in Ghana and Brazil. As I have shown throughout this book, return must become an active politics for negotiating dispossession and subjugation rather than solely concerned with the individualistic repossession of Africa.

In his short story "The Afrolantica Awakening," Derrick Bell crafts a fantastic tale about emigration to a landmass that rises up mystically in the Atlantic Ocean roughly nine hundred miles due east of South Carolina, which reinforces my critique of return.[78] Afrolantica, the pristine island, draws the attention of the U.S. government and other potential colonizers, but the only persons capable of breathing there are Black Americans. Adventurers outfitted in the latest technology that had allowed them to travel to the moon and to explore the depths of the sea were befuddled by their inability to breathe on Afrolantica, stating that attempting to survive there was "like trying to breathe under the burdens of all the world" (33–34). Black Americans begin engaging in the old debates about emigration versus assimilation that had haunted members of their community since the Sierra Leonean and Liberian colonization projects in the early nineteenth century. Regardless of their stance on the issue, the existence of Afrolantica as a place solely habitable by Black Americans increased feelings of racial pride. Those Americans most invested in narratives of progress feared the rise of a radical element that could potentially inspire "other third-world peoples who might conclude that white influence, rather than colored incompetence, was responsible for their poverty and powerlessness" (43). Despite the U.S. government's actions to discourage emigration, including threating to invalidate the citizenship of those who chose to leave, thousands sailed away toward liberty on the Fourth of July. As their ships approached Afrolantica, the landmass that had thrived for a year began to sink into the sea. Rather than grieving at the sight of their imagined promised land disappearing before them,

> they felt deep satisfaction—sober now, to be sure—in having gotten this far in their enterprise, in having accomplished it together. As the great ships swung around in the ocean to take them back to America, the miracle of the Afrolantica was replaced by a greater miracle. Blacks discovered that they themselves actually possessed the qualities

of liberation they had hoped to realize on their new homeland. Feeling this was, they all agreed, an Afrolantica Awakening, a liberation—not of place, but of mind. One returning black settler spoke for all: "It was worth it just to *try* looking for something better, even if we didn't find it." . . . The spirit of cooperation that had engaged a few hundred thousand blacks spread to others, as they recalled the tenacity for humane life which had enabled generations of blacks to survive all efforts to dehumanize or obliterate them. Infectious, their renewed tenacity reinforced their sense of possessing themselves. Blacks held fast, like a talisman, [to] the quiet conviction that Afrolantica had not been a mere mirage—that somewhere in the word *America*, somewhere irrevocable and profound, there is as well the word *Afrolantica*. (45–46)

"Say Me My Name"

GENETIC SCIENCE AND EMERGING SPECULATIVE
TECHNOLOGIES IN THE CONSTRUCTION OF
AFRO-ATLANTIC RECONCILIATORY PROJECTS

Later, in the midnight hour, the missing identity aches.
One can neither assess nor overcome the storm of the middle
passage. One is mysteriously shipwrecked forever, in the Great
New World. The slave is in another condition, as are his heirs:
I told Jesus it would be all right/If He changed my name.
—James Baldwin, *The Price of the Ticket*

We must learn to wear our names within all the noise and
confusion in which we find ourselves. . . . They must become our
masks and our shields and the containers of all those values and
traditions which we learn and/or imagine as being the meaning
of our familial past.
—Ralph Ellison, *Shadow and Act*

Scattered thoughts are framed by very little context, but the sense of loss
is palpable. An iteration of the beloved is crouching among the dead and
nearly dead, yearning for a permanent transition to escape her agony,
when she realizes that such a flight is impossible because "you sleep short
and then return."[1] She is able to rest briefly, but she suddenly awakens amid
hell on earth. Time progresses, but the fates of those who come after her
will include similar impediments in their attempts to access social life.

Standard punctuation is nonexistent in the beloved's narrative, replaced by spaces between sometimes disparate, sometimes seemingly consistent, phrases. The voice that is "heard" by the reader is essentially a series of unspeakable, unspoken thoughts across temporalities that are presented in a lyrical, stream-of-consciousness chapter of Toni Morrison's *Beloved*. Morrison's neo-slave narrative, portions of which have served as an evocative refrain throughout this book, is a meditation on the importance of coming to terms with the trauma endured inside and outside the institution of slavery. A substantial gesture that Morrison makes in the text occurs in a quartet of chapters that are "voiced" by the three major female characters: Sethe, Denver, and Beloved. Each is affected tremendously by a combination of guilt, loneliness, and/or grief, and each is grappling with a lack of and/or desire for recognition and reconciliation. Sethe is a mother who did the best she could with what she knew as an enslaved woman, ushering her children to freedom from slavery, before her world collapses and she commits infanticide. She is so wracked with guilt that she effectively abandons her living daughter, Denver, leaving Denver to deal with the pain of never knowing her father as well as the loss of her grandmother, Baby Suggs, and her brothers, Buglar and Howard, who ran away to escape their melancholic, haunted home and their seemingly homicidal mother. Foremost representative of Sethe's returned, deceased child—until the shift in narrative style in the chapters described above indicate her universality—Beloved does not comprehend Sethe's rationalization that if Sethe had not killed her, "[Beloved] would have died" (236). The vengeful, embodied ghost child reappears to haunt not only Sethe and the inhabitants of 124 Bluestone Road, but also, as the lyrical chapter signals, to serve as a representation of slave descendants and speak for the millions of known and unknown slaves whose fractured lives have gone unrecompensed.

Beloved exemplifies the longing of dispossessed peoples in her affecting utterance that "there is no one to want me to say me my name" (251). Her varied, broken thought pattern resonates her status as a waif overcome by solitude and abandonment. The phrasing of Beloved's succinct thoughts captures aptly the undoneness wrought by slavery. Countless names are unknown and seemingly lost to time. Mothers, fathers, sisters, and brothers on both sides of the Atlantic were filched from their loved ones, never to be seen again. Despite the ramifications of these disconnections, such as the the inability to possess and retain generational knowledge of African ancestral names, geographies, and histories, the U.S. government has yet to formally apologize for the institution of slavery. Nor has the nation engaged in sincere reconciliatory or reparatory measures in the century and a half since slavery ended, a decidedly defiant posture that has led to the derogation of the peculiar institution's significance to the United States' foundation and the subsequent restrictions on Black life.

Much of Morrison's *Beloved* is marked by a tenor of defeat and demoralization, yet there are instances of optimism as conveyed in Baby Suggs's Saturday afternoon ministry. Baby Suggs's brand of eschatological spirituality, which actively elides Western theologies and the social devaluation of Black lives, is ministered in the Clearing, a fantastic, liberatory place in the woods in which Baby Suggs encourages the members of her congregation of to let down their guard by participating in affective performances. She stresses passionately that to truly live, they must dance, laugh, and cry as a community "for the living and the dead" (103). In what is referred to in the text alternatively as her Call or sermon, Baby Suggs urges her congregation to recognize that despite their existence in a divided, nearly insufferable society, they should practice a radical self-love that will enable them to negotiate the world beyond the Clearing: "Here . . . in this here place, we flesh; flesh that weeps, laughs; flesh that dances on bare feet in grass. Love it. Love it hard. Yonder they do not love your flesh. They despise it" (103). The narrator further describes Baby Suggs's theology as one that refigures redemption: "She did not tell them they were the blessed of the earth, its inheriting meek or its glorybound pure. She told them that the only grace they could have was the grace they could imagine. That if they could not see it, they would not have it" (103). Baby Suggs's speculative philosophy, then, holds that former slaves and their descendants should actively envision and actuate grace as a collective rather than anticipating deliverance from dispossession by a religious deity or other powerful outside forces, evoking the imaginary that prompts the extensive flights considered heretofore.

The interview subjects and cultural forms set out in *Afro-Atlantic Flight* have shown that Black Americans have undertaken speculative flights, including revisionist cultural production and actual migrations that privilege return to imagined African homelands, to grapple with perceived cultural loss and also to reject, in a vein similar to Baby Suggs's theological practice, their social alienation from an American society that is almost obsessive in its desire to create and promulgate narratives of progress that absolve the nation of its most egregious sins and hypocrisies regarding liberty and equality. Though Black mobility—the taking back of control of the Black body—is certainly crucial to the assertion of a revolutionary posture, I have shown that literal flights must be informed by a politics that attends to the state of the African descended worldwide. The wide range of material considered in the first chapter of the book illustrated the political turns that Black American cultural production have taken in response to acute and residual forms of social alienation and loss experienced by Black Americans after the passage of the 1960s civil rights legislation. My focus on shame and dispossession as explored in neo-slave narratives and travel accounts illuminated the impetus behind and the imaginary that undergirds the actual renarrativation projects assumed by Black Americans as they endeavor to reclaim imagined ancestral homelands and proxy Africas as well as when they counter master narratives of progress throughout former sites of slavery in the American South.

The second chapter examined the ways that the arbiters of the Ghanaian cultural roots tourist industry attempt to produce return and catharsis for Black American and other Afro-Atlantic travelers by analyzing the limitations of the country's Pan-African triumphalist narrative. I then turned to an investigation of the significance of government-authored kinship scripts to those who decide to become expatriates based on their tourism experiences. Through participant observation and analyses of historical materials, I demonstrated that a set of complicated relations often emerges between those who have remained in the imagined homeland and Black American travelers, as a range of misrecognitions arise that only the development of a neoteric Pan-African politics—one that operates outside the purview of governmental bodies and is developed by African-descended laypersons living under postcolonialism and/or in the aftermath of slavery across the globe—might begin to address.

I considered the creation and performance of Africa by the African-descended population in Bahia, Brazil, in the third chapter to establish how Afro-Bahians' purported possession of Africa helps advance the notion of Brazil as a racial paradise through roots tourism. In my historicization of Black American travel schemes to relocate to Brazil and chart out new lives based on its ostensibly legitimate postracial state, I argued that the Black American consumption of Africa in Bahia actually confirms Afro-Brazilians' flights of the imagination, which they take vis-à-vis mythmaking and their various cultural performances of Africa, while it also sates Black Americans' desire for actual flights to Brazil to repossess linkages to their ancestral pasts. Similar to the letdown that emerges when the pretense is discovered in the roots tourism scripts in Ghana, once Black American travelers realize that advancing beyond race and assuming life in a Bahia-based, primeval Africa are not achievable feats, they become critical of their chosen surrogate homeland and begin taking stock of their new realities to determine whether their limited access to the American Dream in the United States would be a more promising existence. While most travelers in Ghana and Bahia eventually find that living physically and psychically closer to Africa trumps certain dispossession and alienation in the United States, I concluded that their individual ascensions as expatriates do very little to effect changes to the American political landscape or to create broad access to paths toward the Black fantastic.

To address the limitations of attempting to take literal return flights back to Africa, then, the fourth chapter traced the evolving sociopolitical ends of the return migration to the U.S. South and how Black Americans in the region actively renarrativize the lore that has shattered neo-Confederate egos and pushed back against the de facto and de jure forms of oppression that have restricted the mobility of Black Americans in the postbellum period. By participating in acts to disrupt the inglorious Southern geography of silence about slavery and neoslavery, Black Americans have labored to gradually modify what is archived and deemed substantial to the region and, by extension, the nation's historical preservation by struggling for the inclusion of narratives of resistance that were integral to Black Americans' realization of various legislative victories; establishing representative Africas such as Soul City, the Republic of New Africa, and Oyotunji African Village in a violently antagonistic Southern geography; and revising how the region is represented in cultural production. Each of these reconfigurations of Southern master narratives proved imperfect, yet they are categorically more sustainable and group-centered than the individualized travels analyzed in chapters 2 and 3, as they move more closely toward the assertion of a Black politics that is guided by collective, figurative returns to Africa that recognize the transnational stakes of local movements.

One final instance of speculative return caps *Afro-Atlantic Flight*'s analysis: an exploration of African-descended peoples' turn to genetic science and emerging social media technologies to validate their speculations about the ethnic identities of their yearned-for ancestors. The stitching together of ancestral histories by reappropriating the very apparatuses developed to bolster racial science that ostensibly evidenced their inferiority is a decidedly controversial shift in the Afro-Atlantic imaginary. However, in the reimaginings of the purposes of genetic science that follow, there is the possibility of charting an effective path of return that is marked by a desire to show reverence for the past and the promotion of revolutionary potential for the present and future.

The speculative impulse to reconstitute what has been torn apart through contemporary communicative tools is not a new phenomenon. In fact, in the period after slavery, formerly enslaved peoples held out hope of being reconnected with loved ones from whom they had been separated. Facing tremendous odds, including continued limitations on the extent to which they could exercise their mobility, faulty information as to the details of their loved one's sale and location, and the passage of time, some newly freed persons traveled to the last-known sites in which their loved ones lived, while others followed fainter trails, inquiring about their kin using given names that likely changed as they were sold and resold to plantation owners throughout the South. To circumvent such hindrances, many sought out the Freedman's Association for the Restoration of Lost Friends, which assisted them in streamlining their searches by publishing advertisements in local, state, and national church-sponsored newspapers. An advertisement in the *Christian Recorder* from November 18, 1865, for instance, read as follows:

INFORMATION WANTED

Of my mother and father, Caroline and Isaac Denna; also, my sisters, Fanny, Jane and Betsy Denna, and my brothers, Robert R., Hugh Henry, and Philander Denna. We were born in Fauquier Co., Va. In 1849 they were taken from the plantation of Josiah Lidbaugh, in said county, and carried to Winchester to be sold. About the same time I left my home in Clark Co., and have not heard from them since. The different ministers of Christian churches will do a favor by announcing the above, and any information will be gladly received by GEO HENRY DENNA, Galva, Henry Co., Illinois.[2]

It is unknown whether the Denna family was ever reunited, though the severance of Black familial ties in the era of slavery was a permanent fate for most—one that caused some people to have mental breakdowns "because they could not clear their heads of the cries of their lost children" and other loved ones.[3] As I have maintained, the urge to attend to a troubling sense of loss, which commenced with avaricious slave speculators, continues to compel the Black American psyche generations after the initial break. DNA science, along with new technologies and social networks, are gradually becoming central to Black American consumers as they seek new avenues for locating unknown linkages, confirming known kinship ties, and refashioning how they understand the promises of homeland returns. Rather than utilizing science to substantiate racial biometrics, then, these test takers are guided by desires to access ancestral worlds and cultures that predated such categorizations.

On social media sites dedicated to African descendants interested in genealogy and genetic testing, self-described Pan-Africanists located on the African continent have begun encouraging their counterparts to submit DNA samples to various companies that are offering complimentary tests to individuals who have four grandparents from Africa proper—an offer designed to assist the companies by increasing their sample sizes from countries throughout the continent.[4] Believing that they have a duty as Pan-Africanists to assist their diasporan kin in locating their roots, the social media group members actively revise Pan-African responsibility, linking it explicitly with the establishment of biological ties and concerning itself with reconciliation. The popularity of genetic science has increased exponentially due to aggressive advertisement campaigns by online companies and popular television shows that investigate the ancestries of celebrities, including a range of commercials for direct-to-consumer genetic websites and the prominent television series *African American Lives* and *Finding Your Roots*, which are hosted by the African American studies scholar Henry Louis Gates. A pertinent example is a commercial for Ancestry.com that features a Black American man who used the site's electronic databases to access census records and other archival materials to uncover unknown portions of his family's past:

> MAN: I was a little afraid. I mean, as an African American, I knew where my family tree might end up, but I went on ancestry.com anyway, and I found out my great-great-grandfather was born a slave and died a businessman. And that was worth finding.
>
> ANNOUNCER: Visit ancestry.com and discover the world's largest online family history resource.
>
> MAN: You don't have to know what you are looking for. You just have to start looking.
>
> ANNOUNCER: Your discovery starts right now on ancestry.com.[5]

Note the triumphalist narrative promoted by the advertisement and the pride that informs the man's elation at the "discovery" that his ancestor did not "end up" lost to time; nor did his ancestor live a downtrodden life after slavery ended, as most of his counterparts undoubtedly had. In fact, the man's forefather had moved on from a traumatic past in chains to a promising career, which alleviated the man's expressed fear that this particular ancestor might have lived and died a shameful, insignificant death that would not have been "worth finding." The commercial's premise intentionally neglects the reality that most formerly enslaved Black Americans did not have the opportunity to achieve such a professional status in the immediate postbellum period, transmitting a narrative of mobility to attract Black American consumers with similar desires to access their familial histories and find ancestors who somehow evaded unfortunate fates. Several YouTube users satirized this commercial's redemptive plot to point out, in a hyperbolic fashion common to the genre, the absurdity of the commercial's premise, implicitly issuing grave acknowledgments that the slavery-era geography of containment was simply reconfigured after the abolishment of the institution:

> MAN: I was a little afraid. I mean, as an African American, I knew where my family tree might end up, but I went on ancestry.com anyway, and I found out my great-great-grandfather was born a slave but died hanging from a tree with a noose lynched around his neck [and] then burnt to a crisp by the KKK mob. Now that's worth finding.

Visit ancestry.com and discover the world's largest online family resource. The discovery starts now on ancestry.com.[6]

As the satirist's macabre narrative turn indicates, the majority of Black American attempts to unearth long-lost kin will likely turn up evidence that proves just how mundane sadistic violence, the restrictions placed upon Black bodies, and trepidation were to their ancestor's lives. There is, then, a fascinating narrative of doublespeak about the "worth" of the located familial history that surrounds these genealogical quests. Establishing family trees involves a significant amount of time and financial resources, and for those who are consumed by shame and longing, there is very little value to be found in forging linkages without verification that they are connected to enslaved kin who might have, for instance, run away or successfully defied the social order in some grand fashion. For some roots seekers, the gathering of names and the attendant stories that accompanies them suffices. Along with access to census and other governmental records, genealogical sites that offer autosomal genetic testing also aim to match test takers with cousins around the world and help them fill in the gaps that exist in their family trees. Compellingly, some companies are equipped with the ability to show exactly where two or more people match on specific chromosomes, a development that has the potential to lead to the reestablishment of ancient bonds as well as the reconnections of families like the Dennas, who were nonchalantly separated and likely never reunited even after the "lost friends" advertisement was placed.

Beginning in 2010, NBC News's online science column, "Cosmic Log," began its multiyear chronicle of William Holland, a Black American businessman from Atlanta, Georgia, who had been tracing his family's history for nearly a decade using archival materials and family lore before submitting a saliva sample to a DNA testing company with hopes of filling in the gaps regarding what he knew of his ancestry. After Holland uploaded his results into the Sorenson Molecular Genealogy Database, the system identified not just a Y-chromosome connection between him and the peoples in a region in Africa or even a country, but a direct link to a specific group of people in Bamenda, Cameroon. Heartened by the assignment of an ancestral home for one of his forebears, Holland connected with the Cameroonian Fon (king) of the Mankon tribe and later traveled to Bamenda where, "One of the most sobering moments came when the visitors were shown three or four huts where captured [Mankon] Africans were kept prior to their departure for America. . . . Holland said his African hosts stressed that the tribe's long-ago chiefs did not hand over their ancestors for payment, and they hoped that the Americans would not hold their African kin responsible for the horrors of slavery. They posed a disconcerting question to their American cousins: 'How was it not possible to keep your family name?'[7] In a symbolic gesture, the king assigned Holland his father's royal name during an official naming ceremony, a cathartic, redemptive moment for Holland that mitigated the veil of indignity that he felt slavery had cast over his family. Holland elatedly recollected: "Imagine receiving that news, after all these years when you grew up as the son of a sharecropper . . . [e]verybody tells you that you came from slaves, you came from slaves. And now you find out that you came from royalty."[8] The following year, Holland planned a reunion to introduce his Virginia-based family to their royal Mankon kin, but he began to feel uneasy, as many of the Mankon people who were not invited to travel as part of the tribal delegation to the United States expressed displeasure, a sentiment that Holland found curious for a community of people that theretofore had appeared sincere in their efforts to assist him in reestablishing his ancestral heritage.[9]

Subsequent trips to the Central African village validated for Holland that his initial felt connection to the Mankon was a figment of his imagination; his perception had been obscured by his desire to locate cultural roots rather than based on conclusive evidence that precisely corresponded to his earlier historical research. The Mankon tribe had assured Holland that their ancestors had not sold their kin into slavery, but according to the oral tradition passed down by the nearby Oku tribal group, the Mankon were indeed complicit in the trade, acting as middlemen between other African tribes and European traders. The Oku lore held that in the 1700s, seventy members of their tribe were captured as slaves and were presumably sold into transatlantic slavery. The period indicated in the Oku oral history paralleled what Holland knew of his distant great-grandfather who was sold to a Virginia-based plantation owner in the late eighteenth century. This development led Holland to submit his DNA for further genetic testing that would offer a more accurate determination of his connections to the region. Holland ultimately revised his understanding of his Cameroonian lineage and declared that based on the certainty of his DNA matches and the emotional way in which he was welcomed by the Oku ("they were running down the hill to come to meet us"), he is likely descended from the Oku people.[10] To further complicate matters, sometime between Holland's connection with the Mankon and his introduction to the Oku, the Sorenson database was updated with genetic data from new test takers that also connected Holland's distant genetic roots to the royal family of Ghana's Adidokpoe-Battor village, which sits hundreds of miles away from his relatives in Cameroon. While it might appear that matches to persons in two distinct countries would render the genetic information flawed, the historical migrations of peoples throughout this region of the African continent are said to be consistent with Holland's results. Welcomed to Ghana in a similar manner as he had been to the Oku peoples of Cameroon, Holland was given three Ghanaian names in a formal ceremony, one of which is Degboe, meaning a "brave person who went away and returned."[11]

Controversial in its seeming affirmation of race as a biological fact, genetic science offers an avenue for curious global African-descended peoples to attend to the dispossession and shame of not knowing that has consumed them, though as Holland's case proves, African results can be misleading and point test takers in conflicting directions that the technology alone perhaps will never be able to explicate. Given that the discovery of a connection to a specific group of people is likely representative of only a minuscule portion of a test taker's genetic makeup (one out of thousands of ancestors), some geneticists find that such identifications are marginal to the test taker's actual ethnic identity.[12] Furthermore, most, if not all, African-descended test takers' enslaved ancestors were plucked from diverse countries throughout the slave trade, rendering it virtually impossible for them to identify a sole contemporary African village or nation as their home. Not only does genetic science have inherent limitations, then, but also being armed with genealogical records and genetic evidence has no bearing on whether or how particular African groups will receive their distant American kin.

In 2013, Holland traveled back to Cameroon to meet with eight traditional Bakou fons to tour remnants of the slave trade in service of "ameliorating the injurious repercussions of the past."[13] Determined to appease their gods and apologize to Holland and his family for their ancestors' probable role as brokers in the transferral of Holland's Oku ancestors to European traders, the Bakou leaders signed an official statement of expiation written in French, after balking at an English-language declaration that was prepared by Holland for the occasion, as they were concerned about improper inferences of culpability that might have escaped translation. However, the head fon of Bakou, Ngako Ngalatchui, later signed Holland's version, which read:

> We, the local Fons from the Bafang subdivision of Bakou, Cameroon, would like to formally state that we are sorry and issue an official apology for our involvement and the involvement of our ancestors in the horrible institution of transatlantic slavery. The United States of America, France, and the United Kingdom should issue similar formal apologies for this evil institution that broke up families and caused generational hardships that continue to the present day. Our sincere statement should be read to and displayed for thousands of other families who suffered the same fate as the Hollands of Virginia, USA. So say the undersigned on this day Saturday, 26 October 2013, in Bakou, Cameroon.[14]

Regardless of the declaration signed, the Bakou fons ratified the indictment of their forefathers as co-conspirators in the slave trade, signaling the leaders' atonement for what followed the enslaved persons' forced removals: lost familial names and cultures as well as the present-day reverberations of slavery across the Afro-Atlantic. The matter that arises is whether scientific assignments of purported definitive home countries are necessary to the establishment of transnational political linkages. The passage of time and dearth of records render it quite evident that the majority of slave descendants will never possess extensive genealogical records, which suggests the intrinsic inadequacy of the material returns from the unearthing of random, deeply rooted, natal evidence. Despite fascinating strides in genetic research, the increase in cultural roots tourism industries across the Afro-Atlantic and recent resurrections of various nations' wretched histories with transatlantic slavery, acute shame and strategic silence endure, revealing the decidedly persistent nature of the ideologies that bolstered transatlantic slavery.

Efficacious advancements toward worldwide Black social life will depend on strategic flights of the imagination in the development of a sustainable transnational politics.[15] The most essential precept revealed by the myriad post-1965 flights delineated herein is that the Black fantastic is realizable if reconciliatory efforts are coupled with meditations on and strategies to transmute the devastation that transatlantic slavery exacted on both dispersed African-descended populations and those who remained on the African continent proper. Disrupting the effects of dispossession and symbolic annihilation indeed remains a possibility for architects of contemporary Afro-Atlantic speculative flights who return to psychic Africas as they organize locally and globally, imagine pasts and futures in cultural production and roots tourism, and contest contemporary master narratives of progress. To proceed speculatively, indeed, is to live.[16]

Introduction

1. The Zong massacre is examined beautifully in Baucom, *Specters of the Atlantic.*
2. Baraka, *Wise, Why's, Y's* (Africa section). The "Black ivory" sequence was articulated in a live performance, which is printed in the transcript for Bill Moyers's *Fooling with Words* (Part One) television program.
3. My utilization of *haunted* here is inspired by Gordon, *Ghostly Matters.*
4. As retold in Buxton, *Haunted Plantations,* 59–63.
5. Mami Wata also brings weather-related wrath and takes human lives if she is offended. Stories abound in communities on Ghana's coastline about beach-goers being violently grabbed and swept into the ocean as the ancestors' vengeance for the slave trade.
6. See Rediker, *The Slave Ship.*
7. I cite the Middle Passage as a significant moment in the history of Pan-Africanism in which there was an eruption of Black radicalism and to acknowledge the Middle Passage's significance to more recent flights of the imagination. The Flying Africans myth is reimagined in a range of African diasporic literary texts, including Lovelace, *Salt*; Marshall, *Praisesong for the Widow*; Morrison, *Song of Solomon*; and Schwarz-Bart, *Between Two Worlds* and *The Bridge of Beyond.*
8. David Wyatt, quoted in S. Jackson and Moody-Freeman, "The Black Imagination and the Genres," 2.
9. For more on Afrofuturism, see Dery, "Black to the Future"; Nelson, "Introduction"; Womack, *Afro-Futurism.*
10. Gerima and Woolford, "Filming Slavery," 92.
11. In "The Evidence of Felt Intuition," Harper beautifully examines the importance of speculative logic to Black queer and other minoritized subjects who find that they must engage with the fantastic to realize social life.

12. S. Camp, *Closer to Freedom*, 6. Camp credits Houston Baker for coining the phrase "geography of containment," which she goes on to expound upon throughout the book.

13. Douglass, *Narrative of the Life of Frederick Douglass*, 91.

14. Douglass, *Narrative of the Life of Frederick Douglass*, 95.

15. The concept of Black fugitivity has been a topic of much theorization recently (see Best, *The Fugitive's Properties*; Chaney, *Fugitive Vision*; Goffman, *On the Run*; Harney and Moten, *Undercommons*; and Rusert, "Delany's Comet"). Alexis Pauline Gumbs, a scholar producing wonderful work at the intersections of Black feminism and Afro-futurism, recently published an essay that chronicled the Eternal Summer of the Black Feminist Mind's trip to the Lowcountry of South Carolina to commemorate the 150th anniversary of the Combahee River uprising, which was led by Harriet Tubman in 1863. Gumbs discusses a head injury that Tubman experienced at the hand of an overseer that caused Tubman to be "immobilized yet aware of her waking surroundings. Sometimes she went to sleep at night like the rest of us and woke up with important information about the future. . . . [A]bout a year before Harriet Tubman moved to Beaufort, South Carolina, to work and strategize for the Union Army, she had a dream. She woke up triumphant and was reported to have repeated all day with gratitude and wonder a prophecy in the present tense: 'My people are free.' . . . How far could she see?" (Gumbs, "Prophecy in the Present Tense," 143–44).

16. A wealth of literature on the Liberia settlement exists across disciplines. See, for instance, Barnes, *Journey of Hope*; Clegg, *The Price of Liberty*; Crummell, *Destiny and Race*; Delany, *The Condition, Elevation, Emigration, and Destiny of the Colored People of the United States*; Huffman, *Mississippi in Africa*; M. Mitchell, *Righteous Propagation*; and Moses, *Liberian Dreams*.

17. A plethora of texts on Black American migration exists. A wonderful online reference is the Schomburg Center's "The African American Migration Experience," which covers in great detail Black migrations from slavery to the present day.

18. For texts from and about the fugitive slave tradition, see, for example, Bordewich, *Bound for Canaan*; Brown, *The Narrative of William W. Brown*; Craft and Craft, *Running a Thousand Miles for Freedom*; Douglass, *Narrative of the Life of Frederick Douglass*; and Jacobs, *Incidents in the Life of a Slave Girl*.

19. For more on the relations between Black Americans and immigrant Europeans, see Ignatiev, *How the Irish Became White*; Jacobson, *Whiteness of a Different Color*; and Roediger, *Working toward Whiteness*.

20. Extensive analyses of Reconstruction's impact on the Black community can be found in Du Bois, *Black Reconstruction in America*; and Foner, *Reconstruction*.

21. See Archer-Straw, *Negrophilia*; Fabre, *From Harlem to Paris*; Huggins and Rampersad, *The Harlem Renaissance*; D. Lewis, *When Harlem Was in Vogue*; Locke, *The New Negro*; and Stovall, *Paris Noir*.

22. Du Bois, "Returning Soldiers."

23. For an extended analysis of Garvey's movement and impact, see Grant, *Negro with a Hat.*

24. These migrations have been explored brilliantly in Gregory, *The Southern Diaspora*; Grossman, *Land of Hope*; Hahn, *A Nation under Our Feet*; Lemann, *The Promised Land*; Sernett, *Bound for the Promised Land*; and Wilkerson, *The Warmth of Other Suns.*

25. See, for instance, Franklin and Moss, *From Slavery to Freedom*; Kelley, *Freedom Dreams*; and Lee, *For Freedom's Sake.*

26. Dudziak, *Cold War Civil Rights.*

27. See Gaines, *American Africans in Ghana*; and Meriwether, *Proudly We Can Be Africans.*

28. Singh, *Black Is a Country*, 10. The "days of hope" are examined cogently in Sullivan, *Days of Hope.*

29. For more on these trends, see Marable, *How Capitalism Underdeveloped Black America.*

30. L. Johnson, "Commencement Address at Howard University."

31. Marable, *Race, Reform, and Rebellion*, 212.

32. Hartman, *Lose Your Mother*, 87. Excellent discussions about living *otherwise* can be found in Ashon Crawley's important research. See, for instance, Crawley, "Otherwise Movements."

33. For a compelling examination of the ever-expanding U.S. prison-industrial complex, see Gilmore, *Golden Gulag.*

34. Singh, *Black Is a Country*, 220.

35. Quoted in Angelou, *All God's Children Need Traveling Shoes*, 139.

36. X, *The Autobiography of Malcolm X*, 357.

37. C. Robinson, *Black Marxism*, 171. Also see Clifford, *Routes*, 244–77; Edwards, *The Practice of Diaspora*; and Shepperson, "African Diaspora."

38. Echeruo, "An African Diaspora," 13–14.

39. S. Hall, "Cultural Identity and Diaspora," 235–36.

40. S. Hall, "Cultural Identity and Diaspora," 235. Other texts on the transnational defining and redefining of Blackness and Africa include Gilroy, *The Black Atlantic*; and Mudimbe, *The Invention of Africa.*

41. Morrison, *Beloved*, 248–49.

42. Childs offers an impressive reading of the historic restriction of Black American mobility and Paul D's masculinity in *Beloved* by examining Paul D's experiences in relation to the prison-industrial complex. Childs, "'You Ain't Seen Nothin' Yet.'"

43. Clarke, "New Spheres of Transnational Formations," 59.

44. Personal conversation with Fred Moten on July 3, 2013.

45. See Adeleke, *UnAfrican Americans*, and Gruesser, "Afro-American Travel Literature and Africanist Discourse"; and chapter 3 of Tillet, *Sites of Slavery*. For a scathing critique of the mythmaking in Afrocentrism, see C. Walker, *We Can't Go Home Again.*

46. Munoz, *Disidentifications*.

47. Iton, *In Search of the Black Fantastic*, 17.

48. I am indebted to the scholarship presented in Byerman, *Remembering the Past in Contemporary African American Fiction*; Rushdy, *Neo-Slave Narratives*; Spaulding, *Re-Forming the Past*; Wall, *Worrying the Line*; and Woolfork, *Embodying American Slavery in Contemporary Culture*.

49. The texts that I am in conversation with here include Bailey, *African Voices of the Atlantic Slave Trade*; Ebron, *Performing Africa*; Gaines, *American Africans in Ghana*; Hartman, *Lose Your Mother*; Holsey, *Routes of Remembrance*; and Meriwether, *Proudly We Can Be Africans*.

50. This multidisciplinary examination, then, is informed by and in direct conversation with the histories and ethnographies outlined in K. Butler, *Freedoms Given, Freedoms Won*; Capone, *Searching for Africa in Brazil*; Clarke, *Mapping Yoruba Networks*; Hellwig, *African-American Reflections on Brazil's Racial Paradise*; Santana Pinho, *Mama Africa*; and Seigel, *Uneven Encounters*.

51. Hong, "'The Future of Our Worlds,'" 107–8.

52. An important narrative that charts a convincing argument for self-exile because of perpetual disfranchisement is R. Robinson, *Quitting America*. America, Robinson maintains, is where he has lived his life "within the innermost of concentric circles; my comfort, my protection, my psychic security provided by the bold unbroken line of the smaller of the rings. Two *countries*, one within the other. The outer, official, distant, alien, unaffirming, hostile. The other, safe for my spirit's function, respectful of my long-sequestered story, loving of my *me*" (244). No longer feeling safe in an increasingly dangerous, racist United States, Robinson and his family migrate to his wife's native St. Kitts, where Robinson feels fully free for the first time in his life.

1. Fantastic Flights

1. Harris, *É Minha Cara/That's My Face*.

2. Christol, "The African American Concept of the Fantastic as Middle Passage," 165.

3. Christol, "The African American Concept of the Fantastic as Middle Passage," 164–66.

4. Patterson, *Slavery and Social Death*, 5.

5. Rushdy, *Neo-Slave Narratives*, 3.

6. Rushdy, *Neo-Slave Narratives*, 7.

7. Eyerman, *Cultural Trauma*, 1.

8. Patterson, *Slavery and Social Death*, 7.

9. Eyerman, "The Past in the Present," 162. Eyerman is partially quoting from the introduction to Paul Antze and Michael Lambek's edited volume, *Tense Past: Essays in Trauma and Memory* (London: Routledge, 1996).

10. Kaplan, "Souls at the Crossroads," 513–14.

11. Rushdy, *Remembering Generations*, 8.

12. McKoy, "The Limbo Contest," 209–10.

13. Butler, *Kindred*. Subsequent quotes from the novel have page numbers in parentheses in the text.

14. Quoted in Kenan, "An Interview with Octavia E. Butler," 496.

15. Spaulding, *Re-Forming the Past*, 57.

16. Patterson, *Slavery and Social Death*, 12.

17. Salvaggio, "Octavia Butler," 33.

18. A. Mitchell, "Not Enough of the Past," 52.

19. Gerima, *Sankofa*.

20. Kandé and Karaganis, "Look Homeward, Angel," 129.

21. Gerima, *Sankofa*.

22. Quoted in Woolford, "Filming Slavery," 100–102.

23. Douglass, *Narrative of the Life of Frederick Douglass*.

24. Hartman, *Scenes of Subjection*, 3.

25. Hartman, *Scenes of Subjection*, 4.

26. Moten, *In the Break*, 5.

27. Keeling, *The Witch's Flight*, 55.

28. Keeling, *The Witch's Flight*, 60.

29. Kaplan, "Souls at the Crossroads," 519.

30. Marshall, *Praisesong for the Widow*. Subsequent quotes from the novel have page numbers in parentheses in the text.

31. Christian, "Ritualistic Process and the Structure of Paule Marshall's *Praisesong for the Widow*," 75.

32. Christian, "Ritualistic Process and the Structure of Paule Marshall's *Praisesong for the Widow*," 75.

33. Roach, *Cities of the Dead*, 27.

34. Busia, "What Is Your Nation?," 207.

35. My use of "misrecognitions" is inspired by Kenneth Warren's insights about diaspora in "Appeals for (Mis)recognition."

36. See Tillet, *Sites of Slavery*.

37. Hartman, *Lose Your Mother*, 99.

38. Morrison, *Beloved*, 43.

39. Patterson, *Slavery and Social Death*, 98.

40. Gruesser, "Afro-American Travel Literature and Africanist Discourse," 9.

41. Angelou, *All God's Children Need Traveling Shoes*, 22. Subsequent quotes from the book have page numbers in parentheses in the text.

42. See, for example, Hartman, *Lose Your Mother*; and Robinson, *Returning Home Ain't Easy*.

43. Hartman, "The Time of Slavery," 769–70.

44. E. Harris, *Native Stranger*. Subsequent quotes from the book have page numbers in parentheses in the text.

45. His disavowal of and attempt to distance himself from Africa is reminiscent of a controversial Black American travelogue written by Richburg, *Out of America*.

46. Hartman, *Lose Your Mother*, 139.

47. Ashe and McKnight, "'Under the Umbrella of Black Civilization,'" 428–29.
48. Reginald McKnight, *I Get on the Bus*. Subsequent quotes from the novel have page numbers in parentheses in the text.
49. Quoted in Nicholas, "A Conversation with Reginald McKnight," 309.
50. Quoted in Nicholas, "A Conversation with Reginald McKnight," 320.
51. Murray, "Diaspora by Bus," 54. It is interesting to note here the disparate ways in which Evan and Avey in *Praisesong* interpret their personal pain in relation to what the slaves endured. Avey is well on her way to being reborn by the time she is on the boat to the Beg Pardon and she maintains a reverence for the ancestors, while Evan remains *on the bus* and is unable to escape his sense of dispossession.
52. Murray, "Diaspora by Bus," 57.
53. Murray, "Diaspora by Bus," 57.
54. Hartman, *Lose Your Mother*. Subsequent quotes from the book have page numbers in parentheses in the text.

2. The Production of Homeland Returns

1. Following the tradition of reflexive anthropology, I am using the first person here and will use it, where appropriate, in other chapters as well. I am mindful of the risks of the move, but I find it useful in crafting the narrative arcs with which I am engaging. I am guided by such texts as Hartman, *Lose Your Mother*; Kondo, *Crafting Selves*; and Tsing, *In the Realm of the Diamond Queen*.
2. Baldwin, *The Price of the Ticket*.
3. Richards, "What Is to Be Remembered?," 625.
4. Compelling, though pessimistic, cases for mediating diasporan romantic visions and mythologies about Africa are presented in Gruesser, "Afro-American Travel Literature and Africanist Discourse," 9; and C. Walker, *We Can't Go Home Again*.
5. This story is recollected in Campbell, *Middle Passages*, 318–19.
6. Meriwether, *Proudly We Can Be Africans*, 152.
7. Nkrumah, "Ghana is Free Forever."
8. By "diaspora," I am referring to the dispersal of Africans sparked by the transatlantic slave trade as well as to the more recent migration of Africans to other countries around the world.
9. Nkrumah, "Ghana is Free Forever."
10. Quoted in Esedebe, *Pan-Africanism*, 6.
11. For a concise history of Pan-Africanism in addition to Esedebe, *Pan-Africanism*, see Lemelle, *Pan-Africanism for Beginners*.
12. Quoted in Esedebe, *Pan-Africanism*, 44–45.
13. Meriwether, *Proudly We Can Be Africans*, 151.
14. For an extended exploration of Nkrumah's impact on Black American political figures and the U.S.-based Black social movement, see Gaines, *American Africans in Ghana*.
15. Iton, *In Search of the Black Fantastic*, 17.
16. It should be noted that much is at work here to impede unity. The intricacies of how race is understood and functions in Ghana certainly differ from those

of diasporan communities. For a fascinating examination of race in Ghana, see Pierre, *The Predicament of Blackness*.

17. Iton, *In Search of the Black Fantastic*, 199–200.

18. X, *The Autobiography of Malcolm X*, 357.

19. Angelou, *All God's Children Need Traveling Shoes*, 97.

20. Angelou, *All God's Children Need Traveling Shoes*, 97–99.

21. Angelou, *All God's Children Need Traveling Shoes*, 98.

22. Hartman, "The Time of Slavery," 769.

23. This story was recounted to me by a friend who was aboard the plane during this performance. The lyrics are from the third stanza of "Lift Ev'ry Voice and Sing" (lyrics by James Weldon Johnson, music by John Rosamond Johnson, 1900).

24. See Bruner, "Tourism in Ghana," 290–91.

25. Imahküs, *Returning Home Ain't Easy*, 5.

26. Imahküs, *Returning Home Ain't Easy*, 54.

27. Imahküs, *Returning Home Ain't Easy*, 66.

28. Imahküs, *Returning Home Ain't Easy*, 82.

29. Imahküs, *Returning Home Ain't Easy*, 85.

30. Hartman, *Lose Your Mother*, 9.

31. Hartman, *Lose Your Mother*, 27–29.

32. Quoted in Hartman, *Lose Your Mother*, 28–33.

33. Interview with Timothy, March 13, 2007. All interviewees' names have been changed, unless full names are used.

34. Fanon, *Black Skin, White Masks*, 10–11.

35. Fanon, *Black Skin, White Masks*.

36. Patterson, *Slavery and Social Death*, 336.

37. Patterson, *Slavery and Social Death*, 340.

38. These responses are culled from separate interviews with Katherine (May 20, 2005), Nathaniel (December 11, 2007), Vicki (May 16, 2005), Mama Linda (November 15, 2007), and Baba (November 28, 2007).

39. There has been a long-standing community of Caribbean repatriates in Ghana as well, but the migration is smaller and not as stigmatized and researched as the tourism and expatriation of Black Americans. For more on this related Afro-Atlantic movement, see Jennifer Jackson and Cothran, "Black versus Black"; Lake, "A Taste of Life," and "Toward a Pan-African Identity"; and White, "Living in Zion."

40. There is a wide range of interdisciplinary research on these productions, including Bruner, "Tourism in Ghana"; Hartman, "The Time of Slavery"; Hasty, "Rites of Passage, Routes of Redemption"; Holsey, *Routes of Remembrance*; Richards, "What Is to Be Remembered?"; and Schramm, *African Homecoming*.

41. Ebron, *Performing Africa*, 190.

42. Widespread attention was paid to tracing Michelle Obama's roots prior to this trip to Ghana. See, for example, Swarns, "In First Lady's Roots a Complex Path from Slavery."

43. Obama, "Remarks by the President to the Ghanaian Parliament."
44. See "AMA Issues 'Final Warning' to Hawkers, Beggars."
45. In other documents, this event was referred to as the "Press Conference/Orientation for Our African Diasporan Family and International Guests." I have used the name on the signage at the location. The W. E. B. Du Bois Centre is Du Bois's former home; it shares grounds with Du Bois's tomb and the office of the African American Association of Ghana. In 2007, the Black History month events usually offered by the association, such as lecture series, performances, and film showings, were integrated into the larger Ghana@50 program throughout the year.
46. Nii Martey Kwao, extemporaneous remarks at the Press Conference/National Orientation," March 3, 2007. Kwao was also the economic chief of the town of Pram Pram, Ghana, at the time, which was a unique position for an expatriate to hold.
47. This quote is taken from the 2007 "Ghana's Golden Homecoming" program guide.
48. "Ghana@50: President Kufuor's Speech."
49. "Ghana@50: President Kufuor's Speech."
50. Jerome Johnson, extemporaneous remarks at the Ghana@50 UNIA conference, March 7, 2007.
51. Julius Garvey, remarks at the Ghana@50 UNIA conference, March 7, 2007.
52. Jacob Obetsebi-Lamptey, speech given at the Ghana@50 UNIA conference, March 7, 2007.
53. In *African Voices of the Atlantic Slave Trade,* Anne Bailey incorporates oral narratives from the Anlo Ewe society in southern Ghana with existing historical documents to offer a better understanding of the role that the society played in the slave trade and how this participation compromised the livelihood of its people politically, socially, and religiously. Through her examination of shame and silence in the Anlo Ewe example, Bailey concludes that while some African societies were complicit in the sale of other Africans, their partnerships with Europeans were not equal, given that Europeans had never been enslaved on a plantation in the Americas, lending credence to Obetsebi-Lamptey's point that most African societies possess limited oral histories of their ancestors' role in transatlantic and/or domestic slavery. Throughout *African Voices of the Atlantic Slave Trade,* Bailey explains that this legacy of shame has tended to shut down any possibility of a meaningful dialogue within Ghana and other West and Central African nations—let alone between these groups and the diaspora—concerning slavery. Nevertheless, she remains optimistic that formal acknowledgments, governmental apologies, and other forms of reparation on both sides of the Atlantic could lead to reconciliation as long as these actions are tied to efforts to restore historical memory about the slave trade and address its continuing effects on contemporary societies.
54. Gaines, *American Africans in Ghana,* 282.
55. The online transcript of Morrison's interview with Elizabeth Farnsworth can be found at "Toni Morrison."

56. Hartman, *Lose Your Mother*, 218.

57. This discussion about reparations for Ghana and other nations affected by transatlantic slavery is explored aptly in Asare, "The Ghanaian National Reconciliation Commission."

58. Hartman, *Lose Your Mother*, 218.

59. Hartman, *Lose Your Mother*, 218.

60. Clarke, "New Spheres of Transnational Formations."

61. Diaspora African Forum, "Our Mission."

62. Interview with Erieka Bennett, October 30, 2007.

63. See Edozie, "The Sixth Zone."

64. Hartman, *Lose Your Mother*, 165.

65. My thinking about sincerity and authenticity here is guided by John L. Jackson, *Real Black*, 14–15.

66. S. Hall, "Cultural Identity and Diaspora," 237.

67. Wright, *Black Power*, 101.

68. Seestah Imahküs as quoted in Journeyman Pictures, *Coming Home-Ghana*.

69. Quoted in "The Irrepressible Envoy from Ghana," *Ebony*, 74.

70. Tillet, *Sites of Slavery*, 117.

71. Seestah Imahküs as quoted in Journeyman Pictures, *Coming Home-Ghana*.

72. Imahküs, *Returning Home Ain't Easy*, 217.

73. Hartman, *Lose Your Mother*, 123.

74. Hartman, *Lose Your Mother*, 152.

75. Hartman, *Lose Your Mother*, 153.

76. Hartman, *Lose Your Mother*, 133.

77. Bob Marley, "Redemption Song," Island/Tuff Gong, 1980.

3. "We Love to Be Africans"

1. Graden, "An Act 'Even of Public Security,'" 255.

2. Reis, *Slave Rebellion in Brazil*, 91.

3. Schaumloeffel, *Tabom*, 93–95.

4. Interview with Corrine, June 19, 2007.

5. Interestingly, the period that Corrine cites was a sort of changing of the guard in Ghana, when the military dictator Jerry Rawlings was nearing the end of his tenure and the Ghanaian people sought to transition to a democracy. Because Rawlings had been the leader of three bloody attempted coups in the past, it is probable that Black American interests were stunted somewhat during this time, but Ghana generally has been a peaceful nation otherwise.

6. Markowitz, *Homecomings*, 3.

7. S. Hall, "Cultural Identity and Diaspora," 236.

8. Interview with Richard, July 31, 2007.

9. Interview with Aaron, June 22, 2007.

10. Ahmed, "Multiculturalism and the Promise of Happiness," 125.

11. See K. Butler, *Freedoms Given, Freedoms Won*, chapter 6.

12. "Blacks in Brazil."

13. This particular colonization project was headquartered in Topeka, Kansas. As was the case with most colonization schemes, it was not embraced by all, as the emigration of skilled workers was deemed by critics as potentially detrimental to the rebuilding of the South, there was no guarantee that Black Americans would succeed abroad, and many Black Americans were determined to fight for integration and the realization of their civil rights in the United States. The debate is covered in "Discussing the Proposed Exodus"; "An Echo of the Proposed Exodus"; and "Proposed Exodus."

14. See Losch, "Dr. Henry W. Furniss."

15. Quoted in Hellwig, *African American Reflections on Brazil's Racial Paradise*, 28 and 36.

16. For a compelling example of the struggle to maintain a nationwide movement, see the analyses of two iterations of Brazil's Negro Frente in K. Butler, *Freedoms Given, Freedoms Won*, chapters 4 and 5.

17. Quoted in Hellwig, *African American Reflections on Brazil's Racial Paradise*, 45.

18. Hellwig, *African American Reflections on Brazil's Racial Paradise*, 76.

19. Hellwig, *African American Reflections on Brazil's Racial Paradise*, 19 and 57–59.

20. Seigel, *Uneven Encounters*, 213–14.

21. The following texts include excellent critiques of the mammy figure: P. Collins, *Black Feminist Thought*; McElya, *Clinging to Mammy*; and Sanders, *Mammy*.

22. Edwards, *The Practice of Diaspora*, 14–15.

23. For more on their emigrationist positions, see Delany, *The Condition, Elevation, Emigration, and Destiny of the Colored People of the United States*; and Rhodes, *Mary Ann Shadd Cary*.

24. The UNESCO Race Relations Project of the 1950s was actually undertaken to examine the Brazilian model for the world as far as race was concerned. However, the researchers ended up unearthing several patterns of racism and other intersecting forms of oppression throughout the country. For more on these UNESCO studies, see Maio, "UNESCO and the Study of Race Relations in Brazil."

25. Hellwig, *African American Reflections on Brazil's Racial Paradise*, 87.

26. Quoted in Hellwig, *African American Reflections on Brazil's Racial Paradise*, 105.

27. For more about the Estado Novo regime of Getúlio Vargas and its impact on Afro-Brazilian political organizing, see Hanchard, *Orpheus and Power*, chapter 5.

28. Quoted in Hellwig, *African American Reflections on Brazil's Racial Paradise*, 112–13.

29. Hellwig, *African American Reflections on Brazil's Racial Paradise*, 145–58.

30. For examples of such reflections on race and the importance of Black pride, see Hellwig, *African American Reflections on Brazil's Racial Paradise*, 167–258.

31. Hanchard, *Orpheus and Power*, 88–98.

32. For an incisive account of the impact of re-Africanization on Afro-Bahians, see Paschel, "Re-Africanization and the Cultural Politics of 'Bahianidade.'"

33. E. Robinson, *Coal to Cream*, 44–45.

34. As evident in the opinions expressed by Black American journalists and travelers in the early twentieth century and in Robinson's initial emotional fascination during his contact with an imagined paradise, understanding how race is figured in Brazil is complicated and has been the source of great contestation, particularly between U.S. and Brazilian scholars. See, for example, Ferreira da Silva, "Facts of Blackness"; Freyere, *The Masters and the Slaves*; Hanchard, *Orpheus and Power*; and Omi and Winant, *Racial Formation in the United States*. The ongoing discourse is a debate between those who understand racial structures as based mainly on genotype and those who conceive of racial systems primarily based on phenotype and class status. In fact, the 1976 Brazilian Institute of Geography and Statistics (the country's census bureau) collected 134 terms that Brazilians used to identify skin color alone. And though it is projected that at least 40 percent of Brazil's population is of African descent, the racial demographics in the 2010 self-reported census were distributed as follows: 47.7 percent white, 43.1 percent mixed race, 7.6 percent Black, and less than 1 percent Asian or indigenous. These statistics were found at the English version of the Instituto Brasileiro de Geografia e Estatística's, "2010 Population Census." For Black American tourists, who for the most part understand race in U.S. terms where the one-drop rule trumps any arguments one could make about skin tone, Bahia's African-descended population and its seeming lack of racial intolerance are attractive and are cited often as the primary inducements for permanent migration.

35. E. Robinson, *Coal to Cream*, 48.

36. E. Robinson, *Coal to Cream*, 148.

37. E. Robinson, *Coal to Cream*, 123 and 159.

38. E. Robinson, *Coal to Cream*, 203–4.

39. E. Robinson, *Coal to Cream*, 184.

40. "Promoting Afro-Brazilian Trade."

41. Wagner, "Opening Bahia, Brazil, to the U.S."

42. Wagner, "Opening Bahia, Brazil, to the U.S."

43. I draw this conclusion from personal conversations with Silas Silva and César Nascimento of Integrare on July 23–24, 2007.

44. K. Butler, "Afterword," 170.

45. K. Butler, "Afterword," 170.

46. For more about the history of the Mercado Modelo and the "curiosities and legends" that surround the market, see "Mercado Modelo."

47. "Mercado Modelo."

48. In *Shadows of the Slave Past*, Ana Lucia Araujo argues that the mythologizing about slavery at the Mercado Modelo is a form of "memory replacement," which allows the "local Afro-Brazilian population [to deal] with the lack of

visible and official markers indicating the existence of sites remembering the Atlantic slave trade in Salvador," 103.

49. Thomas, *Desire and Disaster in New Orleans*, 5–7.

50. J. Collins, *Revolt of the Saints*, 3.

51. Roach, *Cities of the Dead*, xi–xii.

52. Interview with Joel Gondim, August 2, 2007.

53. All tourist interviewees' names have been changed.

54. For more on the political and social imperatives of the Boa Morte sisterhood, see Caldwell, *Negras in Brazil*; Matory, *Black Atlantic Religion*; and Selka, "Rural Women and the Varieties of Black Politics in Bahia, Brazil" and "The Sisterhood of Boa Morte in Brazil."

55. McDonnell, "Bahia."

56. This is evident in the popularity of tales as expressed in folklore, fugitive slave narratives, and stories about the Underground Railroad.

57. S. Walker, "The Feast of the Good Death," 28.

58. Santana Pinho, *Mama Africa*, 53.

59. For an extended exploration of these contested religious histories, see Capone, *Searching for Africa in Brazil*.

60. Capone, *Searching for Africa in Brazil*, 18.

61. John L. Jackson, *Real Black*, 14–15.

62. Black American businesspeople who split their time between the United States and Bahia, for example, are especially content, and not just financially. Most of them provide tourism services, while others are making plans to build and/or invest in hotels. After the group of full-fledged expatriates, the travel industry migrants are perhaps the most dedicated to living in Bahia. Representative of the sentiments and desires held by the tourism professionals is Richard, a seventy-something retired professor of photography and media, who made his initial trip to Bahia in 1986. Taken by his ability to fit in—to relax without the burden of race weighing him down as it does in the United States, Richard began plotting his return to Bahia by arranging a conference there for an organization to which he belonged. Two years later, he brought over his first tour/conference group of 200 visual artists. This trip began negatively when the tourists, who Richard points out still had the civil rights and Black Power movements fresh on their minds, were informed that poor Afro-Bahians (*pretos*) were not allowed to enter the hotel. The entire group, including Richard, threatened to cancel their reservations, prompting the hotel managers to alter permanently their discriminatory policies. Despite the discrimination witnessed on his second trip and other societal problems that he has discovered in twenty years of traveling to Bahia, Richard has maintained a spiritual connection, choosing to enjoy the cultural positives, while utilizing his business to assist Afro-Brazilian communities in Bahia and Rio de Janeiro through an educational foundation that awards scholarships, supports local schools, and sponsors student exchanges between Bahia and the United States.

63. S. Hall, "Africa Is Alive and Well and Living in the Diaspora," 1.

64. S. Hall, "Cultural Identity and Diaspora," 236.

65. Interview with Tamara, June 24, 2007.

66. Interview with Isaac, June 28, 2007.

67. Hartman, *Lose Your Mother*, 46.

68. Da Silva, "Facts of Blackness."

69. Follow-up interview with Isaac, July 12, 2007.

70. E-mail correspondence, October 3, 2007. Isaac indeed journeyed back to the United States, choosing his Virginia childhood home as a residence before his death less than three years later. Perhaps in that final transition he found home, his paradise, Africa.

71. Quoted in Okpewho, *The African Diaspora*, xxv.

72. The quote is from the expatriate Charles during an interview on July 10, 2007.

73. Interview with Charles, July 10, 2007.

74. Interview with Kevin, June 26, 2007.

75. I should also note here that finances dictate where expatriates can afford to live, and that it is perhaps easier for certain individuals to suspend their awareness of Bahia's impoverishment if they are living a posh or relatively upscale lifestyle. In contrast, those who live among or in close proximity to financially depressed populations have everyday reminders of the malnutrition, disease, and crime that sweep the Afro-Bahian community. Generally, expatriates under fifty tend to live in or frequently visit friends in lower-income Afro-Bahian neighborhoods on the outskirts of the city, where they become active in advocacy programs and personally assist families of which they have become an "adopted" member. Those over fifty, including the retired members of the expatriate community, typically reside in Ondina, Barra, or other exclusive and tourist-heavy areas in the city of Salvador. While some of the members of this latter group have involved themselves in various social causes, they tend to feel defeated or cynical after a short period and do not have the drive to fight what they feel is too arduous battle.

76. Follow-up interview with Isaac, July 12, 2007.

77. Interview with Allen, July 18, 2007.

78. Interview with Donald, July 19, 2007.

79. Iton, *In Search of the Black Fantastic*, 200.

80. Morrison, "The Site of Memory," 192.

81. Jones, *Song for Anninho*, 37.

82. Jones, *Song for Anninho*, 36.

4. Crafting Symbolic Africas in a Geography of Silence

1. For more on these historical claims, see G. Davis, "Afro-American Coil Basketry in Charleston County, South Carolina." Also of interest here is Jones-Jackson, *When Roots Die*.

2. Cheshire, *Moving Midway*.

3. *The House Next Door* interview transcript can be found at HND@Grassroots: Season 2, Episode 2, "Moving Midway."
4. "The Story of the Plantation That Moved Away."
5. "Boone Hall Plantation: About Us." Recently, the plantation has created an exhibit spread throughout eight of its slave quarters that tells its version of Black American history, though it is unclear how much of the Black history at Boone Hall itself is conveyed. See "Boone Hall Plantation: Black History in America."
6. Gordon, *Ghostly Matters*, 6.
7. For more about the contestations over the narratives recited at slave plantations and other sites of slavery, see Battle, "Re-Envisioning the Museum"; Brundage, *The Southern Past*; Hargove, "Mapping the 'Social Field of Whiteness'"; and S. Lewis, "Slavery, Memory, and the History of the 'Atlantic Now.'"
8. Eichstedt and Small, *Representations of Slavery*, 107.
9. "Sanco Pansy's Cottage."
10. Roberts and Kytle, "Looking the Thing in the Face," 647.
11. Roberts and Kytle, "Looking the Thing in the Face," 654.
12. In July 2014, Joseph P. Riley, mayor of Charleston, South Carolina, announced that an International African American Museum will be built at Charleston Harbor, which will complement and expand upon the narratives offered in the Old Slave Mart. See Smith, "Museum to be Built in SC Where Slaves Entered US."
13. See "The Slave Dwelling Project."
14. Quoted in Horwitz, "One Man's Epic Quest to Visit Every Former Slave Dwelling in the United States."
15. Quoted in Horwitz, "One Man's Epic Quest to Visit Every Former Slave Dwelling in the United States."
16. Morrison and Richardson, "A Bench by the Road," 4.
17. For more information about the placement of benches at which to ponder the absences, see Toni Morrison Society, "Bench by the Road Project."
18. The Port Royal Experiment is discussed aptly in Rose, *Rehearsal for Reconstruction*.
19. Quoted in Higginson, "Denmark Vesey," 742.
20. Hunter, "Denmark Vesey Was a Terrorist."
21. Trouche, letter.
22. Parker, "Denmark Vesey Monument Unveiled before Hundreds."
23. The memorialization struggle, including the Angelou quotation controversy, was covered nationally by the Associated Press, "Savannah Divided over Monument"; and "Council Approves African-American Monument."
24. Associated Press, "Council Approves African-American Monument."
25. The litany was printed in the program for the rededication of the commemorative marker at Port Royal, Gullah Festival, May 26, 2013.
26. McHugh, "Black Migration Reversal in the United States," 172.
27. McHugh, "Black Migration Reversal in the United States," 173. For more historical information and statistical data on this reverse migration, also see

Alderman, Morrett, and Tolnay, "Homeward Bound"; Frey, "The New Great Migration"; and Hunt, Hunt, and Falk, "'Call to Home?'"

28. Stack, *Call to Home*, xiv.

29. Stack, *Call to Home*, 196–97.

30. For further critiques of the implications of Black American return migrations to the South, see T. Davis, "Expanding the Limits"; and Woodward, "Look Away, Look Away."

31. Angelou, "Why Blacks Are Returning to Their Southern Roots," 46.

32. Cohn, "Ethnic Identity in New York City," 9.

33. Bonetti, "An Interview with Gloria Naylor," 45.

34. Naylor discusses her cultural nationalism in Bellinelli, "A Conversation with Gloria Naylor," 107.

35. Ashford, "Gloria Naylor on Black Spirituality," 77. In another interview, Naylor explains that the lack of a geographic center "wrecks memory. We have no surviving relatives in the South . . . we seem to have lost an emphasis upon ties—communal ties and spiritual ties. Those things can still be there. Those types of ties can be there regardless of where your spiritual land base might be" (quoted in Bonetti, "An Interview with Gloria Naylor," 45).

36. Naylor, *Mama Day*, 206. Page numbers of references to the novel appear in parentheses in the text.

37. Quoted in Ashford, "Gloria Naylor on Black Spirituality," 78.

38. Quoted in Bonetti, "An Interview with Gloria Naylor," 58–59.

39. The following texts provide excellent analyses of all-Black towns in the United States: Bethel, *Promiseland*; H. Johnson, *Acres of Aspiration*; and Painter, *Exodusters*. See also "The Black Towns Project."

40. Quoted in Rowell, "An Interview with Gloria Naylor," 184–85.

41. Quoted in Bonetti, "An Interview with Gloria Naylor," 107–8.

42. International Black ideologies regarding self-determination, revolt, and rebellion certainly inspired these more radical U.S-based responses to continued oppression as well. See, for instance, James, *A History of Pan-African Revolt*; and Stephens, *Black Empire*.

43. Sherman, "Special Orders Number 15," 61.

44. Tillet, *Sites of Slavery*, 139–40.

45. "Turn toward Freedom."

46. "The Black Declaration of Independence."

47. R. Hall, *Black Separatism in the United States*, 184.

48. "How Did We Get a Government."

49. R. Hall, *Black Separatism in the United States*, 221.

50. In fact, the RNA's former minister of justice, Chokwe Lumumba, was elected as the mayor of Jackson, Mississippi, on June 4, 2013, though he met an untimely death seven months later. The RNA continues to boast a cohort of Black nationalists who are committed to its original charter. Further information can be found at the website, Provisional Government, Republic of New Afrika, http://www.pg-rna.org.

51. Minchin, "'A Brand New Shining City,'" 134.
52. Quoted in Strain, "Soul City, North Carolina," 63.
53. Quoted in Strain, "Soul City, North Carolina," 65.
54. Fergus, "Black Power, Soft Power," 158.
55. Quoted in Strain, "Soul City, North Carolina," 57.
56. Fergus, "Black Power, Soft Power," 180.
57. Strain, "Soul City, North Carolina," 67.
58. "Without 'the Man.'"
59. Adefunmi, "Pay for Slavery."
60. McCarthy, "A Little Bit of Africa."
61. For an insightful analysis of the global enmeshment of U.S. rural queer separatist encampments, see Povinelli, *The Empire of Love.*
62. McCarthy, "A Little Bit of Africa."
63. Clarke, "Transnational Yoruba Revivalism and the Diasporic Politics of Heritage," 724.
64. The Oyotunji African Village maintains a strong online presence. See "Oyotunji"; and Oyotunji African Village USA, "Get to Know Us."
65. Quoted in LeFever, "Leaving the United States," 182.
66. Quoted in LeFever, "Leaving the United States," 182.
67. Quoted in Donohue, "40 Years Later, African Village Still in Sheldon."
68. See, for example, "Africa—American Style"; and "An African Village in South Carolina."
69. Clarke, *Mapping Yoruba Networks*, 297.
70. Quoted in Marble, "Villagers Maintain Traditions."
71. This is not to suggest that the Oyotunji and Gullah peoples maintain a strict separation from each other. As Carl Hunt found, "it was not long before the communities accepted the Villagers warmly, and they soon realized that they had some things in common. The Blacks who live along the Georgia and South Carolina Sea Islands are probably the most voodoo conscious people in the United States. When they learned that the divination and roots medicines were a part of the Yoruba lifestyle, most of their fears disappeared and the villagers began to visit them occasionally and attend their parties, homecomings, funerals, and weddings" (*Oyotunji African Village*, 60).
72. Clarke, *Mapping Yoruba Networks*, 65.
73. Since the group was rushed, I did not receive an explanation as to what held back those who stayed aboard the bus, but it was clear that what they deemed most authentic were the traces of Africa that remained with the Gullah people, not what was fashioned on a plot of land in more recent times.
74. "'In the Name of Jesus.'"
75. This version of Eddy's civil disobedience is drawn from K. Harris, "Black Santa Claus Torches Confederate Flag."
76. Quoted in Taylor, "EXCLUSIVE."
77. Iton, *In Search of the Black Fantastic*, 19.

78. Bell, "The Afrolantica Awakening." Page numbers for subsequent quotes from the story appear in the text in parentheses.

Conclusion

1. Morrison, *Beloved*, 249. Page numbers for subsequent quotes from the novel appear in the text in parentheses.
2. Quoted in Williams, *Help Me to Find My People*, 162.
3. Williams, *Help Me to Find My People*, 12.
4. Several companies, such as Ancestry and 23andMe, began offering free tests partly because they realized that their African-descended customers were complaining about feeling cheated due to the lack of Africans in the companies' databases.
5. "Ancestry.com Black Man's Ancestor Born a Slave."
6. Motown Maurice PANDEMONIUM, "Ancestry.com's Commercial—African Americans."
7. Boyle, "Family Roots Get Tangled Up in Africa."
8. Quoted in Boyle, "DNA Points to Royal Roots in Africa."
9. Boyle, "DNA Points to Royal Roots in Africa."
10. Boyle, "African-American's Roots Revised."
11. Boyle, "Black History Saga Comes Full Circle."
12. In an interview for the British documentary *Motherland*, the biologist Fatimah Jackson surmised that "when they [African diasporans] finish all the searching, they still have to get up in the morning and look in the mirror and be satisfied with who they are. They still have to be confident in their true identity. And that's not going to come from a test tube. It's not going to come from a computer program, a DNA sequencer . . . it's going to come from [within]" (quoted in Baron, *Motherland*).
13. Nelson, "Reconciliation Projects," 20–21. See also Nelson, *The Social Life of DNA*.
14. Quoted in Boyle, "Genetic Quest Leads to African Apology for Role in Slave Trade."
15. Martin Delany averred in a portion of his manifesto on the promises of emigration as an antidote for Black alienation: "Moral theories have long been resorted to by us, as a means of effecting the redemption of our brethren in bonds, and the elevation of the free colored people in this country. Experience has taught us, that speculations are not enough; that the *practical* application of principles adduced, the thing carried out, is the only true and proper course to pursue" (*The Condition, Elevation, Emigration, and Destiny of the Colored People of the United States*, 66–67).
16. The notion of "proceeding speculatively" is borrowed from Philip Harper, who wrote: "for not to proceed speculatively is, to speak plainly, not to live" ("The Evidence of Felt Intuition," 652).

BIBLIOGRAPHY

"2010 Population Census: General Characteristics of the Population, Religion and Persons with Disabilities." Accessed October 29, 2012. http://www.ibge.gov.br /english/estatistica/populacao/censo2010/caracteristicas_religiao_deficiencia /caracteristicas_religiao_deficiencia_tab_pdf.shtm.

Adefunmi, Oseijeman. "Pay for Slavery." Letter. *Charleston News and Courier*, November 13, 1971.

Adeleke, Tunde. *UnAfrican Americans: Nineteenth Century Black Nationalists and the Civilizing Mission.* Lexington: University Press of Kentucky, 1998.

"Africa—American Style: Village in South Carolina Imitates West Africas Culture." *Ebony*, January 1978, 86–88, 90, and 92.

"An African Village in South Carolina." *Jet*, January 3, 1974, 50–52.

Ahmed, Sara. "Multiculturalism and the Promise of Happiness." *New Formations* 63 (Winter 2007–8): 121–37.

Alderman, Robert M., Chris Morrett, and Stewart E. Tolnay. "Homeward Bound: The Return Migration of Southern-Born Black Women." *Sociological Spectrum* 20, no. 4 (2000): 433–63.

"AMA Issues 'Final Warning' to Hawkers, Beggars." Ghanadot, March 1, 2007. Accessed June 13, 2014. http://www.ghanadot.com/news.gna.030107v.html.

"Ancestry.com Black Man's Ancestor Born a Slave." Accessed December 14, 2014. https://www.youtube.com/watch?v=WQQ9gjBby10.

Angelou, Maya. *All God's Children Need Traveling Shoes.* 1986. New York: Random House, 1991.

Angelou, Maya. "Why Blacks Are Returning to Their Southern Roots." *Ebony*, April 1990, 44, 46, and 48.

Araujo, Ana Lucia. *Shadows of the Slave Past: Memory, Heritage, and Slavery.* New York: Routledge, 2014.

Archer-Straw, Petrine. *Negrophilia: Avant-Garde Paris and Black Culture in the 1920s*. London: Thames and Hudson, 2000.

Asare, Abena Ampofoa. "The Ghanaian National Reconciliation Commission: Reparation in a Global Age." *Global South* 2, no. 2 (2008): 31–53.

Ashe, Bertram, and Reginald McKnight. "'Under the Umbrella of Black Civilization': A Conversation with Reginald McKnight." *African American Review* 35, no. 3 (2001): 427–37.

Ashford, Tomeiko. "Gloria Naylor on Black Spirituality: An Interview." *MELUS* 30, no. 4 (2005): 73–87.

Associated Press. "Savannah Divided over Monument." *Los Angeles Times*, February 10, 2001. Accessed April 3, 2014. http://articles.latimes.com/2001/feb/10/news/mn-23539.

Bailey, Anne C. *African Voices of the Atlantic Slave Trade: Beyond the Silence and the Shame*. Boston: Beacon, 2005.

Baldwin, James. *The Price of the Ticket: Collected Nonfiction, 1948–1985*. New York: St. Martin's, 1985.

Baraka, Amiri. *Wise, Why's, Y's: The Griot's Song Djeli Ya*. Chicago: Third World, 1995.

Barnes, Kenneth C. *Journey of Hope: The Back-to-Africa Movement in Arkansas in the Late 1800s*. Chapel Hill: University of North Carolina Press, 2004.

Baron, Archie, dir. *Motherland: A Genetic Journey*. London: Takeaway Media Productions, 2003.

Battle, Mary. "Re-Envisioning the Museum: Developing the International African American Museum in Charleston, South Carolina, during an Economic Crisis." *International Journal of the Inclusive Museum* 5, no. 1 (2013): 11–24.

Baucom, Ian. *Specters of the Atlantic: Finance Capital, Slavery, and the Philosophy of History*. Durham, NC: Duke University Press, 2005.

Bell, Derrick. "The Afrolantica Awakening." In Derrick Bell, *Faces at the Bottom of the Well: The Permanence of Racism*, 32–46. New York: Basic, 1993.

Best, Stephen. *The Fugitive's Properties: Law and the Poetics of Possession*. Chicago: University of Chicago Press, 2004.

Bethel, Elizabeth R. *Promiseland: A Century of Life in a Negro Community*. 1981. Columbia: University of South Carolina Press, 1997.

"The Black Declaration of Independence." Aset Books. n.d. Accessed March 3, 2014. http://www.asetbooks.com/us/AsetU/Courses/BlackGovernment101/BkDeck.html.

"Blacks in Brazil." *North Star*, July 13, 1849.

"The Black Towns Project." Accessed September 23, 2015. www.blacktownsproject.org.

Bonetti, Kay. "An Interview with Gloria Naylor." In *Conversations with Gloria Naylor*, edited by Maxine Lavon Montgomery, 39–64. Jackson: University Press of Mississippi, 2004.

"Boone Hall Plantation: About Us." Accessed April 11, 2010. http://boonehallplantation.com/about.php.

"Boone Hall Plantation: Black History in America." Accessed April 11, 2010. http://boonehallplantation.com/black_history.php.

Bordewich, Fergus. *Bound for Canaan: The Epic Story of the Underground Railroad, America's First Civil Rights Movement.* New York: HarperCollins, 2005.

Boyle, Alan. "African-American's Roots Revised." NBC News, May 14, 2012. Accessed December 14, 2014. http://cosmiclog.nbcnews.com/_news/2012/05/14/11690543-african-americans-roots-revised.

Boyle, Alan. "Black History Saga Comes Full Circle." NBC News, February 28, 2011. Accessed December 14, 2014. http://cosmiclog.nbcnews.com/_news/2011/02/28/6156374-black-history-saga-comes-full-circle?lite.

Boyle, Alan. "DNA Points to Royal Roots in Africa." NBC News, September 8, 2010. Accessed December 14, 2014. http://cosmiclog.nbcnews.com/_news/2010/09/08/5070972-dna-points-to-royal-roots-in-africa.

Boyle, Alan. "Family Roots Get Tangled Up in Africa." NBC News, February 1, 2011. Accessed December 14, 2014. http://cosmiclog.nbcnews.com/_news/2011/01/25/5916155-family-roots-get-tangled-up-in-africa.

Boyle, Alan. "Genetic Quest Leads to African Apology for Role in Slave Trade." NBC News, October 27, 2013. Accessed December 14, 2014. http://www.nbcnews.com/science/science-news/genetic-quest-leads-african-apology-role-slave-trade-f8C11467842.

Brown, William Wells. *The Narrative of William W. Brown, A Fugitive Slave.* 1816. Whitefish, MT: Kessinger, 2004.

Brundage, William. *The Southern Past: A Clash of Race and Memory.* Cambridge, MA: Belknap Press of Harvard University Press, 2005.

Bruner, Edward. "Tourism in Ghana: The Representation of Slavery and the Return of the Black Diaspora." *American Anthropologist* 98, no. 2 (1996): 290–304.

Busia, Abena P. A. "What Is Your Nation? Reconnecting Africa and Her Diaspora through Paule Marshall's *Praisesong for the Widow.*" In *Changing Our Words: Essays on Criticism, Theory and Writing by Black Women*, edited by Cheryl A. Wall, 196–212. New Brunswick, NJ: Rutgers University Press, 1989.

Butler, Kim D. "Afterword." In *Afro-Brazilian Culture and Politics: Bahia, 1790s–1990s*, edited by Hendrick Kraay, 158–76. New York: M. E. Sharpe, 2002.

Butler, Kim D. *Freedoms Given, Freedoms Won: Afro-Brazilians in Post-Abolition São Paulo and Salvador.* New Brunswick, NJ: Rutgers University Press, 1998.

Butler, Octavia. *Kindred.* 1979. Boston: Beacon, 2008.

Buxton, Geordie. *Haunted Plantations: Ghosts of Slavery and Legends of the Cotton Kingdoms.* Charleston, SC: Arcadia, 2007.

Byerman, Keith. *Remembering the Past in Contemporary African American Fiction.* Chapel Hill: University of North Carolina Press, 2006.

Caldwell, Kia. *Negras in Brazil: Re-Envisioning Black Women, Citizenship, and the Politics of Identity.* New Brunswick, NJ: Rutgers University Press, 2007.

Camp, Stephanie M. H. *Closer to Freedom: Enslaved Women and Everyday Resistance in the Plantation South.* Chapel Hill: University of North Carolina Press, 2004.

Campbell, James T. *Middle Passages: African American Journeys to Africa.* New York: Penguin, 2007.

Capone, Stefania. *Searching for Africa in Brazil: Power and Tradition in Candomblé.* Durham, NC: Duke University Press, 2010.

Chaney, Michael A. *Fugitive Vision: Slave Image and Black Identity in Antebellum Narrative.* Bloomington: Indiana University Press, 2009.

Cheshire, Geoffrey, dir. *Moving Midway.* New York: First Run Features, 2007. DVD.

Childs, Dennis. "'You Ain't Seen Nothin' Yet': *Beloved*, the American Chain Gang, and the Middle Passage Remix." *American Quarterly* 61, no. 2 (2009): 271–97.

Chomsky, Marvin, John Erman, David Greene, and Gilbert Moses, dir. *Roots.* 1977. Burbank, CA: Warner Home Video, 2007. DVD.

Christian, Barbara. "Ritualistic Process and the Structure of Paule Marshall's *Praisesong for the Widow*." *Callaloo* 18 (Spring–Summer 1983): 74–84.

Christol, Hélène. "The African American Concept of the Fantastic as Middle Passage." In *Black Imagination and the Middle Passage*, edited by Maria Diedrich, Henry Louis Gates Jr., and Carl Pederson, 164–82. New York: Oxford University Press, 1999.

Clarke, Kamari Maxine. *Mapping Yoruba Networks: Power and Agency in the Making of Transnational Communities.* Durham, NC: Duke University Press, 2004.

Clarke, Kamari Maxine. "New Spheres of Transnational Formations: Mobilizations of Humanitarian Diasporas." *Transforming Anthropology* 18, no. 1 (2010): 48–65.

Clarke, Kamari Maxine. "Transnational Yoruba Revivalism and the Diasporic Politics of Heritage." *American Ethnologist* 34, no. 7 (2007): 721–34.

Clegg, Claude A. *The Price of Liberty: African Americans and the Making of Liberia.* Chapel Hill: University of North Carolina Press, 2004.

Clifford, James. *Routes: Travel and Translation in the Late Twentieth Century.* Cambridge, MA: Harvard University Press, 1997.

Clifton, Lucille. "why some people be mad at me sometimes." In Lucille Clifton, *NEXT: New Poems*, 20. Rochester, NY: BOA Editions, 1989.

Cohn, Sandra. "Ethnic Identity in New York City." MA thesis, New York University, 1973.

Collins, John F. *Revolt of the Saints: Memory and Redemption in the Twilight of Brazilian Racial Democracy.* Durham, NC: Duke University Press, 2015.

Collins, Patricia Hill. *Black Feminist Thought: Knowledge, Consciousness, and the Politics of Empowerment.* New York: Routledge, 2000.

"Council Approves African-American Monument." SavannahNow, January 12, 2001. Accessed April 3, 2014. http://savannahnow.com/stories/011201/LOCcitycouncil.shtml#.Vyx8EfkrLIU.

Craft, William, and Ellen Craft. *Running a Thousand Miles for Freedom*. 1860. Athens: University of Georgia Press, 1999.

Crawley, Ashon. "Otherwise Movements." New Inquiry, January 19, 2015. Accessed April 30, 2016. http://thenewinquiry.com/essays/otherwise-movements/.

Crummell, Alexander. *Destiny and Race: Selected Writings, 1840–1898*. Edited by Wilson Jeremiah Moses. Amherst: University of Massachusetts Press, 1992.

Da Silva, Denise Ferreira. "Facts of Blackness: Brazil is Not (Quite) the United States . . . And, Racial Politics in Brazil?" *Social Identities* 4, no. 2 (1998): 201–34.

Davis, Gerald L. "Afro-American Coil Basketry in Charleston County, South Carolina." In *American Folklife*, edited by Don Yoder, 151–84. Austin: University of Texas Press, 1976.

Davis, Thaddeus M. "Expanding the Limits: The Intersection of Race and Region." *Southern Literary Journal* 20, no. 2 (1988): 3–11.

Delany, Martin R. *The Condition, Elevation, Emigration, and Destiny of the Colored People of the United States and Official Report of Niger Valley Exploring Party and Their Legacy in Liberia Today*. Edited by Toyin Falola. Amherst, NY: Humanity, 2004.

Dery, Mark. "Black to the Future." In *Flame Wars: The Discourse of Cyberculture*, edited by Mark Dery, 179–222. Durham, NC: Duke University Press, 1994.

Diaspora African Forum. "Our Mission." Accessed July 4, 2016. http://www.audaf.org/about-daf.html.

"Discussing the Proposed Exodus." *Huntsville Gazette*, February 11, 1888.

Donohue, Patrick. "40 Years Later, African Village Still in Sheldon." *Beaufort Gazette*, November 19, 2010.

Douglass, Frederick. *Narrative of the Life of Frederick Douglass, An American Slave*. 1845. New York: Modern Library, 2000.

Du Bois, W. E. B. *Black Reconstruction in America, 1860–1880*. New York: Free Press, 1935.

Du Bois, W. E. B. "Returning Soldiers." *Crisis*, May 1919, 13.

Du Bois, W. E. B. *The Souls of Black Folk*. 1903. New York: Penguin, 1989.

Dudziak, Mary. *Cold War Civil Rights: Race and the Image of American Democracy*. Princeton, NJ: Princeton University Press, 2000.

Ebron, Paulla. *Performing Africa*. Princeton, NJ: Princeton University Press, 2002.

Echeruo, Michael J. C. "An African Diaspora: The Ontological Project." In *The African Diaspora: African Origins and New World Identities*, edited by Isidore Okpewho, 3–18. Bloomington: Indiana University Press, 1999.

"An Echo of the Proposed Exodus." *Huntsville Gazette*, May 26, 1888.

Edozie, Rita Kiki. "The Sixth Zone: The African Diaspora and the African Union's Global Era Pan-Africanism." *Journal of African American Studies* 16, no. 2 (2012): 268–99.

Edwards, Brent Hayes. *The Practice of Diaspora: Literature, Translation, and the Rise of Black Internationalism*. Cambridge, MA: Harvard University Press, 2003.

Eichstedt, Jennifer L., and Stephen Small. *Representations of Slavery: Race, Ideology and Southern Plantation Museums*. Washington: Smithsonian Institution Press, 2002.

Ellison, Ralph. *Shadow and Act*. 1953. New York: Vintage, 1995.

Esedebe, P. Olisanwuche. *Pan-Africanism: The Idea and the Movement, 1776–1991*. Washington: Howard University Press, 1994.

Eyerman, Ron. *Cultural Trauma: Slavery and the Formation of African American Identity*. Cambridge: Cambridge University Press, 2001.

Eyerman, Ron. "The Past in the Present: Culture and the Transmission of Memory." *Acta Sociologica* 47, no. 2 (2004): 159–69.

Fabre, Michel. *From Harlem to Paris: Black American Writers in France, 1840–1980*. Urbana: University of Illinois Press, 1991.

Fanon, Frantz. *Black Skin, White Masks*. Translated by Constance Farrington. New York: Grove, 1967.

Fergus, Devin. "Black Power, Soft Power: Floyd McKissick, Soul City, and the Death of Moderate Black Republicanism." *Journal of Policy History* 22, no. 2 (2010): 148–92.

Foner, Eric. *Reconstruction: America's Unfinished Revolution, 1863–1877*. New York: Harper and Row, 1988.

Fooling with Words (Part One): Amiri Baraka. Accessed July 5, 2016. http://billmoyers.com/content/fooling-with-words-part-i/

Franklin, John Hope, and Alfred A. Moss. *From Slavery to Freedom: A History of African Americans*. 8th ed. Boston: McGraw-Hill Higher Education, 2000.

Frey, William H. "The New Great Migration: Black Americans Return to the South, 1965–2000." Washington: Brookings Institution, 2004. Accessed April 30, 2016. http://www.brookings.edu/~/media/research/files/reports/2004/5/demographics%20frey/20040524_frey.

Freyre, Gilberto. *The Masters and the Slaves: A Study in the Development of Brazilian Civilization*. 2nd rev. ed. Berkeley: University of California Press, 1987.

Gaines, Kevin K. *American Africans in Ghana: Black Expatriates and the Civil Rights Era*. Chapel Hill: University of North Carolina Press, 2006.

Gerima, Haile, dir. *Sankofa*. Washington: Mypheduh Films, 1993. DVD.

Gerima, Haile, and Pamela Woolford. "Filming Slavery." *Transition* 64 (1994): 90–104.

"Ghana@50: President Kufuor's Speech." Accessed July 4, 2016. http://www.ghanaweb.com/GhanaHomePage/NewsArchive/Ghana-50-President-Kufuor-s-Speech-120567.

Gilmore, Ruth Wilson. *Golden Gulag: Prisons, Surplus, Crisis, and Opposition in Globalizing California*. Berkley: University of California Press, 2007.

Gilroy, Paul. *The Black Atlantic: Modernity and Double Consciousness*. Cambridge, MA: Harvard University Press, 1993.

Goffman, Alice. *On the Run: Fugitive Life in an American City*. Chicago: University of Chicago Press, 2014.

Gordon, Avery. *Ghostly Matters: Haunting and the Sociological Imagination.* Minneapolis: University of Minnesota Press, 1997.

Graden, Dale T. "An Act 'Even of Public Security': Slave Resistance, Social Tensions, and the End of the International Slave Trade to Brazil, 1835–1856." *Hispanic American Historical Review* 76, no. 2 (1996): 249–82.

Grant, Colin. *Negro with a Hat: The Rise and Fall of Marcus Garvey.* New York: Oxford University Press, 2008.

Gregory, James N. *The Southern Diaspora: How the Great Migrations of Black and White Southerners Transformed America.* Chapel Hill: University of North Carolina Press, 2005.

Grossman, James R. *Land of Hope: Chicago, Black Southerners, and the Great Migration.* Chicago: University of Chicago Press, 1989.

Gruesser, John C. "Afro-American Travel Literature and Africanist Discourse." *Black American Literature Forum* 24, no. 1 (1990): 5–30.

Gumbs, Alexis Pauline. "Prophecy in the Present Tense: Harriet Tubman, the Combahee Pilgrimage, and Dreams Coming True." *Meridians* 12, no. 2 (2014): 142–52.

Hahn, Steven. *A Nation under Our Feet.* Cambridge, MA: Belknap Press of Harvard University Press, 2003.

Haley, Alex. *Roots: The Saga of an American Family.* 1976. New York: Vanguard Books, 2007.

Hall, Raymond L. *Black Separatism in the United States.* Hanover, NH: University Press of New England, 1978.

Hall, Stuart. "Africa Is Alive and Well and Living in the Diaspora." Paris: UNESCO, 1975.

Hall, Stuart. "Cultural Identity and Diaspora." In *Theorizing Diaspora: A Reader,* edited by Jana Evans Braziel and Anita Mannur, 233–46. Malden, MA: Blackwell, 2003.

Hanchard, Michael George. *Orpheus and Power: The Movimento Negro of Rio de Janeiro and São Paulo, 1945–1988.* Princeton, NJ: Princeton University Press, 1994.

Hargove, Melissa. "Mapping the 'Social Field of Whiteness': White Racism as Habitus in the City Where History Lives." *Transforming Anthropology* 17, no. 2 (2009): 93–104.

Harney, Stefano, and Fred Moten. *Undercommons: Fugitive Planning and Black Study.* Brooklyn, NY: Autonomedia, 2013.

Harper, Philip Brian. "The Evidence of Felt Intuition: Minority Experience, Everyday Life, and Critical Speculative Knowledge." *GLQ* 6, no. 4 (2000): 641–57.

Harris, Eddy L. *Native Stranger: A Black American's Journey into the Heart of Africa.* New York: Simon and Schuster, 1992.

Harris, Kenneth A. "Black Santa Claus Torches Confederate Flag." *The State* (Columbia, SC), April 18, 2002.

Harris, Thomas Allen, dir. *É Minha Cara/That's My Face.* 2001. New York: Fox Lorber, 2004. DVD.

Hartman, Saidiya. *Lose Your Mother: A Journey along the Atlantic Slave Route.* New York: Farrar, Straus, and Giroux, 2007.

Hartman, Saidiya. *Scenes of Subjection: Terror, Slavery, and Self-Making in Nineteenth-Century America.* New York: Oxford University Press, 1997.

Hartman, Saidiya. "The Time of Slavery." *South Atlantic Quarterly* 101, no. 4 (2002): 757–77.

Hasty, Jennifer. "Rites of Passage, Routes of Redemption: Emancipation Tourism and the Wealth of Culture." *Africa Today* 49, no. 3 (2002): 47–76.

Hellwig, David J. *African-American Reflections on Brazil's Racial Paradise.* Philadelphia, PA: Temple University Press, 1992.

Higginson, Thomas Wentworth. "Denmark Vesey." *Atlantic Monthly*, June 1861, 728–44.

HND@Grassroots: Season 2, Episode 2, "Moving Midway," with Godfrey Cheshire (Transcript Included). Accessed July 18, 2014. http://www.slantmagazine.com /house/article/hndgrassroots-season-2-episode-2-20-moving-midway-with -godfrey-cheshire-transcript-included.

Holsey, Bayo. *Routes of Remembrance: Refashioning the Slave Trade in Ghana.* Chicago: University of Chicago Press, 2008.

Hong, Grace Kyungwon. "'The Future of Our Worlds': Black Feminism and the Politics of Knowledge in the University under Globalization." *Meridians* 8, no. 2 (2008): 95–115.

Horwitz, Tony. "One Man's Epic Quest to Visit Every Former Slave Dwelling in the United States." *Smithsonian*, October 2013. Accessed April 4, 2014. http://www .smithsonianmag.com/history/one-mans-epic-quest-to-visit-every-former-slave -dwelling-in-the-united-states-12080/?no-ist.

"How Did We Get a Government?" Republic of New Africa: Short Official Basic Documents. Accessed July 7, 2016. http://collections.msdiglib.org/cdm/ref /collection/tougaloo/id/208.

Huffman, Alan. *Mississippi in Africa: The Saga of the Slaves of Prospect Hill Plantation and Their Legacy in Liberia Today.* New York: Gotham, 2005.

Huggins, Nathan, and Arnold Rampersad. *The Harlem Renaissance.* Oxford: Oxford University Press, 2007.

Hunt, Carl M. *Oyotunji African Village: The Yoruba Movement in America.* Washington: University Press of America, 1979.

Hunt, Matthew O., Larry L. Hunt, and William Falk. "'Call to Home?' Race, Region, and Migration to the U.S. South, 1970–2000." *Sociological Forum* 27, no. 1 (2012): 117–41.

Hunter, Jack. "Denmark Vesey Was a Terrorist." *Charleston City Paper*, February 10, 2010. Accessed June 6, 2014. http://www.charlestoncitypaper.com /charleston/denmark-vesey-was-a-terrorist/Content?oid=1756179.

Ignatiev, Noel. *How the Irish Became White.* Milton Park, UK: Routledge, 1995.

Imahküs, Seestah. *Returning Home Ain't Easy, but It Sure Is a Blessing.* Cape Coast, Ghana: One Africa Tours and Specialty Services, 1999.

"'In the Name of Jesus!': Activist Takes Down Confederate Flag from SC Statehouse." Accessed July 6, 2016. https://www.youtube.com/watch?v =KzxXuLHEDA4.

"The Irrepressible Envoy from Ghana." *Ebony*, November 1970, 68–74.

Iton, Richard. *In Search of the Black Fantastic: Politics and Popular Culture in the Post–Civil Rights Era*. New York: Oxford University Press, 2008.

Jackson, Jennifer, and Mary Cothran. "Black versus Black: The Relationship among African, African American, and African Caribbean Persons." *Journal of Black Studies* 33, no. 5 (2003): 576–604.

Jackson, John L. *Real Black: Adventures in Racial Sincerity*. Chicago: University of Chicago Press, 2005.

Jackson, Sandra, and Julie Moody-Freeman. "The Black Imagination and the Genres: Science Fiction, Futurism and the Speculative." In *The Black Imagination: Science Fiction, Futurism and the Speculative*, edited by Sandra Jackson and Julie Moody-Freeman, 1–14. New York: Peter Lang International Academic Publishers, 2011.

Jacobs, Harriet. *Incidents in the Life of a Slave Girl*. 1861. New York: Modern Library, 2000.

Jacobson, Matthew Frye. *Whiteness of a Different Color: European Immigrants and the Alchemy of Race*. Cambridge, MA: Harvard University Press, 1999.

James, C. L. R. *A History of Pan-African Revolt*. 1938. Oakland: PM, 2012.

Johnson, Hannibal. *Acres of Aspiration: The All-Black Towns in Oklahoma*. Austin, TX: Eakin, 2003.

Johnson, Lyndon B. "Commencement Address at Howard University: 'To Fulfill These Rights': June 4, 1965." Accessed April 30, 2016. http://www.lbjlib.utexas .edu/johnson/archives.hom/speeches.hom/650604.asp.

Jones, Gayl. *Song for Anninho*. Boston: Beacon, 2000.

Jones-Jackson, Patricia. *When Roots Die: Endangered Traditions on the Sea Islands*. Athens: University of Georgia Press, 1987.

Journeyman Pictures. "Coming Home-Ghana." Accessed January 16, 2010. https:// www.youtube.com/watch?v=4jFviE37E2Y.

Kandé, Sylvie, and Joe Karaganis. "Look Homeward, Angel: Maroons and Mulattos in Haile Gerima's *Sankofa*." *Research in African Literatures* 29, no. 2 (1998): 128–46.

Kaplan, Sara Clarke. "Souls at the Crossroads, Africans on the Water: The Politics of Diasporan Melancholia." *Callaloo* 30, no. 2 (2007): 511–26.

Keeling, Kara. *The Witch's Flight: The Cinematic, the Black Femme, and the Image of Common Sense*. Durham, NC: Duke University Press, 2007.

Kelley, Robin D. G. *Freedom Dreams: The Black Radical Imagination*. Boston: Beacon, 2002.

Kenan, Randall. "An Interview with Octavia E. Butler." *Callaloo* 14, no. 2 (1991): 495–504.

Kondo, Dorinne. *Crafting Selves: Power, Gender, and Discourses of Identity in a Japanese Workplace*. Chicago: University of Chicago Press, 1990.

Lake, Obiagele. "A Taste of Life: Diaspora African Repatriation to Ghana." PhD diss., Cornell University, 1990.

Lake, Obiagele. "Toward a Pan-African Identity: Diaspora Repatriates in Ghana." *Anthropological Quarterly* 68, no. 1 (1995): 21–36.

Lee, Chana Kai. *For Freedom's Sake: The Life of Fannie Lou Hamer*. Urbana: University of Illinois Press, 1999.

LeFever, Harry G. "Leaving the United States: The Black Nationalist Themes of Orisha-Vodu." *Journal of Black Studies* 31, no. 2 (2000): 174–95.

Lemann, Nicholas. *The Promised Land: The Great Black Migration and How It Changed America*. New York: Knopf, 1991.

Lemelle, Sid. *Pan-Africanism for Beginners*. Danbury, CT: Writers and Readers, 1992.

Lewis, David Levering. *When Harlem Was in Vogue*. New York: Penguin, 1997.

Lewis, Simon. "Slavery, Memory, and the History of the 'Atlantic Now': Charleston, South Carolina and Global Racial/Economic Hierarchy." *Journal of Postcolonial Writing* 45, no. 2 (2009): 125–35.

Locke, Alain. *The New Negro: Voices of the Harlem Renaissance*. New York: Touchstone, 1992.

Losch, Paul S. "Dr. Henry W. Furniss, Cônsul Afro-Norte-Americano na Bahia, 1898–1905." *Afro-Ásia* 40 (2010): 223–58.

Lovelace, Earl. *Salt*. London: Faber and Faber, 1996.

Maio, Marcos Chor. "UNESCO and the Study of Race Relations in Brazil: Regional or National Issue?" *Latin American Research Review* 36, no. 2 (2001): 118–36.

Marable, Manning. *How Capitalism Underdeveloped Black America: Problems in Race, Political Economy and Society*. Updated ed. Cambridge, MA: South End, 2000.

Marable, Manning. *Race, Reform and Rebellion: Second Reconstruction in Black America, 1945–82*. 1984. Jackson: University Press of Mississippi, 2002.

Marble, Laura. "Villagers Maintain Traditions." *Beaufort Gazette*, June 1, 2003.

Markowitz, Fran. *Homecomings: Unsettling Paths to Return*. Lanham, MD: Lexington, 2004.

Marshall, Paule. *Praisesong for the Widow*. New York: Plume, 1983.

Matory, Lorand J. *Black Atlantic Religion: Tradition, Transnationalism, and Matriarchy in Afro-Brazilian Candomblé*. Princeton, NJ: Princeton University Press, 2005.

McCarthy, Rebecca. "A Little Bit of Africa—Controversial Oyotunji Village Bringing Voodoo and Tourists to S.C. Lowcountry." *Atlanta Journal and Atlanta Constitution*, September 11, 1988.

McDonnell, Patrick J. "Bahia: Brazil's Cultural Link for African Americans." *Los Angeles Times*, September 23, 2007.

McElya, Micki. *Clinging to Mammy: The Faithful Slave in the Twentieth Century*. Cambridge, MA: Harvard University Press, 2007.

McHugh, Kevin E. "Black Migration Reversal in the United States." *Geographical Review* 77, no. 2 (1987): 171–82.

McKnight, Reginald. *I Get on the Bus*. Boston: Little, Brown, 1990.

McKoy, Sheila Smith. "The Limbo Contest: Diaspora Temporality and Its Reflection in *Praisesong for the Widow* and *Daughters of the Dust.*" *Callaloo* 22, no. 1 (1999): 208–22.

"Mercado Modelo." Accessed June 14, 2014. http://www.mercadomodelobahia .com.br/english/Mercado/.

Meriwether, James H. *Proudly We Can Be Africans: Black Americans and Africa, 1935–1961.* Chapel Hill: University of North Carolina Press, 2002.

Minchin, Timothy J. "'A Brand New Shining City': Floyd McKissick Sr. and the Struggle to Build Soul City, North Carolina." *North Carolina Historical Review* 82, no. 2 (2005): 125–55.

Mitchell, Angelyn. "Not Enough of the Past: Feminist Revisions of Slavery in Octavia Butler's *Kindred.*" *MELUS* 26, no. 3 (2001): 51–75.

Mitchell, Michele. *Righteous Propagation: African Americans and the Politics of Racial Destiny after Reconstruction.* Chapel Hill: University of North Carolina Press, 2004.

Morrison, Toni. *Beloved.* 1987. New York: Vintage, 2004.

Morrison, Toni. "The Site of Memory." In *Inventing the Truth*, edited by William Zinsser, 83–102. New York: Houghton Mifflin, 1995.

Morrison, Toni. *Song of Solomon.* New York: Random House, 1977.

Morrison, Toni, and Robert Richardson. "A Bench by the Road." [*Unitarian Universalist*] *World*, January–February 1989, 4.

Moses, William Jeremiah. *Liberian Dreams: Back-to-Africa Narratives from the 1850s.* University Park: Pennsylvania State University Press, 1998.

Moten, Fred. *In the Break: The Aesthetics of the Black Radical Tradition.* Minneapolis: University of Minnesota Press, 2003.

Motown Maurice PANDEMONIUM. "Ancestry.com's Commercial—African Americans." Accessed December 14, 2014. https://www.youtube.com/watch?v =ANf4098LZ-E.

Mudimbe, Valentin Y. *The Invention of Africa: Gnosis, Philosophy, and the Order of Knowledge.* Bloomington: Indiana University Press, 1988.

Munoz, José E. *Disidentifications: Queers of Color and the Performance of Politics.* Minneapolis: University of Minnesota Press, 1999.

Murray, Rolland. "Diaspora by Bus: Reginald McKnight, Postmodernism, and Transatlantic Subjectivity." *Contemporary Literature* 46, no. 1 (2005): 46–77.

Naylor, Gloria. *Mama Day.* New York: Vintage, 1988.

Nelson, Alondra. "Introduction: Future Texts." *Social Text* 20, no. 2 (2002): 1–15.

Nelson, Alondra. "Reconciliation Projects: From Kinship to Justice." In *Genetics and the Unsettled Past: The Collision of DNA, Race, and History*, edited by Keith Wailoo, Alondra Nelson, and Catherine Lee, 20–31. New Brunswick, NJ: Rutgers University Press, 2012.

Nelson, Alondra. *The Social Life of DNA: Race, Reparations, and Reconciliation after the Genome.* Boston: Beacon, 2016.

Nicholas, Xavier. "A Conversation with Reginald McKnight." *Callaloo* 29, no. 2 (2006): 304–21.

Nkrumah, Kwame. "Ghana is Free Forever." Accessed July 4, 2016. http://www .bbc.co.uk/worldservice/focusonafrica/news/story/2007/02/070129_ghana50 _independence_speech.shtml.

Obama, Barack. "Remarks by the President to the Ghanaian Parliament." July 11, 2009. Accessed May 2, 2016. https://www.whitehouse.gov/the-press-office /remarks-president-ghanaian-parliament.

Okpewho, Isidore. *The African Diaspora: African Origins and New World Identities.* Bloomington: Indiana University Press, 1999.

Omi, Michael, and Howard Winant. *Racial Formation in the United States.* New York: Routledge, 1994.

"Oyotunji." Accessed July 3, 2014. https://www.youtube.com/user/Oyotunji.

Oyotunji African Village USA. "Get to Know Us." Accessed July 3, 2014. http:// www.oyotunji.org/.

Painter, Nell Irvin. *Exodusters: Black Migration to Kansas after Reconstruction.* 1977. New York: W. W. Norton, 1992.

Parker, Adam. "Denmark Vesey Monument Unveiled before Hundreds." *Charleston Post and Courier*, February 16, 2014.

Paschel, Tianna. "Re-Africanization and the Cultural Politics of 'Bahianidade.'" *Souls* 11, no. 4 (2009): 423–40.

Patterson, Orlando. *Slavery and Social Death: A Comparative Study.* Cambridge, MA: Harvard University Press, 1982.

Pierre, Jemima. *The Predicament of Blackness: Postcolonial Ghana and the Politics of Race.* Chicago: University of Chicago Press, 2012.

Povinelli, Elizabeth A. *The Empire of Love: Toward a Theory of Intimacy, Genealogy, and Carnality.* Durham, NC: Duke University Press, 2006.

"Promoting Afro-Brazilian Trade." *New Pittsburgh Courier.* May 21, 2003, City Edition.

"Proposed Exodus. Scheme for [Colonizing] Colored Laborers in South." *Huntsville Gazette*, February 4, 1888.

"Provisional Government—Republic of New Afrika." Accessed May 4, 2014. http:// www.pg-rna.org/.

Rediker, Marcus. *The Slave Ship: A Human History.* New York: Viking, 2007.

Reis, João José. *Slave Rebellion in Brazil: The Muslim Uprising of 1835 in Bahia.* Baltimore, MD: Johns Hopkins University Press, 1993.

Rhodes, Jane. *Mary Ann Shadd Cary: The Black Press and Protest in the Nineteenth Century.* Bloomington: Indiana University Press, 1998.

Richards, Sandra. "What Is to Be Remembered? Tourism to Ghana's Slavecastle-Dungeons." *Theatre Journal* 57, no. 4 (2005): 617–37.

Richburg, Keith B. *Out of America: A Black Man Confronts Africa.* New York: Basic, 1997.

Roach, Joseph. *Cities of the Dead: Circum-Atlantic Performance.* New York: Columbia University Press, 1996.

Roberts, Blain, and Ethan J. Kytle. "Looking the Thing in the Face: Slavery, Race, and the Commemorative Landscape in Charleston, South Carolina, 1865–2010." *Journal of Southern History* 78, no. 3 (2012): 639–84.

Robinson, Cedric J. *Black Marxism: The Making of the Black Radical Tradition.* 1983. Chapel Hill: University of North Carolina Press, 2000.

Robinson, Eugene. *Coal to Cream: A Black Man's Journey beyond Color to an Affirmation of Race.* New York: Free Press, 1999.

Robinson, Randall. *Quitting America: The Departure of a Black Man from His Native Land.* New York: Dutton, 2004.

Roediger, David. *Working toward Whiteness: How America's Immigrants Became White: The Strange Journey from Ellis Island to the Suburbs.* New York: Basic, 2005.

Rose, Willie Lee. *Rehearsal for Reconstruction: The Port Royal Experiment.* 1964. Athens: University of Georgia Press, 1998.

Rowell, Charles H. "An Interview with Gloria Naylor." *Callaloo* 20, no. 1 (1997): 179–92.

Rusert, Britt. "Delany's Comet: Fugitive Science and the Speculative Imaginary of Emancipation." *American Quarterly* 65, no. 4 (2013): 799–829.

Rushdy, Ashraf H. A. *Neo-Slave Narratives: Studies in the Social Logic of a Literary Form.* New York: Oxford University Press, 1999.

Rushdy, Ashraf H. A. *Remembering Generations: Race and Family in Contemporary African American Fiction.* Chapel Hill: University of North Carolina Press, 2001.

Salvaggio, Ruth. "Octavia Butler." In *Suzy McKee Charnas, Octavia Butler, and Joan D. Vinge,* edited by Marleen S. Barr, Ruth Salvaggio, and Richard Law, 1–44. Mercer Island, WA: Starmont House, 1986.

"Sanco Pansy's Cottage." Prospect Hill Bed and Breakfast. Accessed March 5, 2014. http://www.prospecthill.com/rooms_sanco.htm.

Sanders, Kimberly Wallace. *Mammy: A Century of Race, Gender, and Southern Memory.* Ann Arbor: University of Michigan Press, 2008.

Santana Pinho, Patricia de. *Mama Africa: Reinventing Blackness in Bahia.* Durham, NC: Duke University Press, 2010.

Schaumloeffel, Marco Aurelio. *Tabom: The Afro-Brazilian Community in Ghana.* Lexington, KY: Custom Books, 2009.

Schomburg Center for Research in Black Culture. "The African American Migration Experience." New York Public Library. 2005. Accessed April 30, 2016. http://www.inmotionaame.org/home.cfm;jsessionid=f8301619831461995158607?bhcp=.

Schramm, Katharina. *African Homecoming: Pan-African Ideology and Contested Heritage.* Walnut Creek, CA: Left Coast, 2010.

Schwarz-Bart, Simone. *Between Two Worlds.* London: Heinemann, 1992.

Schwarz-Bart, Simone. *The Bridge of Beyond.* London: Heinemann, 1982.

Seigel, Micol. *Uneven Encounters: Making Race and Nation in Brazil and the United States.* Durham, NC: Duke University Press, 2009.

Selka, Stephen. "Rural Women and the Varieties of Black Politics in Bahia, Brazil." *Black Women, Gender and Families* 3, no. 1 (2009): 16–38.

Selka, Stephen. "The Sisterhood of Boa Morte in Brazil: Harmonious Mixture, Black Resistance, and the Politics of Religious Practice." *Journal of Latin American and Caribbean Anthropology* 13, no. 1 (2008): 1–35.

Sernett, Milton. *Bound for the Promised Land: African Americans' Religion and the Great Migration.* Durham, NC: Duke University Press, 1997.

Shepperson, George. "African Diaspora: Concept and Context." In *Global Dimensions of the African Diaspora*, edited by Joseph E. Harris, 46–53. Washington: Howard University Press, 1982.

Sherman, William Tecumseh. "Special Orders Number 15." In *War of the Rebellion: Official Records of the Union and Confederate Armies*, vol. XLVII, edited by Daniel S. Lamont, George B. Davis, Leslie J. Perry, and Joseph W. Kirkley, 60–62. Washington: Government Printing Office, 1895.

Singh, Nikhil. *Black Is a Country: Race and the Unfinished Struggle for Democracy.* Cambridge, MA: Harvard University Press, 2004.

"The Slave Dwelling Project." Accessed May 2, 2014. http://slavedwellingproject .org/.

Smith, Bruce. "Museum to be Built in SC Where Slaves Entered US." *The State* (Columbia, SC), July 15, 2014.

Spaulding, Timothy. *Re-Forming the Past: History, the Fantastic, and the Postmodern Slave Narrative.* Columbus: Ohio State University Press, 2005.

Stack, Carol. *Call to Home: African Americans Reclaim the Rural South.* New York: Basic, 1996.

Stephens, Michelle. *Black Empire: The Masculine Global Imaginary of Caribbean Intellectuals in the United States, 1914–1962.* Durham, NC: Duke University Press, 2005.

"The Story of the Plantation That Moved Away." National Public Radio, May 23, 2009. Accessed July 18, 2014. http://www.npr.org/templates/story/story.php ?storyId=104494296.

Stovall, Tyler. *Paris Noir: African Americans in the City of Light.* Boston: Houghton Mifflin, 1996.

Strain, Christopher. "Soul City, North Carolina: Black Power, Utopia, and the African American Dream." *Journal of African American History* 89, no. 1 (2004): 57–74.

Sullivan, Patricia. *Days of Hope: Race and Democracy in the New Deal Era.* Chapel Hill: University of North Carolina Press, 1996.

Swarns, Rachel L. "In First Lady's Roots a Complex Path from Slavery." *New York Times*, October 7, 2009.

Taylor, Goldie. "EXCLUSIVE: Bree Newsome Speaks for the First Time after Courageous Act of Civil Disobedience." Blue Nation Review, June 29, 2015. Accessed September 1, 2015.https://www.bluenationreview.com/exclusive-bree -newsome-speaks-for-the-first-time-after-courageous-act-of-civil-disobedience /#ixzz3oxwTa9R4.

Thomas, Lynnell L. *Desire and Disaster in New Orleans: Tourism, Race, and Historical Memory.* Durham, NC: Duke University Press, 2014.

Tillet, Salamishah Margaret. *Sites of Slavery: Citizenship and Racial Democracy in the Post–Civil Rights Imagination.* Durham, NC: Duke University Press, 2012.

"Toni Morrison." *PBS NewsHour.* Accessed July 4, 2016. http://www.pbs.org /newshour/bb/entertainment-jan-june98-morrison_3-9/.

Toni Morrison Society. "Bench by the Road Project." 2008. Accessed July 18, 2014. http://www.tonimorrisonsociety.org/bench.html.

Trouche, Michael. Letter. *Charleston Post and Courier.* February 24, 2014.

Tsing, Anna L. *In the Realm of the Diamond Queen.* Princeton, NJ: Princeton University Press, 1993.

"Turn toward Freedom." Republic of New Africa leaflet. Accessed May 3, 2014. http://cds.library.brown.edu/projects/FreedomNow/do_search_single.php ?searchid=30&x=37&y=34.

Wagner, Phillip. "Opening Bahia, Brazil, to the U.S." Accessed July 5, 2016. http:// www.brazzil.com/2004/html/articles/apr04/p113apr04.htm.

Walker, Clarence E. *We Can't Go Home Again: An Argument about Afrocentrism.* New York: Oxford University Press, 2001.

Walker, David. *Walker's Appeal, in Four Articles; Together with a Preamble, to the Coloured Citizens of the World, but in Particular, and Very Expressly, to Those of the United States of America, Written in Boston, State of Massachusetts, September 28, 1829.* Accessed May 2, 2014. http://docsouth.unc.edu/nc/walker /walker.html#n33.

Walker, Sheila. "The Feast of the Good Death: An Afro-Catholic Emancipation Celebration in Brazil." *Sage* 3, no. 2 (1986): 27–31.

Wall, Cheryl. *Worrying the Line: Black Women Writers, Lineage, and Literary Tradition.* Chapel Hill: University of North Carolina Press, 2005.

Warren, Kenneth W. "Appeals for (Mis)recognition: Theorizing the Diaspora." In *Cultures of U.S. Imperialism,* edited by Amy Kaplan and Donald E. Pease, 392–406. Durham, NC: Duke University Press, 1993.

White, Carmen. "Living in Zion: Rastafarian Repatriates in Ghana, West Africa." *Journal of Black Studies* 37, no. 5 (2007): 677–709.

Wilkerson, Isabel. *The Warmth of Other Suns: The Epic Story of America's Great Migration.* New York: Random House, 2010.

Williams, Heather Andrea. *Help Me to Find My People.* Chapel Hill: University of North Carolina Press, 2012.

"Without 'the Man.'" Editorial. *Charleston News and Courier,* November 9, 1971.

Womack, Ytasha. *Afro-Futurism: The World of Black Sci-Fi and Fantasy Culture.* Chicago: Lawrence Hill, 2013.

Woodward, C. Vann. "Look Away, Look Away." *Journal of Southern History* 59, no. 3 (1993): 487–504.

Woolfork, Lisa. *Embodying American Slavery in Contemporary Culture.* Urbana: University of Illinois Press, 2009.

Wright, Richard. *Black Power: A Record of Reactions in a Land of Pathos.* Westport, CT: Greenwood, 1954.

X, Malcolm. *The Autobiography of Malcolm X: As Told to Alex Haley.* 1965. New York: Ballantine, 1987.

Note: Page numbers followed by *f* indicate a figure.

expatriates in Ghana, 55–59, 65–66, 70, 82–87, 103, 225; citizenship and visa status of, 111–13, 115–17; contemporary controversies of, 108–20, 242n53; misconceptions of contemporary African reality of, 16–18, 54–55, 91–98; reimagined Pan-Africanism of, 115–20. *See also* Pan-Africanism

family trees, 226–32, 251n4
Fanon, Frantz, 94–95
Federal Bureau of Investigation (FBI), 113
Finding Your Roots, 226
flight. *See* expatriates; imagining flight; migrations of Black Americans
Flying Africans tale, 2–4, 43, 51, 119, 235n7
Franklin, Aretha, 37
Freedman's Association, 226
Furniss, Henry, 132

Ga Mashie, 128
Garvey, Julius, 105–6
Garvey, Marcus, 10, 94, 103, 106, 122
Gates, Henry Louis, 226
genetic science, 226–32, 251n4
geography of containment, 7, 10, 33, 183, 228, 236n12
Gerima, Haile, 6, 20–21, 27, 35–43, 52
Ghana, 21, 80–85, 213, 224–25; Angelou in, 55–56, 85, 108; Black American expatriates in, 56–58, 70, 82–87, 90–98, 103; Caribbean expatriates in, 241n39; citizenship and visa status of expatriates in, 111–13, 115–17; controversies on the slave trade in, 108–20, 242n53; debt of, 102; economic development goals of, 105–14, 116; flag of, 103; in Gerima's *Sankofa*, 35–38; Ghana@50 celebration of, 80, 101–8, 113, 242n45; in Hartman's *Lose Your Mother*, 69–72; homeland tourism to, 75–122, 243n5; independence of, 21, 80–82,

84; Joseph Project of, 106–7, 111, 113, 116; Obama family's visit to, 19, 80, 98–100, 101*f*; Pan-African Historical Theatre Festival (PANAFEST) in, 76, 98, 100, 120, 122; popularity as tourist destination of, 21, 84; repatriated Afro-Brazilians (Tabom people) in, 125–29; slave castles of, 1, 2*f*, 56–57, 69–72, 75–79, 87–91; spiritual practices in, 47; tourist industry of, 87–90, 98–104; triumphalist independence narrative of, 42, 81, 115–16; understandings of race in, 240n16. *See also* homeland and cultural roots tourism
"The Ghosts of Charleston" tour, 173–74
Gold Coast, 75. *See also* Ghana
Gondim, Joel, 149–52, 155
Gorée Island slave castle, 62, 67–68
Great Migration, 10, 189–90
Greusser, John, 55
griots, 28
Gullah culture, 22–23, 174, 180–81, 188–89, 194, 209, 250n71, 250n73

Haley, Alex, 107, 190
Hall, Stuart, 14–15, 114, 129, 158
Hanchard, Michael, 137–38
Harlem Renaissance, 9
Harris, Eddy L., 27, 59–63, 68, 239n45
Harris, Thomas Allen, 20–21, 25–26, 45, 48–53; personal history of, 48–49; spiritual quest in Bahia of, 50–53
Hartman, Saidiya, 12–13, 80; on homeland travel, 59, 62, 109–10, 113–14; imaginings of slavery of, 118–20; on sexual violence of slavery, 40; travel narrative of, 17–18, 20–21, 69–72, 91–93, 97
Helms, Jesse, 201–2
Holland, William, 229–32
Holshouser, James, 200
homeland and cultural roots tourism, 4–5, 15, 20, 59, 224–26; to Bahia,

Marable, Manning, 12
Marley, Bob, 122
Marshall, Paule, 27, 44–53, 72, 240n51
Mary Ellen (Black American expatriate in Ghana), 91–93, 97, 109
Mayfield, Julian, 108
McGill, Joseph, 185–86
McKissick, Floyd, 199–203
McKnight, Reginald, 21, 27, 91
Middle Passage and slavery: in Afro-Atlantic folklore traditions, 2–3, 235n7; *Beloved*'s remembering of, 15–16; cultural trauma of, 29–30; dehumanized machinelike Black bodies of, 38–39; Door of No Return of, 79, 88–89, 101*f*, 115, 117, 169; sexual violence and shame of, 39–42. *See also* Bahia; Ghana; slave castles; U.S. South
migrations of Black Americans: to Bahia, 129–30, 136–37, 158–69, 224–25, 246n62; décalage and, 135–37; early nineteenth-century colonization projects and, 8, 10, 94, 103, 113, 218; to Ghana, 55–59, 65–66, 70, 82–87, 90–98, 103, 108–14, 224–25; Great and Second Great Migrations of, 10, 189–90; return migration to the South, 22–23, 174, 189–90, 225–26; as self-exile, 23–24, 238n52. *See also* Middle Passage and slavery
Mills, John Evans Atta, 99, 100*f*
misnaming, 108–9
misrecognition in the homeland, 84, 239n35; expatriate experiences of, 113, 116, 168; Hartman's witnessing of, 70, 118; neoteric Pan-Africanism and, 224; tourist encounters of, 89–90, 108–9, 154
Mississippi Democratic Freedom Party, 196
mobility, 8–13. *See also* homeland and cultural roots tourism; migrations of Black Americans

Morrison, Toni, 54, 221–23; on literary archeology, 169; on paradises, 109; on Reconstruction, 15–16; on slave memorials, 186
Moseley, Ira, 141
Moten, Fred, 16
Mother Emanuel African Methodist Episcopal Church (Charleston, SC), 214
Moving Midway (Cheshire), 175–80
Muñoz, José E., 17
mythmaking process, 6
myth of the Flying Africans. *See* Flying Africans tale

NAACP (National Association for the Advancement of Colored People), 10
Nascimento, César, 141–42
National March on Washington of 1963, 11
Native Stranger (E. Harris), 27, 59–63, 68, 239n45
Naylor, Gloria, 191–95, 249nn34–35
Nelson, Donovan, 4*f*
neoliberalism, 12
neo-slave narratives and travel, 3–4, 26–30. *See also* homeland and cultural roots tourism; speculative texts
neoteric Pan-Africanism, 13–20, 84–85, 120, 224; definition of, 18–19; myth-making and psychic freedom in, 17, 19–20
New Economic Partnership for African Development, 104
New Patriotic Party (NPP) (Ghana), 101–2
Newsome, Brittany "Bree," 213–17
Ngalatchui, Ngako, 232
Nixon, Richard, 80–81, 198, 201
Nkrumah, Kwame, 11, 21, 93–95, 99, 101, 108; coup and deposition of, 113, 116; Ghana's independence and, 81; Pan-Africanism of, 81–82, 84

roots tourism. *See* homeland and cultural roots tourism

Rougeau, Weldon J., 141

Rushdy, Ashraf, 28

Sankara, Thomas, 93

Sankofa (Gerima), 20–21, 27, 35–43, 52

Santana Pinho, Patricia de, 156–57

saudade, 128–29, 136, 152–53, 169–71

Scenes of Subjection (Hartman), 40

Schuyler, George S., 137

Second Great Migration, 10

segregation, 9–10, 80–81, 135, 139–40, 184

Seigel, Micol, 134–35

self-exile, 23–24, 238n52

Senegal: Black American expatriates in, 65–66; Gorée Island slave castle of, 62, 67–68; McKnight's fictionalized travel memoir of, 63–69

separatist communities, 196–203, 249n42; in Naylor's *Mama Day*, 191–95, 249nn34–35; Oyotunji Village, 22–23, 189, 194, 203–13, 217; Port Royal Experiment, 194; Republic of New Africa plans for, 197–99, 249n50; Soul City project's democratization of, 199–203

Sherman, William Tecumseh, 186, 197

Singh, Nikhil, 13

slave castles, 1, 56–57, 59, 62, 67–68; archived accounts of, 118–20; Door of No Return of, 79, 88–89, 101*f*, 115, 117, 169; in Eddy Harris's travel memoir, 62; in Gerima's *Sankofa*, 35–38; in Hartman's *Lose Your Mother*, 69–72, 118–20; historical preservation of, 75; homeland tourism to, 75–79, 85–91; officials' living spaces in, 77, 87; photos of, 2*f*, 76*f*, 78*f*, 79*f*, 101*f*; tour guide scripts at, 78–79, 87–88, 98, 115–16; as UNESCO World Heritage sites, 75, 117

Slave Dwelling Project, 185–86

slavery. *See* Middle Passage and slavery; U.S. South

Smith, Clarence, 141

Song for Anninho (Jones), 169–71

Sorenson Molecular Genealogy Database, 229, 231

Soul City, 199–203

the South. *See* U.S. South

South Carolina, 173–74; Bench by the Road project in, 186; Boone Hall Plantation in, 180–81, 182*f*, 248n5; celebrations of emancipation in, 183–84, 188; Gullah culture in, 22, 174, 180–81, 188–89, 194, 209, 250n71, 250n73; Oyotunji Village in, 22–23, 189, 194, 203–13, 217; Port Royal Experiment in, 186, 194, 197; preservation of sites of slavery in, 140, 146, 174, 180–89; proposed African American museum in, 248n12; Statehouse Confederate flag in, 213–17; white heritage tourism in, 181–85

speculative texts, 5–6, 25–74, 235n11; ancestral past in, 26–30, 44–45; Bell's "The Afrolanitca Awakening," 218–19; Butler's *Kindred*, 27, 30–35, 41; chaotic temporality in, 30; Gerima's *Sankofa*, 20–21, 27, 35–43, 52; of griots, 28; Hartman's *Lose Your Mother*, 17–18, 20–21, 69–72; in homeland travel memoirs, 54–69; Jones's *Song for Anninho*, 169–71; as literary archeology, 169; Marshall's *Praisesong for the Widow*, 27, 44–53, 72, 240n51; McKnight's *I Get on the Bus*, 21, 27, 63–69; Morrison's *Beloved*, 15–16, 54, 186, 221–23; Naylor's *Mama Day*, 191–95; spiritual healing in, 49–53; tropes of travel and flight in, 20–21, 26–27, 221–23

Stewart, Ollie, 136–37

Stinson, L. H., 133–34

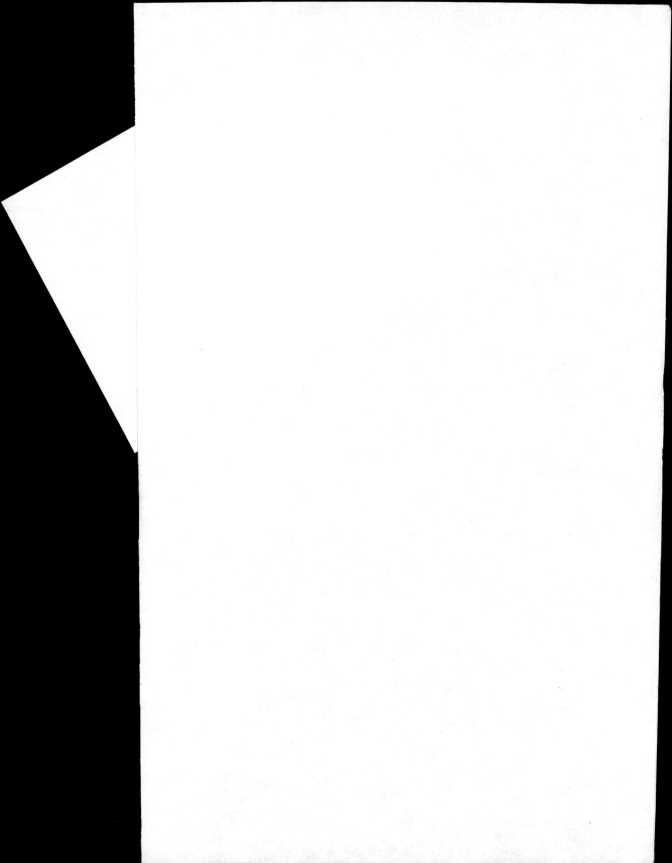

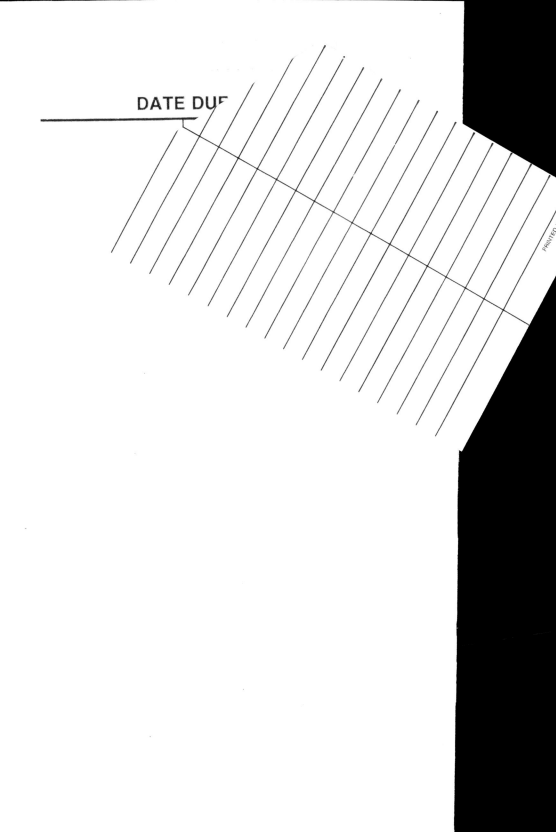

DATE DUE